KYRA'S STORY

KYRA'S STORY

Reminiscences of a Girlhood in Revolutionary Russia

by Kyra Karadja

With a Preface by Margaret Mead

WILLIAM MORROW AND COMPANY, INC.

NEW YORK   1975

92
K18k

Library of Congress Catalog Card Number 75-14314
ISBN 0-688-02939-6

Book design by Helen Roberts

To Del

Preface

by Margaret Mead, author of *Coming of Age in Samoa*

This moving story of a revolutionary childhood admits the reader to events behind the Russian Revolution which have never before been presented in just this way. Although half the human race has lived through revolutions during the 20th century, we in America, far from revolutionary struggles, fighting wars only on other shores, have very little conception of what such scenes have meant to the children and adolescents of the world.

Kyra's Story is written with the freshness of a young woman looking back to her own past as a basis for reminiscences of rare charm and honesty.

Elements of the fate of the privileged after the Russian Revolution are here as well as unique experiences—the memories of a glamorous childhood where the little girl had a preview (never to be realized) of what balls would be like when she grew up, the terrors of the Revolution, the flight with the faithful old nurse to the Caucasus, the death of the father in the typhus epidemic, the years of famine, the troubled and confused struggles of a group of alienated young people in a drug scene that provides a strange preview of the drug scene in the United States after World War II, and the astounding court-

7

ship by a fierce mountaineer. All of these are seen through the sensitive writing of Kyra Karadja.

When this manuscript first came to my attention, I was able to compare it with studies and interviews with Russian refugees from that by-gone world; I found it entrancing, with episodes which continued to haunt me with the vividness of their imagery.

Today we are emphasizing the importance of giving young people access to the real world, not only the real world as seen by adults, but the real world as it appears to a growing child and emerging adolescent. *Kyra's Story* does this. Americans who have been spared the horrors of war and revolution can experience what they meant—and did not mean—to a Russian child who had fled to the Caucasus.

Because all Russians carry with them a continuing sense of kinship with their native country and to those they left behind, the writer uses a pseudonym, not to disguise, but to protect.

Kyra's Story makes us see the Russia of fifty years ago, vividly, nostalgically, warmly.

Contents

PART I

1. Summer of 1914

That year, as in other years, they left St. Petersburg early to spend the summer at their country estate, Slavnoe. The season began with the village priest coming to bless the black naked earth, the shining plows, the workmen, and the horses. Kyra and Tassia, still in warm coats and felt boots, drove out to the fields with their parents. Squinting in the sun, solemn, they stood, crossing themselves while the priest knelt in the field damp from the winter snows, and the choir of peasant boys chanted praises to God and a plea for a good harvest. It seemed to Kyra that the new spring brightness about her was itself full of joyful singing and humming and ringing. Shrill, tiny golden bells dangled in the sun, oddly fashioned booming ones crouched in the gullies where the unmelted snow still lay, and even the snorting of the plow horses rising in white vapor curled itself into pools of sound. It was a marvelous world!

The children played in the park and among the tall silver birches of the avenue which led to the flower garden. They built houses under the birches of pebbles and moss with gates of crossed twigs to shut out the world. Kyra milked cows in her house, but that was a secret. When she balanced the heavy pail, careful not to spill the foaming whiteness inside it, Tassia would call out plaintively, asking what she was carrying. But Kyra never told her. She steadily milked cow after cow, and all the time Pavla was there watching her, Pavla praising and admiring her. And after Kyra got through with the bad black cow who kicked naughtily and nearly up-set the milk pail, Pavla declared that she herself could hardly do as well and that she was, in truth, afraid of that cow. But Kyra was afraid of no cow in her house under the birches. Then she and Pavla sat together and ate strawberries and cream because Kyra had done all Pavla's work and now Pavla was free and no one would call her away. Pavla had the gray shawl about her head and shoulders which always enchanted Kyra. It was full of friendly smells of the dairy and of hay and of warmth, and it had a long fringe all around which was such fun to braid into a row of tight little tails. Pavla liked the braids and she smiled; then serious again, she asked Kyra's advice in the matter of naming the newborn calves. Kyra considered the problem carefully and suggested beautiful names, but she knew all along that the finest calf would be called by Pavla "Kyrka" in her honor. Tassia, too, could have a calf named after her, a fat white calf with round brown eyes—but they did not have to decide that just yet. For in Kyra's house, Pavla paid attention only to her.

In sad reality, Pavla had no time to spare for Kyra. Around the hour when Alexis, the white-bearded head coach-man, Peter, the jovial gardener, and Pavla, who was in charge of the dairy, came to Kyra's father for their daily orders, Kyra perched on the fence between the garden and the yard and watched for them impatiently. If, after crossing the yard, Pavla had to wait in the yellow-painted hall, Kyra hurried to join her there. She jumped around Pavla and hung on her arm, but Pavla, preoccupied and business-like, was not quite the perfect companion of Kyra's imaginings. All too soon the door of her father's study opened and either Alexis or Peter bowed himself out, and then it was Pavla's turn. Kyra skipped back to her post on the fence, for much as she would have liked to, she did not dare follow Pavla beyond the door of her father's study. Little girls must not be a nuisance. Sideways, from the fence, she caught glimpses of her father's green belted tweed jacket bending over the huge desk by the window. Down in the yard, in the shade of the linden tree, a group of peasants stood waiting. But after Pavla had left and was walking slowly back toward the cow barns, Kyra seldom stayed long enough to watch the peasants talking to her father. When he came out and stood on the step, tall and erect in his riding boots, the peasants moved forward slowly and ceremoniously, caps in hand, those who were older ahead of the others. It took them ever so long to ask what it was they had come for—medicine or lumber or work. They tugged at their beards and they scratched their heads and they shifted their weight from foot to foot. Kyra, growing impatient long before they were through, would run off to rejoin Tassia and nyanya.*

At Slavnoe nyanya always wore a white kerchief around her head. The many wrinkles about her eyes reminded Kyra of a pattern in cross-stitch, but her cheeks were rounded and pink. She was soft to press against, and when she moved it was unhurriedly and smoothly, first turning her head and shoulders, then slowly the rest of her body in its broad starched apron. There was room for both Tassia and Kyra to lean against her in comfort, even when her hands were holding her knitting over her lap. When nyanya began a story, she spoke in an even, singsong voice, and the stories were spellbinding.

"Beyond thrice-nine lands, in the thrice-tenth kingdom, there once lived a czar who had three doughty sons, but his favorite was the youngest, Ivan Czarevitch. This czar had a marvelous garden and in it grew many rare trees. The rarest among them all was an apple tree with apples of pure gold. The czar loved this apple tree and took much pride in it. It so happened that the Firebird began coming at night to the garden and she would sit on the apple tree and pluck down

* The Russian equivalent of nanny.

the golden apples. The feathers of this bird shone as bright as the red sun and her eyes were like precious jewels . . ."

Kyra knew it all by heart, but nevertheless, she shivered in expectation of the fearful part:

"And as Ivan Czarevitch went on the road and way, going whither his eyes gazed—it may be far, it may be near, it may be high, it may be low; the tale is soon told, but the deed is not soon done—he came at last to an open field where three roads crossed. And as he stood at the crossroad, considering which road to choose, he noticed a column of stone, and on that column these words were written: 'Whosoever goes on straight from this column, he shall have hunger and cold; whosoever goes to the right, shall have his horse slain; and whosoever goes to the left, he shall himself be slain.' "

Huddling close against nyanya on the low, old-fashioned Russian stove which ran the width of the room, the children stared fearfully into the shadows gathered in the corners of the nursery and at the deepening darkness beyond the window. Baba-yaga, the bloodthirsty witch, rode in her mortar, stomping the ground with the pestle, toward her hut, standing on cocks' legs, deep in the forest, ready for feasting on human flesh, sniffing and crying out loudly: "Fee, fi, fo, fum, I smell the blood of a Christian!" and Koshchey the Deathless, the hateful magician, held a fair maiden imprisoned in his fastness beyond unfordable rivers, impenetrable forests, and unpassable mountains; and worst of all, the cunning Leshi wandered in the woods where one could meet him at any time.

"Nyanya, tell me, Nyanya," Kyra whispered under her breath, "how can one tell if one meets a witch in disguise? Maybe the stableboy, Vanka, is a werewolf. How can I tell?"

Nyanya let her knitting rest in her lap, pulled her slipping kerchief lower over her forehead, and sighed deeply.

"I don't know that there's any way to tell for sure, Kyrochka, but it helps to make the sign of the cross three times . . . There are many evil forces about and, ignorant peasant that I am, I know little save what I've heard said, what every Christian soul either fears or praises. So pray to God and His Saints with all your heart that protection and mercy may be granted you."

After she had been tucked in bed, Kyra watched nyanya make the sign of the cross over her cot, straighten the small icon of her guardian saint on the wall above her head, then fill the little oil lamp in the icon corner of the room and slowly kneel down to pray. Nyanya prayed diligently and at length, crossing herself with the broad gestures of a village woman, bowing down till her kerchief touched the floor, raising her head slowly to fix her eyes on the dark silhouette of the Savior, hands folded humbly on the white apron over her voluminous skirts. To the sound of whispered prayers, Kyra fell asleep . . .

Suddenly she opened her eyes. She saw huge shadows on the wall, and the yellow glow of the lamp before the icons and the night lurking beyond the windows. Stillness lay upon everything. She heard creaking, then the faint bark of a dog. Once more it was quiet. Then there was the creaking again on the stairs. Kyra's breath caught, she dared not move an eyelid. Mortal terror clamped her body as if in an iron mold. There was something right behind the door now, something which caused the shadows to sway along the wall. Oh, what would it be? Kind God, don't let it happen, don't let it happen! Was that the breathing of the domovoi? The house-demon's hairy grasp would be upon her this very second, weighing her down, strangling her. No—it was the ghost of the Tartar which had stopped by the nursery door. A breath of cold was already drifting toward her. He was coming in! Unmoving, breathless, surrendered, Kyra waited. And all of a sudden, she was able to scream. Her scream broke the tension and she lay limp and crying, still terrified but knowing that the worst was over.

"God be with you, Kyrochka, what is the matter?" Nyanya lifted herself up in bed, peering in the direction of Kyra's cot.

"He's standing by the very door!"

Cautiously nyanya got up, walked barefoot to the middle of the room and stood listening and crossing herself.

"It's the dead Tartar and I heard his chains clink," Kyra whispered just audibly.

And in silence they waited, Kyra stifling her sobs, straining to catch any movement outside, nyanya heavy and square in her stiff nightgown in the middle of the floor, Tassia, half-awake, sitting up in bed, beginning to whimper. And then a cock crowed in the barnyard, reassuringly and cheerfully. The square of the window was graying visibly, the curtains moving softly to a breeze which was bringing the promise of dawn into the room.

"You must have been mistaken, Kyrochka, or else he's gone by now. Hear the cock? Cross yourself, dear, and go to sleep."

Yawning, nyanya tucked Kyra in again, and Kyra wriggled herself into a comfortable little ball, glancing gratefully at the paling window before she closed her eyes.

Kyra sat in the sunshine. The sand on the paths glistened and looked white, and the huge round flowerbeds rose in a daze of color from the forget-me-nots and pansies around the border to the towering tiger lilies in the center of the bed. The air was still and hot and scented, full of the incessant twittering of birds in the linden trees bordering the garden. A sparrow dropped down from somewhere, hopped busily along the path, took wing once again and, with a soft flutter, alighted on Kyra's head. Kyra felt its tiny claws pressing tentatively into her hair. She gasped with delight, but the sparrow seemed not to notice, its firm compact weight settling trustingly on her crown.

"Look, look, Nyanya, there's a sparrow sitting on Kyra!"

Kyra felt the touch of a wing, then nothing. The bird was gone. She ran toward the verandah, wild with joy and excitement, but also angry at Tassia's loud cry.

"Without a doubt it's a sign something out of the ordinary is about to happen," nyanya prophesied.

That afternoon their mother told Kyra and Tassia that an English governess was coming to look after them, in place of nyanya. They were getting to be big girls, and besides, nyanya would be needed to take care of a new brother or sister who would soon be sent to them.

Kyra clung to nyanya's side, sorrowful and angry by turns, throwing herself at nyanya's neck in sudden violent anguish. Red-eyed, the ends of her kerchief damp from wiping tears, nyanya tried to comfort her little girls.

"You'll be growing up, and an unlettered old peasant like me isn't good enough for you. Maybe that English one won't be so bad, maybe she'll take pity on me and let me see my little angels sometimes. Don't fret so, my precious ones. I'll tell you a story. Shall it be the one about the Fisherman and the Little Gold Fish?"

"Tell us about when you were a little girl, Nyanya."

"What's there to tell, Kyrochka? I was a country lass like any other . . . They sent me out with the geese, and was I frightened at first! The geese would come screaming and thrashing their huge wings about and straight toward me . . . And it happened a thunderstorm would come while I was alone in the meadow. . . ."

"And afterward?"

"And afterward I was given in marriage. I was going on sixteen, I reckon."

"And then?"

"Well, my babies died one after the other. It was at haymaking time that some illness went through the village. It was God's will, may their innocent souls rest in peace. Then my man got called up to fight Japan. I wasn't too sorry to see him go, and he never came back. Afterward the lady from our neighboring estate took me to look after her little boy."

"Did you like him as much as us?"

"He was a good, obedient boy, Vovochka, and the mistress was kind enough, and was she a beauty! Like a swan sailing about!"

"Like Mother? Will I be like that when I grow up? Tell me, Nyanya." Kyra jumped up and down in her impatience.

"You'll be a grand lady some day, to be sure, Kyrochka.

But, you take after your father. Tall and proud and willful you'll be, and your eyes flashing . . . See how they flash even now, and your mouth curving and moving like it was alive by itself."

"And me?" Tassia cajolingly rubbed her face against nyanya's apron.

"It's hard to tell much of a child of not even three years—" nyanya stroked Tassia's hair thoughtfully—"but you've got the disposition of your mother, calm and sweet, and your dimples always show as if nothing should make you unhappy for long."

Kyra and Tassia dashed into the drawing room and climbed onto the sofa over which hung a gilded mirror. Leaning against the sofa's back, they stared solemnly at their reflections in silence. They did not look alike. Dark-haired Kyra, almost five, had a small, narrow face with high cheek bones, a straight nose, and deep-set eyes which were neither brown, nor yellow, nor yet green, but a mixture of the three. Pug-nosed, round-faced Tassia looked like a little boy, with short silvery blonde hair, dimples, and huge brown eyes like ripe cherries.

Just before tea time on a stuffy, parched afternoon, Kyra and Tassia started down the road with their mother to meet the carriage which had been sent to the station for Miss Mildred Jenkins. Kyra felt sullen and miserable, and she pinched and poked Tassia to make her miserable too, for Tassia kept chattering cheerfully and did not seem really to mind anyone's coming. The soft dust of the road powdered their shoes, the grass on either side looked limp and bruised, and the trees of their park beyond the tall fence which ran alongside the highway were dark and unhappily bowed. It was no help for Kyra that her mother talked of some island called England and the long journey which the horrible intruder had had to make, or that the new governess would read stories to her about a round table and a king and his knights just as soon as Kyra learned to understand English. And when they finally did sight the carriage which carried Miss Jenkins and it had stopped to pick them up, her mother would not let Kyra climb onto the box next to Alexis, the way she always did when they met the carriage. Instead of the glory of holding the reins and learning from Alexis how to handle a pair, Kyra was made to sit politely at Miss Jenkins' side and listen to the ugly, non-sensical sounds which her mother and the new woman were making.

Kyra and Tassia did not understand a word that "Miss" said, and she did not look like anyone they had ever known. Though she was young, she was all stiff white waist and high collar and longish, thin nose and straight tight hair, and it seemed to Kyra that if one were to lean against her, she would feel hard and cool and insecure like a folding card table.

That summer of 1914 had been their last in Slavnoe, which they were never to see again.

2. The Diary

Kyra lay wide-awake watching the slowly graying darkness about her, waiting for the pale streak between the drawn window curtains to grow brighter. Presently she reached for her flannel bathrobe at the foot of her bed, threw back the blankets, got out of bed, and crept barefoot across the room. At the open door of Miss Jenkins' bedroom she paused. Miss Jenkins was breathing slowly, rhythmically, with an occasional brief, gurgling snore. Kyra crept on toward the nursery bookcase and, lying flat on her stomach in front of it, pulled her diary from its hiding place. She then sidled up to the window and wormed her way cautiously between the long curtains so as not to push them too far apart. She scrambled onto the windowsill, hunched herself up comfortably, shivering a little from the cold which came through the double windows. She pulled her flannel robe down over her feet and tucked it under her toes.

Suddenly lazy, she sat staring at the broad, icebound expanse of the Volga, and the heavy mass of the monastery walls and domes on the opposite bank. Beyond the monastery the sky was streaked with dim yellow, but the monastery itself still looked dark and grim, very different from the warm whiteness it had when the sun shone on it. In a little while, Kyra knew, she would hear the tolling of bells and perhaps catch a glimpse of the nuns in their long black robes. The banks of the Volga looked steeper and higher in the grayness, and Kyra wondered how it was that in the daytime she and Tassia tobogganed so gaily down this forbidding hill. As yet she could hardly discern the path which was broken by peasant sleighs all day long as they crept to and fro across the river, between their town and the villages on the other side. Only a dark break in the otherwise endless smoothness showed where the snow had been flung up, then trampled, yellowed, and beaten in to form a dirty curving ribbon through the sugary sparkling plain of white.

Kyra turned around with a jerk. A sudden sharp sound had come from the direction of Miss Jenkins' room. Kyra listened, holding her breath, then peered through the curtains. All was still again. Miss Jenkins must have sneezed in her sleep, or her bed had creaked. Settling back, Kyra opened her diary and put her hand in the pocket of her dressing gown for the pencil she had hidden there the evening before. She had so much to write about and so little time—the light of the February dawn was so long in coming. Before long there would be Dunia's steps as she came with an armful of logs to start the stoves going.

In the daytime Kyra did not touch her diary because she wanted no grown-up to suspect its existence. Only in Tassia did she confide, by way of comforting her for the loss of their ponies, Orlik and Mamay, that last summer at Slavnoe. It was really then that Kyra first thought of keeping a diary, and the first thing she put down in it was that Orlik and

Mamay had been sent to war. Tassia and Kyra had tried to be brave about it—their father had told them he expected it of them—but when alone they had cried and cried, for Orlik and Mamay had been their very own, and were so gentle and beautiful with their white tails and manes. Kyra had painstakingly described the blue August morning when the drafted peasants and the horses alike were gathered in the village churchyard to receive the priest's blessing before starting on their way to war. Kyra and Tassia had stood on the church steps, staring into the misty candle-lit interior, listening to the chanting and weeping. Outside larks had soared and tumbled in the sunlit sky over the golden cross of the church dome. The air had smelled of hay and incense.

They were never to return to Slavnoe, for after the winter in St. Petersburg—since the war renamed Petrograd, Russian style—they had gone to live in a provincial capital on the Volga where their father had been posted.

To Kyra life became confusing. It was not even and simple as it had been before she began to keep her diary and to think about what she wrote in it, the good things and bad things and things that baffled her. For instance, there were the refugees. Everyone felt great pity for them. They were forever complaining and tearful, and they were dirty. Kyra's mother had supervised the building of log dormitories on the outskirts of the town. She had taken Kyra there the day before the refugees moved in. The buildings smelled of freshly cut pine wood and small yellow drops of gum still clung to the walls. Flowers had been planted and benches put up in the shade of trees. A few weeks later, as she happened to be driven by, Kyra saw the flower beds trampled and the fresh wood walls wretchedly spattered. And one afternoon, as she was about to run down the stairs from her nursery on the third floor, she saw her mother standing below, talking to a woman wearing a black cloak and torn shoes held together with string. The woman snatched her mother's hand and kissed it. Then descending two steps and bending low, she picked up the hem of Mother's skirt and kissed that too, muttering blessings.

Mother, whose voice quivered, could not stop her. Kyra became all hot, and, her head against the banister, she burst into tears, too.

Then there was the morning in the Cathedral on the occasion of the Czar's birthday. They stood in the front row, their father in his sparkling parade uniform, their mother in white velvet, she and Tassia and their little sister Sonia in lace dresses and new hats with tiny blue cornflowers. She and Tassia, together with Olga and Kitty, the daughters of the Governor of the province, were to pass the collection plates around. The proceeds would go to the Red Cross. They came up to the altar steps for the Bishop's blessing, and an attendant handed each a silver platter. Kyra felt good and pure and joyful, the way she felt after Holy Communion. One after the other, slowly, they started to move through the crowd, and coins tinkled against the platters. At the back of the Cathedral were grouped the children from the city orphange, and as Kyra approached, she saw them staring with wide-open eyes, all leaning forward a bit in their clumsy gray dresses with the white pinafores freshly starched. A stout woman began thrusting the orphan girls roughly out of the way.

"Watch out, don't push the barishni!" she hissed, and the gray figures huddled together apprehensively. To herself Kyra whispered vehemently: "They're not pushing at all, you old witch," but she dared say nothing aloud to the stout woman. By the glare in Olga's eyes, she knew Olga had heard it, too. Bending low over the platter to hide her ashamed face, she hurried past the orphans. When she came back to stand at her parents' side, the mood of goodness and gladness had left Kyra. She squirmed and fidgeted unhappily through the rest of the service.

Even at her mother's charity bazaar a wicked thing had happened. The bazaar was to include a children's corner where they would "fish" for masquerade costumes. Most of the costumes were made in their parents' drawing room which had been turned into a workroom for refugee women, to sew and paste and make artificial flowers. Madame Popov, a hired assistant from among the refugees, supervised the women's work. She let the children stand about and watch.

"Now tell me, dears, which costumes do you find the most lovely, which do you fancy?" she asked them insistently.

Kyra and Tassia admired the Indian outfits: bows that shot arrows, spears, and crowns of feathers. Little Sonia liked the spring goddess' long gown and veil, sprinkled with little flowers. When they answered Madame Popov she nodded and smiled as if she were sharing a secret with them. Then at the bazaar when it was their turn to cast the long rod over the screen, Kyra heard Madame Popov whisper to someone out of sight, "Those bundles over there are the outfits for His Excellency's daughters." Kyra and Tassia fished out the Indian outfits and Sonia the gown with the flowers. When Kyra at last found her mother she threw herself at her in tears. She loved the bow and arrow, but how could she keep them when she got them in such a bad, unfair way. Horrid, beastly Madame Popov!

. . . The monastery bells were beginning to chime. The sky was turning blue and the monastery walls were taking on a pale pink glow. Frowning impatiently, Kyra quickly turned the pages of the diary. This way she'd never get started this morning, her fingers were already stiff with cold. And she had to write about last week's dancing lesson at the palace because, as luck would have it, she had been paired off with Olga, whom Kyra idolized. Usually Olga, two years older than she, did not condescend to notice her. But that day, pointing with her chin at the other dancing children, Olga had whispered: "We cannot talk with all those about, but I'll get Mademoiselle to take us to your house very soon so we can plan what to do about your horrid Madame Popov." Olga had added: "Don't answer me now." So Olga had understood her tears at the bazaar and instead of scorning her childishness, was firmly taking her side!

3. Too Early One Morning

Very early one morning, her mother stood, fully dressed, in the doorway between Kyra's and Miss Jenkins' rooms. The room was dark but for the candle her mother held. Kyra thought she might be dreaming, then instantly she knew that she was awake and that something had happened. Her mother was talking in an odd, jerky way, and the candle flame twitched and twisted, throwing unsteady shadows along the wall. Kyra leaned far out of bed and, beyond her mother, caught a glimpse of Miss Jenkins sitting up in bed, pulling the blankets up to her chin. All of a sudden Miss Jenkins let the blankets drop, her legs in the long nightgown swung out from under them and landed with a thud on the floor.

"Mother," Kyra called, sliding back onto her pillow. Her mother turned and came toward her.

"Hurry up, darling, hurry up and get dressed. Hurry as much as you can, and don't turn the light on. I'll leave this candle."

"But I'm so sleepy still . . ." The expression in her mother's eyes, and on her strangely stretched mouth, made Kyra sit up immediately. It was cold in the room, the stove hadn't yet been lit, and Kyra shivered and yawned and tried to stop feeling sleepy.

"Why are we getting up, Mother?" But without answering, her mother hurried out of the room.

Kyra reached out for her clothes on the chair by her bed and started to pull on a sock. Miss Jenkins rushed in, and snatching the sock, thrust woolen stockings at her. And because everything was so strange and dark and quiet as in a dream, Kyra did not protest, though she hated woolen stockings for they tickled on the inside of her knees. Buttoning her dress, Tassia came in.

"I think something has happened," she said.

"Of course, stupid."

"Stupid yourself. Tell me what's happened."

"Probably somebody died."

"Who died?"

"How would I know?" They stared at each other crossly.

"Nyanya is crying," Tassia said presently.

"What's she crying about?"

"She's just crying. I asked her, I don't think she knows. She said: 'Lord have mercy, what is happening, what is happening.' "

Hats, coats, galoshes in her arms, Miss Jenkins rushed in again.

"Hurry up, children, hurry."

"But where are we going? What's happened, please tell us what's happened."

"It's a revolution," Miss Jenkins said.

"What's that?"

Miss Jenkins did not explain.

Down the dark stairs they groped their way and into the dining room where Sonia sat drinking milk. There were two candles on the table and the shutters remained closed. In her coat, a shawl about her head, nyanya came in with more hot milk for Kyra and Tassia.

"Everybody's gone except Masha," nyanya said and started to cry again.

Blowing at the skin to keep it away from her lips, Kyra gulped the boiled milk uncomplainingly. After a glance at her, Tassia drank too. Their mother came in with a bundle of papers which she handed to Miss Jenkins who, turning aside, stuffed them into her petticoat pocket. Tassia caught hold of her mother's sleeve and as she tugged at it, stretching out across the table, she upset Sonia's cup. While Sonia whimpered, Tassia kept asking:

"Mother, what's happened, what's happened, Mother, tell me—"

"We have to go immediately."

Suddenly the doorbell was ringing; it kept on ringing. The children fell silent abruptly, Sonia with her mouth still open petulantly, Tassia with her arm outstretched. Nyanya, bending over Sonia to wipe up the milk, remained shoulders bent, napkin in midair. Miss Jenkins' hands were clutching her skirt. Kyra stared at her mother and remembered a frozen bird she had once found in the snow. There was banging and a crash. Boots thudded up the stairs and a gruff voice called for their father.

Making the sign of the cross, their mother stepped forward at last. Now she was running toward the dining room door and opening it. Above her head appeared the gray cap of a soldier. Their mother stood blocking the door and the soldier peered over her shoulder.

"Where is His Excellency?"

"He isn't here. I'm alone with the children. You can search the house. He left for Petrograd yesterday morning."

Kyra knew her mother was not telling the truth, for she had kissed her father good night. Suddenly she began to tremble. The soldier pushed back his cap, scratched his head.

"We'll find out soon enough . . ." he spat loudly, turned away, and his boots thudded down the staircase.

A loud echoing crack came from the street. Again Kyra saw her mother standing as if suddenly frozen. Masha, the maid, ran in screaming.

"He shot Vassili, Vassili, our policeman. He's lying there right in front of the house—"

"Barinia, oh my Barinia!" wailed nyanya.

"Remain here with the children . . . I must see— We're leaving . . ."

Kyra sprang to her feet. Paying no attention to Miss Jenkins' calls, she dashed from the dining room, up the stairs, into her nursery. She turned on the light. She stood in the middle of the room, mouth open, panting. Everything was as always: books and copybooks on the table, neatly stacked, her toys in the cupboard with the glass doors and others heaped in front of cupboard, the box with the wooden animals she had been coloring for the refugee children. Suddenly she was rushing here and there, snatching up her balalaika, her large white teddy bear, the bow and arrows, her diary, *Little Lord Fauntleroy* with the pictures. Then, on her knees by her bed, she thrust each toy under the bed just as far as she could reach.

"You wicked, wicked, disobedient girl." Miss Jenkins' hand grabbed her shoulder.

Desperately Kyra glanced around the blue-walled nursery with its row of little cats and dogs high up by the ceiling and, as Miss Jenkins was dragging her out, she managed to reach out for her tiniest yellow bear and hide him under her coat.

They left the house through the kitchen and the back door and went across the yard and the garden. The snow looked blue; it was stiff and creaked with every step. They passed the rabbits and guinea pigs in their hutches.

"Who's going to feed them today? Will I be back in time?" Tassia asked Miss Jenkins.

They passed the swings and the summerhouse where the children kept their spades and sleds and skates, and then they reached the garden wall where their mother unlocked the gate to the street. They went a little way down the small street and the sun began to rise from beyond their garden. To the right stood the church, the churchyard and the priest's house, white and squat, with a red slanting roof. Their mother went up to the door of the priest's house and pulled the heavy bell. Kyra saw her glance once back toward their own house, then she merely stood, her eyes fixed on the door, waiting for it to open.

The huge dented samovar's singing on the round table, voices exclaiming, voices never ceasing, her mother's white face and her hands always moving at her throat—beyond those things, at first, Kyra did not grasp anything. They kept on drinking tea, the priest's wife filling and refilling their cups and offering fat hunks of bread and strawberry jam. After the third cup Kyra began to feel better.

Though she tried hard, Kyra could not understand most of what the priest and her mother said. Then they talked about her father.

"If only His Excellency had time to leave town . . ." the priest kept repeating. "If he reached the station in time . . ."

But what had her father done that he had to go away? Why did they have to leave home and come here? Who could be after them?

"The townsfolk will help His Excellency, there's not a doubt. He's much loved here. All know he is a just, good man. The Lord grant that he does not fall into the hands of those wild ones . . . They'd tear anyone apart without so much as finding out whom they are murdering."

"But, Mother, what have we done?" Kyra cried out in despair.

"Don't interrupt your mother," Miss Jenkins said sternly. "If you've finished your tea, go and sit on that couch over there, and quietly, please. Sonia, don't forget to say thank you."

On the couch they began talking about what they would do when they got home. Kyra said she would show Tassia how to play the balalaika. Tassia said that both Kyra and Sonia could help her feed her white rabbits. Sonia kept asking in wonderment, "You mean me, too, me, too?" for her sisters seldom included her in their games and projects. From a distance they heard shouts and dry crackling thuds which they knew were shots, for the priest had said so. He kept listening, trying to guess what part of town they were shooting in. Their mother now sat looking into space.

Presently nyanya came in from the kitchen and said a man had come with a message for their mother. She brought the man in and he stopped near the door, cap in hand. He had come with a little scribbled note from their father. Their mother first read the note to herself, then stared at it a long time, her mouth stretching at the corners. When her mouth became steady, she read the few sentences aloud. Their father was safe in somebody's house on the outskirts of town and said they had better not try to rejoin him as his presence might add to their danger.

"The Lord save and protect him," the priest said.

The man who brought the note was crumpling his cap in both hands and looking up, then back at the floor, then again into their mother's face.

"I was passing by your house just now," he finally said.

"Yes," said their mother.

"Well, I don't like to tell you this, Barinia, but they have made a mess of things. Like a storm had been through that place, every window smashed and the front door torn clean away, and furniture and things thrown into the street . . . Just like a hurricane had been through, Barinia, and left everything wrecked. I picked this up, Barinia . . ." From inside his coat the man pulled out a small toy elephant and a silver spoon.

"Thank you," said their mother.

"That's my Timour," Tassia exclaimed, then squeezing the toy to her chest, she began to sob.

Sonia, too, started to wail, and nyanya had her apron over her face. But Kyra did not feel like crying. With clenched fists and narrowed eyes she stood by her mother, her body very rigid.

In the afternoon they went to sit in the hall because the shooting was loud and very near. There were no windows in the hall and it was dark but for a small kerosene lamp in the corner. Kyra and Tassia shared a hard chair, their mother and nyanya took turns holding Sonia on their knees. The priest and his family sat along the opposite wall. No one spoke. Even the priest's children were quiet. The gray hall, the enormous shadows silhouetting bodies and chairs, the white splotches which were faces and hands, terrified Kyra. And the listening, cowering stillness within the house. Something within her was clutching, then expanding, then clutching again. She was sure she was going to be sick. If only she did not have to sit still . . . Suddenly as the roar of shouting and stamping and shooting seemed to roll up to the very walls of the house, she could not bear it any longer. With a strange thin scream she sprang up and ran from the hall, across the living room and up to the window. She saw soldiers and she saw other men, and several lay oddly on the opposite pavement. She saw a soldier holding a gun to his shoulder. Then the gun fell and the soldier himself staggered and fell backward, his hands grabbing the cobblestones.

Her mother jerked her back, grabbing her dress. Still holding on to her so tightly that it hurt, she pushed Kyra into the hall and there swung her around. She forced Kyra to look up into her eyes. She spoke to her in French so that no one else would understand.

"I expected more of my daughter. Don't you understand that a stupid action like that can be very dangerous? And not only to you, but to all of us and the kind Father who took us in? You might have been seen and recognized. Try not to be thoughtless again. You can be calm and brave, can't you, Kyra?"

"Yes, Maman," Kyra whispered.

She made her way back to Tassia and the chair, head down, damp hands pressed against her sides. But she felt neither sick nor terrified any longer. She perched on the very edge of the chair. After a while, Tassia nudged her.

"Did you see anything out of the window?"

"Yes," Kyra whispered back.

"What did you see?"

"I think some men were dead . . . I don't know."

"Kyra, sit farther back on the chair, you're going to fall off," Miss Jenkins interrupted briskly.

The priest's children were staring at her mockingly. Kyra blushed, tried to stare back with unconcern. There were four of them, all four yellow-haired and light-eyed, three boys and a girl. The girl's name, Kyra knew, was Grusha, for she was the most mischievous and scolded of them all. She wore a

long pink cotton dress and black stockings which were all
twisted and loose about her skinny legs. A round comb held
down her hair, but every time she shook her head the comb
slid back and a short lock escaped and fell over her left eye.
It was Grusha who, as time dragged on, started the kicking
and fidgeting, but her brothers did not seem to mind when
the priest, losing his patience, ordered all four to stand against
the wall. Kyra's own legs had become numb from sitting still
on the hard chair and she, too, could not help squirming and
leaning back against Tassia.

"Oh, when are we going home?" they whispered to one
another every few minutes.

When evening came at last the streets quieted down,
and the priest's wife went to the kitchen. Once again they all
sat at the round table, nyanya carrying things to and from
the kitchen and mashing up Sonia's potatoes for her. Kyra
felt more tired than she had ever felt after a whole afternoon
of tobogganing. She stared at the wallpaper, brown with
bunches of pink roses and gold leaves, at the lamp low over
the table and its dangling multicolored strings of beads, at
Miss Jenkins' hair unbrushed since morning, at Sonia's frowning sleepy face. Then chairs were being moved, the table itself was pushed into a corner, voices interrupted each other,
exclaiming persuasively. Kyra heard her mother say with
finality: "No, really. I can't allow you to . . . The children
are so tired, they'll fall asleep any place. You've done enough
for us already."

Mattresses were carried in and armfuls of blankets and
pillows. Trying to keep out of the way, Kyra, Tassia, and Sonia
slunk into corners, silent and oppressed. Nyanya came forward
for Sonia and started to undress her. Sonia's bed was made
of two armchairs and a straight chair between them, their
legs fastened together with string. Miss Jenkins called Tassia
to brush her hair. Still Kyra waited, not wholly resigned, unable to obey Miss Jenkins' "hurry up and take off your dress."
After nyanya had put Sonia to bed, she took Kyra by the hand
and led her away to a washstand. Big girl that she was, Kyra

stood gratefully still while nyanya's rough hands patted water onto her face. She and Tassia shared the sofa in the living room. They kept their knickers and bodices on, and Kyra felt the buttons pressing into her, whichever way she turned. Tassia kept rolling against her back, breathing hotly, and tickling her with her hair. The blanket tickled too, as there was no sheet. From the three mattresses on the floor rose unpeaceful sounds. Her mother was twisting about, awake; Miss Jenkins was muttering and gulping; nyanya was snoring.

In the morning they hadn't time to sit down and eat breakfast as noise in the street began with the late winter daylight. The children, their mother, and Miss Jenkins went down a ladder into the cellar. In order to descend, a plank in the kitchen floor had to be lifted, and when they were in, the priest dragged a sack of potatoes and firewood and placed them over that plank. The priest's wife had wailed and swung her arms, and her hair was loose down her back. The priest himself had hardly spoken, though his lips had moved. Kyra guessed he was praying. Sitting in the cellar, Kyra tried to pray too, first properly saying a prayer from beginning to end, then just making up her own to ask that her father stay safe. But it was difficult to pray in such a cold dark place and, climbing down the ladder, she had seen a large spider hanging on the wall. The priest had said: "They must be thinking His Excellency is here, too." And her mother had answered that she was glad of it, for at least it kept them off the right track.

Kyra knew what was happening in the street but kept seeing how yesterday the soldier had fallen backward. What was going on today was more difficult to imagine. She knew that there was a large mob in the street who were trying to break into the priest's house and that other men were trying to prevent them.

The priest had handed a small mattress down into the cellar and they sat on it back to back, knees drawn up. Miss Jenkins was sneezing and worrying that she sneezed too loud. Their mother said she could bundle her face in her skirt if necessary. Kyra and Tassia grew apprehensive lest they, too, took to sneezing, for they wore such short skirts. They snuggled against each other for warmth, and even Sonia sat patiently, her back pressed against Kyra's. Dull, thudding sounds came from the street.

Right between her knees Kyra found a hole in the mattress. She poked a finger in and worked it around till she could squeeze in two fingers and drag out lumps of cotton. She wished nyanya had come down into the cellar too, but their mother had said that, if it came to the worst, nyanya was better off above where she'd be taken for a member of the priest's household. Miss Jenkins, of course, looked too unlike other people and she still could hardly speak Russian, so she couldn't be passed off for a relative of the priest . . . At last Kyra could stuff all her hand save the thumb into the hole in the mattress.

Suddenly there was no more noise. After a while the sack of potatoes and the firewood were dragged from over them and the plank lifted up. The priest helped them to scramble out of the cellar. "They have all gone," he told them and hurried their mother off into the living room. The children were left behind. They slunk about the dark shuttered dining room with the priest's children. From the living room came the sound of voices, unfamiliar men's voices talking with their mother.

Grusha said, "The parlor windows are all broken. Now we'll be catching colds. And it's on account of you."

One of the boys, the biggest, came up to Kyra.

"If I wanted to, I could tell you a secret," he said.

"What?" Kyra did not especially want to hear a secret.

"Something you're not supposed to know. They won't tell you because you'd be scared. It happened just now. It happened when all those men who were fighting by our house suddenly all rushed away. A man who had seen it came to tell your mother. They're all talking about it now with your mother. But you'd be scared."

Kyra said nothing. She stared at the boy. He was very

broad though not more than a head taller than Kyra. He was probably thirteen and she just nine. She wanted to hit him.

"Now they're scared for your father."

"All right, tell me," Kyra said.

"What'll you give me? Will you give me one of your white rabbits? I've seen them in your yard."

"They're not mine, they're my sister's."

"You can fix that up with her."

"All right," said Kyra.

"Say 'swear to God.' "

"No, I'll say 'word of honor.' "

"That's not enough."

"Yes, it is."

"All right, come in the corner and I'll whisper. But sure you won't tell on me?"

"Word of honor."

They went over into the corner. The boy cupped his hands around his mouth and spoke into Kyra's ear.

"They killed the Governor in the palace. They caught him somewhere and dragged him back to the palace and they beat him and beat him for over two hours till he died, and all his family were made to look on, and that was why all the people who were fighting here all suddenly went away, because they wanted to be there when they heard the Governor'd been caught and—"

"You're lying, you're a liar," Kyra said loudly and pressed her fists to her ears. It couldn't be true. Of course it couldn't be true because the Governor was the father of Olga and Olga's sisters. Kyra wanted to rush to her mother, but didn't. Instead she went to stand in the corridor. She waited till nyanya was alone in the kitchen.

"It is true, Kyrochka, may his soul rest in peace, and the barinia and barishni were present."

"So," whispered Kyra, and went out of the kitchen. But she went back presently. "What did they beat him with?"

"The butts of their rifles, Kyrochka."

"Did he scream?"

"He must have, how could he have helped it, now?" Nyanya wiped her eyes with her apron.

Kyra crept away to hide in the darkest nook of the corridor.

Men called again the next day and talked behind closed doors. There was no noise outside; sun poured in through the windows laying neat, precise shadows; sparrows chirped, water gurgled down gutters, drops plopped from the roof; the empty street looked warm and slushy. After the men had left, their mother came out to the children.

"Father is under arrest. He's given himself up. I don't yet know just where he is, he's being held in one of the municipal buildings. But it's really better, he's safer this way." Her eyes were red, but she repeated, "He's safer this way."

The priest said, "While the townspeople are keeping watch over him, you need have no fear. They'll see that no harm befalls him. With them he is safe from the Governor's fate."

A single buff-gray newspaper sheet lay spread out on the dining room table; across the top in huge heavy letters were the words: CZAR ABDICATES IN FAVOR OF GRAND DUKE MICHAEL WHO REFUSES THRONE. GOVERNMENT TAKEN OVER BY DUMA OF STATE. Over her mother's bent shoulders Kyra read carefully, pausing at every difficult word, shaking her head when her mother sighed. Pulling at his beard, his head resting on a fist, the priest murmured to himself, then repeated aloud, "Under God we walk, His will be done, but what's to become of us now?"

Kyra's mother only said, "Poor Russia."

On the tenth day of their stay at the priest's house, as they were finishing their supper, their mother said suddenly:

"Children, you are going away tonight," and for a moment she did not add anything more.

"You are leaving for Petrograd to stay with Aunt Liza and Uncle Alek. From there you'll go to the Caucasus as soon as it can be arranged. You are going with Miss Jenkins and nyanya."

"And you, Mother, and you, aren't you coming with us?"
Their mother shook her head.

"Oh, please, please—" They jumped off their chairs and
clung to her desperately. "Mother, Mother!"

She was crying. "I can't come, I can't leave Father."

"Then we'll stay with you, we want to stay with you . . ."
Their mother tried to stop crying. She got up and led
the children to the living room sofa.

"No, my darlings, I want you to be where it is safest.
You will like the Caucasus, it's all mountains and very beautiful, and I'll know that you are safe. I'll join you very soon,
just as soon as Father is freed. Then we'll all be together again.
Don't cry, my little ones. Kyra, you're the eldest, show how
brave you can be. It cannot be otherwise, and you have to
be brave."

Nyanya persuaded Sonia to go to sleep for a while, and
even Tassia dozed with her head in her mother's lap. Motionless against her mother, Kyra listened to her last instructions
to Miss Jenkins and nyanya. At midnight the bell rang shrilly.
Nyanya opened the door to Yakim, their father's valet, but
now he was wearing a soldier's green shirt.

Their mother said good-bye to Kyra, Tassia, and Sonia,
making the sign of the cross over them, and kissing them as
if she could not let go of them in this last moment. Sobbing,
nyanya tried to catch their mother's hand to kiss it, while
Miss Jenkins blew her nose, repeating over and over that she
would take good care of the girls. They left the priest's house.
At the end of the street a country wagon was standing, the
horses tied to a tree. Yakim was the driver. Crossing the
square in front of the palace, Yakim pointed with his whip.

"See that dark round spot? It's the Governor's head on
the flagpole."

Miss Jenkins told the children not to look.

4. A Difficult Journey

No sooner had they crossed the threshold of the apartment in Petrograd than Aunt Liza fell to anxiously questioning Miss Jenkins. Kyra wanted to listen, but little Alek dragged his cousins off to his nursery and immediately began a long lamentation. "See those cupboards in front of each window? That's because the panes have been broken by shooting, and now I can't see out. I have to sit here and Mamma won't even let me watch the processions. I just hear drums and people shouting. I'm not taking walks anymore, not even to the Summer Garden. Mamma's cross all the time and cries and listens to the doorbell all day and mostly all night. She's afraid soldiers will come for Father. Father doesn't sleep at home, he only comes to see us once in a while. I'm always left by myself. Even nurse does not stay with me all the time because Mamma sends her to stand in food lines as the cook alone is not enough."

"We had to hide in the priest's house, and they took Father to prison—" Tassia interrupted excitedly, then stopped short, her mouth trembling. Turning quickly away, Kyra pretended to be engrossed in tracing with her fingertip every curlicue in the design of the oilcloth on the nursery table. They continued to sit on the low white chairs around the table, occasionally glancing at one another incuriously, each child preoccupied with his own loss. Then Sonia climbed up onto a rocking horse and rocked herself slowly, listening to its rhythmic squeaking.

Kicking into space with a bored air, Alek slid down in the chair till his white sailor blouse was hitched up under his armpits.

"Are you staying long? You know what? I'm glad you came. At least I won't be alone all the time."

"But I want to go home and get Matresha, darling Matresha," Sonia's chubby arms were hugging the horse's neck for comfort.

"Don't be such a baby, Sonia. Your Matresha is only a doll, she can't feel anything, but the poor rabbits and guinea pigs—there's no one to give them even a little food. Oh, I wish I never had any rabbits!" Tassia squeezed her hands despairingly. "I just can't bear to think about them."

"Did you have so many?" Alek stared at Tassia's struggling hands.

"They had babies," Tassia whispered.

"I should think you'd feel worse about Father . . ." Kyra began and stopped in mid-sentence.

"But, you see, if I'd never asked to be given some rabbits, well, then they would not be there to starve, and that makes it so very much worse."

Kyra, too, could not bear to think of the baby rabbits dying slowly from hunger and thirst, with no way to get out of their pen. She could not bear to think, though it forced itself on her again and again, of the Governor's head over the palace roof, of Olga and Kitty being forced to be present at the murder.

The blue nursery suddenly became too small to hold the four children. Alek shifted about uncomfortably. Then, jumping up, took hold of his rocking horse's tail.

"Look out, Sonia, I'll tip you in a minute. Get off my horse." Sonia began to howl, loudly and with relish, plainly glad of the excuse. Tassia closed her ears with her fists. Kyra dragged her struggling sister off the rocker and gave Alek a sharp slap.

Sometimes Kyra went to sit on the trunk in the dark corridor and think. She thought of all kinds of things. There were suddenly lots of things she wanted to know. Aunt Liza had said during lunch:

"It's Alek's birthday on Saturday. I don't see how we're going to celebrate it, my poor Alek."

Kyra asked idly, "Aunt Liza, how was Alek born?"

"The postman brought him."

Kyra became curious.

"How did he know you wanted Alek? Was there a tag or something to show that he was meant for you?"

"Yes."

"But where did Alek come from?"

"Yes, Mother, where did I come from?" Alek joined in.

"Kyra, this is no time to bother your aunt with silly questions," Miss Jenkins had interrupted sternly.

Kyra had not meant to be silly. She simply wanted to know because she'd never thought about it before. Tassia'd been found under a Christmas tree just when the tree was about to be taken down the day after New Year's. She herself had been found on the chaise longue in her mother's bedroom. Sonia had come with a box of flowers. She'd been told that a long time ago and she'd never wondered about it. But she did not believe this about the postman, for Aunt Liza had looked funny saying it. Maybe Alek did not belong to Aunt Liza? But where did babies suddenly appear from, anyway?

Aunt Liza had frowned when she heard Kyra saying, "My father is in jail."

"Your father was arrested," Aunt Liza corrected her, "only criminals are put in jail."

But what did that mean? That her father had done no wrong? Someone must have thought otherwise or he would not be shut up. Tassia had said that she thought that everything had simply turned upside down and now the bad people were punishing the good ones because people who chased you from home and shot in the streets and killed must be bad people. Tassia kept wondering how it was that the bad people suddenly got all the power. Miss Jenkins said it was the "mob" against the "authorities" and that discipline was broken and that it could never happen in England. It was too bad that no one had ever warned them about such a thing as a revolution.

Even in nyana's fairy tales, so full of extraordinary happenings, revolutions had never occurred.

And now that there was a revolution on, the grown-ups were too preoccupied and upset to answer questions properly. Uncle Alek came home for a few hours a day and then he was usually busy discussing things with Aunt Liza. Kyra watched patiently for her opportunity. When no one was watching she slipped into the study where her uncle sat alone, smoking and looking through some papers. Resolutely, Kyra leaned against his knees, trying to attract his attention. Uncle Alek was good-natured and cheerful, but it was not his custom to bother much with the children. After he had patted her hair absentmindedly, Kyra knew he expected her to run away, but she kept on looking up fixedly, and he turned to her at last and smiled, his hands still turning the papers on the desk.

"Well, green-eyed niece, what is it you want? Quarreled again with Alek? It must be dreary for you children to be shut in like this in the house. Can't be helped, though. Are you homesick?"

Intent only on questioning her uncle, Kyra shook her head. She drew back a little from his knees, stood upright the better to face him.

"Uncle Alek, how long does a revolution last?"

Her uncle stopped fingering the papers, took off his pince-nez, breathed on the lenses, and polished them with the handkerchief from his breast pocket.

"Well, my dear, once it's gone this far, there's no telling. It might last another month, or two, or three, maybe much longer. There's dissatisfaction and unrest everywhere—the people, the army. They're tired of the war. There's not enough food. God alone knows how it's all going to end."

"Why do soldiers like shooting in the streets better than shooting at the Germans?"

"You see, they've been told we're their enemies and not the Germans and Austrians. It's propaganda by the Bolsheviks."

"But why have they put Father in prison? Is he an

enemy? Everybody always loved him and Mother, and then suddenly . . ." Kyra grabbed her uncle's hand. "Please tell me, Uncle Alek."

"Your father is a rare man, the soul of honor. There're not many like him. But those things are not taken into consideration. He's just one of us who will bear the responsibility, the result of—But don't worry, child, he'll probably be freed soon. Now run along. You're too young to understand."

"Uncle Alek, have we done anything wrong?"

Thrusting back his chair, her uncle stared ahead, beyond Kyra.

"We may not have been wise . . ." He sat very straight in the chair. "We believe in our oath of allegiance, in loyalty to our allies, we believe in Russia and in honor, we will die, believing it. There are many who have been led to think otherwise. But you can't possibly understand all of this, child. Now run along, I have work to do and I must leave in a very little while."

"Yes, Uncle Alek," Kyra turned slowly away.

"You see, it is not very clear to me either why all this is happening," her uncle added apologetically.

Despite the prohibition, Kyra sat in the dining room staring out of the window. Across the street was a wall pasted over with proclamations, some looking fresh and neat in the morning sunlight, others with torn corners sagging and flapping untidily. Try as she might, Kyra could not distinguish the words printed on them. Four soldiers with rifles across their backs and red bands around their sleeves stopped by the wall, talking among themselves, then marched briskly across the street, disappearing from view under her window.

The front doorbell rang. She heard Aunt Liza's quick steps in the hall, the door chain jangling, then men's loud, peremptory voices. She started off her chair, then stood, one hand clutching its back. She wanted to run. She thought of hiding behind the cupboard at the nursery window. Instead she just stood. The long sunny dining room and herself, alone, in a corner of it, were taking on an unreality, an apartness, that was worse than whatever was taking place elsewhere. Abruptly she dashed forward and ran toward the drawing room where she heard voices and the stamping of feet. Near the door, which was ajar, she pulled herself up, crept a few steps sideways, and looked in.

Aunt Liza was in the middle of the room, surrounded by the four soldiers. Aunt Liza kept crying out again and again, "He is not living here, I tell you, he is not living here." One of the soldiers, his arms akimbo, hid her aunt's face from Kyra, and Kyra was glad of it because the voice rang so crazily, so loudly. Tassia, Sonia, and Alek stood pressing close to the servants in a corner. Sonia and Alek were wailing. The soldier nearest to them took a step in their direction, a scowl on his pug-nosed, round face. Immediately they fell silent. Kyra slipped into the room on tiptoe and, eyes downcast, moved along the wall toward her sisters.

"Who's that?" a voice snapped.

Kyra crouched. When at last she dared to look up, no one was paying any further attention to her. She squeezed in between Tassia and Sonia and took hold of their hands, as cold and sticky as her own. Her heart was thumping so that she thought Tassia could hear it.

"It's only my heart," she whispered to her.

Rifles in hand, three of the soldiers stamped to the door of the study, Aunt Liza following them. From the study came banging and thumping and ripping, but in the drawing room everyone stood so still that the ticking of the small onyx clock could be heard distinctly. The maid and the cook, Alek's nurse and their own, all stood with their hands folded over their aprons, their eyes fixed on some spot in front of them. Bright color had appeared on Miss Jenkins' cheeks; she obviously was doing her best to keep her indignation under control. Occasionally Tassia, Sonia, and Alek shifted their weight from foot to foot. Kyra squinted at the soldier who had been left to keep guard over them. Leaning against the piano, rifle in one hand, he was busy scratching the back of his neck with the other. He had a pockmarked face and a scraggly beard, like many of the peasants at Slavnoe.

The banging and thumping moved from room to room. After a while Aunt Liza came back and stopped in front of Alek. For a moment she stared at him, then went to a chair and sat down. One by one the soldiers reappeared.

"He's gone, all right, the devil take him, and no firearms hidden anywhere," they told each other as they entered.

"And who could that scarecrow be?" said one, thrusting his chin in Miss Jenkins' direction.

"I've seen them better," another answered, winking.

They seemed ready to go. They moved about uncertainly, buttoning up their overcoats, adjusting their rifles. They were still grumbling about leaving empty-handed. The young pug-nosed one strode up to the mantelpiece and lifted the heavy velvet drapes drawn over it. Leaping aside with a yell, he dropped the drapes which slid back into place.

"There he is," he shouted. "There, there"

Pushing each other, swearing, clumsy in their haste, the men unslung their rifles, swung them forward, lifted them. They moved forward, shouting:

"Come out, you there, you accursed bourgeois, you Judas, drop your gun and come out, or you'll get a bullet through you."

Rifles aimed, they sidled to the walls, not drawing too near. A chair overturned and crashed to the floor. Instantly, louder, another crash followed, and the grinding ring of glass. It was the young soldier who had fired. In the grayish smoke all four men sprang forward. They tore at the drapes. Something jangled and crunched, then the drapes came tumbling to their feet. Behind, over the mantel, was a huge mirror smashed in the middle.

Aunt Liza had slid from her chair and lay crookedly, her hair touching the floor. Tassia and Sonia wriggled and twisted, and Kyra, dropping their hands, pressed hers to her mouth to hold back a sound, neither sob nor laughter, which came from somewhere within her. Nyanya had her apron over her face and her free arm hugged Sonia. Just back of Kyra, Alek's nurse kept up a moaning chant: "Lord preserve Thy humble servants, the lovely mirror, oh, the lovely mirror . . ." Miss Jenkins stepped forward, stopped, then without a glance at the soldiers, strode resolutely to the unconscious Aunt Liza. Crying, Alek ran after her and threw himself at his mother.

"Oh, sit up, sit up, Mother," he wailed.

The young soldier snickered, rubbed his nose against his sleeve and avoided looking at anyone. Kicking at the drapes, the others grumbled about never knowing what to expect from the lousy bourgeois. Then they moved toward the front door, jostling one another, their rifles catching in the folds of the portiere.

Kyra snatched her sisters roughly by the arms. Dragging them out of the room and down the corridor, she muttered, "Nothing has happened to us, nothing has happened . . ." She swung them onto the trunk and pressed herself close between them. They sat silent in the semidarkness, shivering, staring ahead at the gray wall and the hard outline of the mat on the floor.

Weeks went by before Aunt Liza managed at last to get tickets for a southbound train. It was to leave Easter night. In the cab going to the station, Kyra sat squeezing her aunt's hand.

"Auntie, do tell Mother not to leave us alone too long."

The streets were dark and empty—so different from other Easter eves—the horses' hooves on the cobblestones hammering through the stillness. And in rhythm to the swinging carriage, again and again, Kyra implored:

"You'll tell Mother, won't you?"

When they drew up at the station there was sudden bright light and a dense untidy crowd struggling forward, swinging angrily back, noisy, jostling, cursing. Holding on tightly to the children, Aunt Liza, Miss Jenkins and nyanya began squeezing their way onto the platform. Just ahead of Kyra a peasant with a bulging sack on his back was elbowing his way, and whenver the mob thrust him backward, the heavy sack hit Kyra's head. Halfway across the platform Kyra stumbled over the trailing shawl of a woman who was hunched up on a bundle and wailing shrilly and horribly, calling out for her little son who must have got lost. No one seemed to care. Shocked, Kyra saw that even Aunt Liza, usually so very kind-hearted, pushed by without stopping to help. Amid cursing and struggling, trunks and bags were being hoisted in through the windows of the train. Soldiers hung on the steps, packed the entrance and corridor. When Miss Jenkins had grimly fought their way to the compartment, reserved and supposedly locked, they found two stout women already inside, firmly settled, their baskets and bundles occupying most of the narrow space. Aunt Liza managed to waylay a conductor, but in answer to her complaint about the intruders, he only waved his arms rudely at her as if she were a chicken that he was shooing away.

As the station clock struck twelve, church bells boomed powerfully and joyfully somewhere, for a moment drowning out the yelling and banging in the train.

"Jesus has risen!" Aunt Liza said, and began to cry.

The two peasant women, clumsy in their sheepskins, were crossing themselves with broad slow gestures, then, untying a bundle, they brought forth bright-hued Easter eggs and hunks of black bread with garlic. Hurriedly, Aunt Liza hugged and blessed the children and began squeezing her way out of the train. They caught a last glimpse of her as she reached the platform.

Voices raised in unison woke Kyra up. From her corner of the upper berth, through a narrow triangle of windowpane, she glimpsed bright sunlight and a stretch of a brown plowed field. Blackbirds circled lazily over the field, now sweeping down into her view, now disappearing beyond the top of the window. Kyra became aware that the train was standing still. She wriggled to the edge of the berth. Down below Tassia and

Sonia were combing and braiding their hair with nyanya's help, tugging at her impatiently when she paused to lean over and speak to the two peasant women. It was plain that some mutual grief or grievance had started a new friendship.

"What's happened, Baboushka?" Kyra called out.

By the startled way nyanya looked up at her, Kyra guessed that she had already forgotten the role she was supposed to assume.

"It's all right, Kyrochka," nyanya muttered in confusion, "you don't have to call me grandmother in front of these good women, simple women like myself who wish you no harm. Old stupid that I am, I clean forgot."

The women nodded and smiled reassuringly.

"That's right, Barishnia, we wish you no harm."

Kyra was furious that she had been caught pretending and to have to be reassured by those fat stupids. She would not call nyanya Baboushka again, whatever happened.

Just then Miss Jenkins stalked in crossly, toothbrush and soap in hand, a towel over her shoulder. "Such a pigsty already! Soldiers pushing in—but I gave them a piece of my mind. And no explanation why the train stopped in the middle of this particular field!"

In some vague way Miss Jenkins' indignation was comforting. However topsy-turvy things might be, Miss Jenkins in her tweed skirt, her starched white waist with the little gold pin at the neck, could be counted upon to keep on insisting on order and decency. It made one feel more secure.

The train hissed, sputtered, jerked, and crept forward. When presently it pulled up by a water pump, a crowd from a nearby station rushed in. Men, mostly army deserters to judge by their ragged uniforms, hoisted themselves onto the roofs of the cars, hung onto buffers, clung to the steps. Late that evening, outside some town, the train was fired upon, bullets hitting the cars with a rapid pattering sound accompanied by the ringing of broken panes. Afterward, to avoid the smashed glass splinters, the windows had to be kept open which let the reek of sheepskins, sweat, garlic, and clogged drains drift out and away. One day it was discovered that the tracks just ahead had been torn up. Half a day passed before the train could proceed, and Miss Jenkins took the children walking in a birch grove where they raced each other among the trees. As the train whistle blew, they rushed back with their hands full of snowdrops which even the two peasant women sniffed at, calling them God's little flowers. The women and nyanya had had to remain in the car for fear of losing their seats.

Halfway south, the train began to empty, its roof no longer padded with huddled deserting soldiers who evidently had reached the vicinity of their respective villages; the corridors became less and less cluttered with trunks and sacks so that it was now possible to walk freely through. Shouting blessings and good wishes, the two peasant women dragged their belongings out onto a small station platform. With the excitement gone, the children grew restless. In rhythm to the chugging and clogging, they made up monotonous chants: from the North, to the South, to the war, back from war, into jail, out of jail, bang, bang, bang, you're shot dead, I shot you, you shot me, bang, bang, bang . . . Miss Jenkins complained it gave her a headache. For hours at a time they drank tea. Aunt Liza had given them a huge wicker basket, packed with chickens and a ham and dozens of boiled eggs and apples, and now that the stations were orderly and quiet, nyanya would go with a kettle in search of hot water, fresh bread, sausage or cheese. Miss Jenkins grumbled that they would all die of indigestion, but nyanya kept handing around hunks of black country bread and salted cucumbers.

"Eat, little angels, it's good for Russian stomachs," she muttered reproachfully.

An excited yell from Tassia woke them one morning. She stood by the window in her nightgown, pointing. Beyond the window, the land through which they were moving had changed so surprisingly in appearance that Kyra thought at first that she might still be dreaming. From her upper berth she saw glittering sand and when she had scrambled down, there was more sand stretching far, far to the right and the left, while in front of them, beyond the sand, pale water shimmered hazily.

"It's the desert and the Caspian Sea," Miss Jenkins explained.

The train overtook a caravan emerging slowly from around a dune, the long-legged camels rocking gently under their burdens. Then in the distance they saw dark mountains rising into the sky, ranges upon ranges, seemingly shutting out everything. The train sped them toward those mountains.

On the eighth day of their journey they arrived in Tiflis.

PART II

5. Royal Hotel

In Tiflis the mountains, the streets and houses, the people, all seemed to Kyra to be as brightly colored as Easter eggs. Roofs and pavements shone dazzlingly except when the brilliant sunlight blurred their outlines momentarily in a yellow shimmer. From the broad terrace onto which their rooms opened, the children watched handsome, swarthy men in strange costumes and high, shaggy hats sauntering about proudly and lazily, and tiny brown donkeys trotting with lowered heads under their burdens, and half-naked beggar children tugging after every passerby with bunches of pink violets, and peddlers carrying earthen jars or trays atop their heads. Long-drawn guttural cries and the tinkling of bells rose to the terrace with the fragrance of mimosa and peaches and almonds in bloom. The children loved it, just as their mother had promised.

Nyanya disapproved of Tiflis immediately. "It's a heathen place, there's not a doubt. Now why would a decent God-fearing man have a dagger dangling from his belt in broad daylight? Brigands they look like, every single one of them, rich or poor. Rolling their black eyes and hanging around street corners as if they had nothing better to do. And I saw some women with my own eyes whose trousers were hanging from under their skirts. Haven't the decency to hitch them

up, the immodest ones! Gold coins in their ears, and all
around their necks and arms and their faces half-hidden.
Well they might hide them in shame. Pure idols!"

Miss Jenkins told the children firmly, "I won't have you
sitting out on that terrace all day just staring. We'll regulate
the day in our usual way—lessons in the morning, then a good
long walk, and I'll ask the hotel manager to have our meals
sent to our rooms. The fewer innovations, the better. Let us
see if we can continue just as if we were elsewhere."

The children, of course, could not pretend that they were
"elsewhere." Both the hotel and the town enchanted them.
On their way out they went down wide, carpeted corridors
with many doors opening onto them, and caught glimpses of
strangers moving inside the rooms. They crossed the hotel
lobby with its pale marble columns and potted palms, which
adjoined a verandah where an orchestra played music unlike
any they had heard before, slow, plaintive, repetitive, then
unexpectedly breaking out furiously, recklessly, until one's
very heart pounded. Men stood about in white, black, gray
cherkesskas,* many with jeweled daggers attached to belts
wrought of gold and silver and gold-tipped cartridges in a
row across their chests. Miss Jenkins stalked past them, her
mouth tight, her glance rigidly set. They stepped out into the
street and the sunlit town was all about them and ascending
the surrounding hills in every direction. In the far distance
shone a snow-covered peak. They followed a broad tree-lined
avenue with white balconied houses. They passed a massive
yellow cathedral and a pink palace within a pink-walled park.
Off the avenue, streets ran crookedly, some uphill toward the
steep naked mountain of St. David, others down toward a
rushing, winding river. There were light neat streets with
lovely wrought iron gates leading to gardens and yards, and
there were narrow, tangled streets with tiny shops opening
onto the sidewalk, uneven, jutting houses and dark gateways.
But Miss Jenkins led the children straight to the public gar-

* Cherkesska: tightly belted tunic-like garment worn by men with riding
breeches and soft knee-high boots.

dens which the hotel manager had pointed out to her. Around the flower beds and the fountains they strolled as primly as they had once strolled in the Tavrichesky Garden in Petrograd.

It had become very hot in Tiflis. Day by day Miss Jenkins grew crosser. She was very concerned. Pinned to her corset she wore a linen bag with the money entrusted to her. Steadily the linen bag grew less bulky. One evening, as she unpinned the bag to slip it under her pillow for the night, she discovered it contained but a few five-rouble bills. The children saw Miss Jenkins turn pale. This was peculiar; usually red blotches appeared on her face in moments of anger or dismay. Over and over Miss Jenkins murmured hoarsely, "Good heavens, good heavens." Nyanya looked out of the adjoining room which she shared with Sonia.

"The Lord have mercy!" she cried out as soon as she saw Miss Jenkins' face. "Has one of the children taken sick?"

Wordlessly, Miss Jenkins thrust toward her the empty bag and the five-rouble bills. For a minute nyanya fingered them tentatively. It always took her a moment to recognize the value of bills, and while she gazed at them, she muttered, "Still, if the children haven't taken sick—"

Suddenly Miss Jenkins got very angry. Slapping the palms of her hands against her petticoat, hunching her shoulders so that her corset puckered up, she spoke rapidly and loudly, panting between broken sentences.

"Had I but known, I would not have set foot out of England. My job is to educate those children, not to worry myself blue how to keep them alive. And when can one expect their parents? How is one to know? Starting this revolution! What am I supposed to do in the meantime; what in the world am I supposed to do now?"

"Poor little forsaken children, what will become of you?" nyanya wailed into her apron.

Next morning Miss Jenkins went down to explain the situation to the manager who suggested that they move from their expensive suite into one modest room. For the last time the children wandered out onto the terrace which overlooked the city and through the two huge rooms with the tasseled brocaded furniture. They hadn't paid attention to any of it before they had seen their new room, dim and cluttered with cots, overlooking the kitchens and the back yard. And it had but one narrow window.

Heat and cooking smells rose from the hotel yard and settled in their room, and there was no escape from them. The little girls could not bear wearing their dark woolen dresses so they stayed undressed all day long, doing nothing. Even the daily walk was given up. For long hours nyanya knelt in the corner in front of the icons, bowing her head to the floor and murmuring her prayers half aloud. Every once in a while Miss Jenkins attempted to show that she had not lost control of the situation. Clapping her hands, she would briskly announce that it was time for an English lesson. Over and over she read about a little boy, Dan, who went walking in a meadow looking for a lost lamb until he fell into a pit. There in the pit Dan found his lost lamb, but he could not climb out without a helping hand. Each time Miss Jenkins reached this part of the story, Kyra felt like screeching. She hated the "helping hand" with unreasoning fury. It had become a fat hand with stubby pink fingers like that of Madame Popov, the fingers moving slowly and methodically as had Madame Popov's when smoothing out the work of the refugee women.

Sonia spent hour after hour talking to herself and whimpering. She whimpered about her doll and wanting chocolate. If anyone approached her, Sonia only kicked, and her face was continually wet with swollen eyes and a nose like a shiny bright radish. Tassia, on the other hand, kept very still. She lay on one of the cots, her hands pressed together, her face hidden in the pillows. When she did raise her face, Kyra did not like to look at it. She knew when Tassia lay with eyes closed, she was imagining her mother sitting at her side; when she threw out her arms hugging the pillow, it was her mother she was trying to hug. In desperation, Kyra had asked, "What do you think of like that all the time?" And after a while, Tassia had answered, "Of someone who is not here." Another time Tassia said, "You know, I'd be willing to eat nothing but eggs and milk, the way we do now, forever and ever, if only—" And though she did not go on to finish her sentence, Kyra sensed that she had tried to say, "If only Mother would come." At night Tassia called out in her sleep and muttered very rapidly, as if she were remonstrating or pleading. It terrified Kyra who shared her bed. Afraid to touch her sister, she would lie very still, feeling utterly helpless. But if she heard Miss Jenkins getting up to come over and comfort Tassia, she would bounce on the bed and tug at the bedclothes so as to wake her up. She could not bear to have Tassia waking suddenly, mistaking Miss Jenkins for her mother.

To pass the long hours, Kyra took to telling stories to her sisters. She knew most of nyanya's by heart and she invented others. When one was making up a story, it was not possible to think of anything else. One morning when she was sitting cross-legged in her petticoat on the bed, reciting in a singsong voice, ". . . And then he was finally able to enter the gleaming palace. A lovely young princess came forward to greet him, and such was her beauty that it can neither be told of in a tale nor described with a pen . . ." she suddenly became aware of a gray-bearded old man standing at their door.

Bowing solemnly to Miss Jenkins and the children and even to nyanya, the old man advanced into the room, while Kyra and Tassia scrambled to reach for the sheet and drape themselves with it. He had come with a message, the old man announced, a message from his mistress, the Princess Kazbekiani. The princess wished to see the children of whom she had heard from a relative who had recently returned from the North. Miss Jenkins told Kyra to inquire politely who Princess Kazbekiani was. Apparently greatly surprised at their ignorance, the old servant replied that his mistress was noble and rich and young, and well known to everyone in Georgia.

"She's one of those Georgians then?" Nyanya could not refrain from interrupting, although, of course, she had not meant to be rude.

"She most certainly is," affirmed the old man, and aware now of the complete ignorance of these "foreigners," he began telling them of the illustrious family of the princess, of her forefathers famed for their valor in war and their hospitality in peacetime, of the ancestral castle up in the mountains facing the mighty Kazbek. Summer, as well as winter, Kazbek's peaks were snow-covered, but on the estate of the princes of the Kazbekiani family, there were vineyards and apricot orchards, and there grazed many hundreds of sheep.

Draped in the sheet, Kyra and Tassia leaned forward on their bed, afraid terribly lest Miss Jenkins or nyanya interrupt the old man. But even Miss Jenkins looked impressed. She was rubbing the tip of her nose the way she always did when trying hard to follow a conversation in Russian, in this case made more difficult by the guttural Georgian accent and the interspersed Georgian words. Sonia was not listening. With a preoccupied face, she was burying her fingers in the shaggy papaha, the hat the servant had placed on a chair when he had entered, and she was trying to reach for his dagger, sheathed in black leather, shiny against the duller black of his tunic.

Timidly, Tassia asked, "And you said the princess is beautiful?"

"Yes, little mistress," the servant bowed in her direction. "She certainly is. Her eyes are like pools in the mountainside and her hair darker than night. You will see for yourselves, little ladies."

Tassia was eager to ask many more questions, but Kyra silenced her. She knew the questions would not be appropriate because Tassia longed to know about the castle and how one reached it and what was the attire of the princess— a stiff white veil on her head or all in soft silk, as their own mother had become clothed in Tassia's imagination.

After the servant left, they sat about waiting for the appointed time to call on Princess Kazbekiani. Miss Jenkins was plainly unnerved. Kyra and Tassia kept still, immersed in reveries. Suddenly Kyra noticed her appearance—her shabby dirty brown flannel dress with a large grease spot right under the collar; holes at the elbows, darned and torn through again; one cuff so frayed that nyanya had cut it off.

She cried out wildly, "I can't go, oh, I can't go!"

She stood in front of Miss Jenkins. "I cannot go in this dress. It's torn and dirty and horrid. I won't go to the princess! And Tassia and Sonia can't go in their dresses. Theirs are even worse than mine. We just can't go."

As she stared defiantly into Miss Jenkins' face, expecting the usual "Do as you are told." she grew aware that incredibly, shockingly, Miss Jenkins had nothing to say. In the pale eyes lifted to hers, Kyra saw resignation. After a long silence, Miss Jenkins got up. "Well, if you would rather not go," she said quietly, "for the honor of your parents, I cannot blame you. You are unfit to be seen. I suppose I had better go and explain things. I don't know that there is anything else I can do."

Neither nyanya nor the children spoke much while Miss Jenkins combed her hair and brushed her old gray suit. When Miss Jenkins was ready to leave, Kyra rose from her cot and, for the first time, went up to her to embrace and kiss her on the cheek. Surprisingly, Miss Jenkins hugged her in response.

Nyanya was slicing bread for breakfast, the knife at regular intervals hitting the table with a soft little thud, and muttering to herself as usual. Inside the screen around the washstand, Kyra combed her hair wearily, putting down the comb and stretching herself, then picking it up again and running it slowly through the two plaits, one down each shoulder. Leaning over the washbasin, Tassia splashed water on her face, with Sonia tugging at her to hurry her up, and Miss Jenkins grumbling at Sonia. Despite the closed windows and drawn curtains, heat hung already heavily in the room.

They heard steps along the corridor, hurrying heavy steps which paused briefly at their door. There was a loud knock and immediately the door was pushed open. They heard nyanya gasp and cry out and her bread knife clatter to the floor. For a second Kyra could not stir, knowing and yet not believing, trembling and weak as in a nightmare. Pushing against Tassia, sobbing violently, she jumped from behind the screen and ran headlong into her father. She felt herself being picked up and kissed all over her face, then the roughness of tweed against her cheek as her father bent to Tassia and Sonia. Kyra pressed her face into the tweed, squeezing herself closer and tighter, clutching with her fingers, her whole body intent on holding and never letting go. She hung on, not listening or looking till her father pulled her back a little.

"Now stop crying, all of you, or you'll drown me before I've had a good look at you." Her father was smiling but his voice rang strangely.

Kyra laughed and cried, and said over and over, "Father, Father." Behind her apron, nyanya sobbed louder than ever, while Miss Jenkins, red with joy, chattered incessantly and pushed chairs forward and brought glasses of water.

"Father, where's Mother?" Tassia suddenly asked.

Everyone was quiet while their father answered, "You'll go to Mother tomorrow. She's waiting for you. You see, Mother isn't quite well. She has been so worried about you, children, and about me during those months of detention. It exhausted her."

"Oh, why couldn't she have come with you?"

"We didn't know where you were exactly, so it was better for Mother to stay quietly in the country while I found you. Well, here you are, a little pale and thin, but you've been brave girls. Now we'll all be together. Do you remember Russudanna Georgievna? You, Kyra, probably remember her son Tenghis. He came to play with you in Petrograd. About your age. Well, it's at the country place of Russudanna Georgievna and her family that we're going to stay. They've been kind enough to let us rent part of the house."

Vaguely Kyra remembered Russudanna Georgievna, a tall dark widow about whom the maid Masha had once said to nyanya, "She'd flatter and worm her way into the devil's own confidence if there was any profit to be had, but our kindhearted Barinia pities her and showers her with gifts. It's a shame, that's what it is."

"Aren't we ever going home?"

"Maybe some day, but not yet, Kyra."

"All this time I so wanted to go home," Tassia whispered sadly.

Their father pulled the children toward him again.

After a while they sat down to the breakfast table, Miss Jenkins pouring the tea with a proud satisfied air, nyanya hovering behind their father's chair, and the children all of a sudden ecstatically happy, chattering all three at once about Princess Kazbekiani and their dirty dresses and about how their money had come to an end.

6. In Other People's Houses

In the crowded house of Russudanna Georgievna, Kyra seldom found her mother alone. When she did she would fling herself onto the sofa where her mother lay and snuggle against her, pressing her face into the warmth of her mother's shoulder. She kept very still, feeling so much love that often she cried without knowing it till the dampness of her mother's dress under her face made her aware of her trickling tears. Her mother, too, would lie quietly, her arms tightening around Kyra in comfort. If they talked it was about Tenghis' naughtiness or about Russudanna Georgievna and her young brothers Illarion and Levan and old Keto, the grandmother. One must be polite and patient in other people's houses, her mother said.

A few days after their arrival at the country place, just as the sun was beginning to slide behind a mountain, everyone descended into the yard to meet a slowly approaching arba.* Skipping about at her father's side, Kyra wasn't much interested in the homecoming of Tamara, the wife of old Keto's eldest son Nikolai, who was away fighting on the Turkish front. But when she caught sight of the young woman in the arba, she stopped skipping abruptly. Tamara looked exactly as Princess Kazbekiani should have looked. Dark huge eyes shone in a pale face and her hair was black and she was smiling softly. Around her neck was a heavy necklace of amber, and the arba was full of embroidered cushions.

Kyra tugged at Miss Jenkins' elbow. "She's like Princess Kazbekiani, isn't she, isn't she? Tell me, that's the way Princess Kazbekiani looked?"

"Come to think of it, well, they're both dark-eyed like all the Georgians. I did not stay at the Princess' very long and one does not stare at people."

Dazedly, Kyra followed into the house and waited by a closed door, and later on the verandah when Tamara rested in an armchair surrounded by the family, Kyra perched on the balustrade beyond the circle of light cast by the lamp. Old Keto's black figure, swaying in a rocker, occasionally cut Tamara from her view, and with angry impatience Kyra then glared at the sallow face until it receded. Russudanna Georgievna, her fingers hurrying over some sewing, asked questions in her usual shrill, fussy way. Behind Tamara, Illarion and Levan, her brothers-in-law, sat tensely on a bench. Kyra was grateful to them for keeping still, and for somehow, in their dark young manly way, providing a fitting background for Tamara.

---

* Arba: two-wheeled heavy cart drawn by a pair of bullocks, with driver guiding them with a long pole. For short hauls and heaviest work, water buffaloes were used.

In a low voice Tamara answered Russudanna's questions. She told of her pilgrimage to the distant monastery, of her long prayers to St. Nikolas, of how she had crawled on her knees three times around the church and burned many a thick candle at the altar. And the monks, to whom she had brought two fat sheep as an offering, promised her that her husband would return safe from war. Yet, her trip home had been an anxious one. In one of the villages where they had stopped to rest, they had been warned of a band of brigands in the neighborhood. Only a few days previously a rich merchant, Tiflis bound, had been robbed and had staggered naked into the village. Herds of sheep had been driven away and their shepherds slain. But the saints had evidently watched over her.

Fabulous worlds were being opened to Kyra. Slipping down from the verandah, she crept away from the house into the darkness of the orchard. She followed the path farther and farther, walking with head tilted upward, staring into the bottomless black of the Southern sky with the myriads of stars which pierced it without giving any light. The heavy fragrance of the apricot trees closed in on her from either side of the path. Within Kyra something was expanding so hugely that her body seemed too small to hold it all. Then she began to sing, slowly and gloriously, making up the words as she went along.

"Yellow amber and sky as black velvet
silken cushions piled up in the arba
dark monasteries high up in the clouds
old monks who accept offerings of sheep
brigands swooping down like the Persians and Turks
swooping in the blackness of night . . ."

Afterward all the stories she told herself were about Tamara. Kyra knew that Tassia, too, was daydreaming about Tamara. She could tell by the intent, reckless expression on her sister's face when Tassia suddenly paused in the midst of gathering apricots under the trees or when she trotted by on Tenghis' donkey with a twig thrust in the belt of her dress.

One glaring afternoon, in the early fall, the children, their mother, Miss Jenkins, and nyanya went back to Tiflis, to a small apartment in the town house of old Keto. Their father had preceded them. Up the steep street the izvozchik * climbed, just off the main avenue where they had gone walking while living at the hotel, and stopped in front of a sprawling white house with two small, round balconies overhanging the sidewalk and a locust tree leaning against the roof. Their father met them at the front door and led them across the hall into the rooms in the rear. He was smiling and talking in a light, easy way as if, Kyra thought, he was trying to make them believe that everything was as it should be. But Kyra could not imagine that they were really going to live in those rooms with the bare, faded walls and floors on which the paint was peeling off in ugly splotches. They gathered in the larger one and turned about uncertainly. There were a kitchen table, some hard chairs, and, on the window-sill, a small kerosene cooking stove. Their father busied himself with the stove, showing nyanya how to pump it and how to raise the wick. Watching him, everyone was silent; only Miss Jenkins sighed discontentedly as she rubbed the tip of her nose. Kyra crossed the room to the window and pressed her face against the glass. The yellow brightness of the afternoon had vanished; it was graying outside. The window overlooked a broad, low porch with steps leading down into a yard where some children were playing.

Turning, Kyra saw that a kettle had been placed on the primus stove and that her mother was preparing cups and plates. Sad-eyed and sleepy, Tassia and Sonia leaned with their elbows on the table, and for once no one was telling them to sit up straight. Sonia's pink hair ribbon had come untied, the ends dangling down her face, but no one took

* Izvozchik: horse-drawn cab.

notice. Suddenly, wholly disheartened, Kyra cried out, "How long do we have to live here?"

Her father laid his hand on her head. He meant her to understand something, Kyra knew, which he would not put into words. And presently she began to feel comforted. During tea he talked to her as if she were the person who really mattered.

"First of all, we'll cover this table with a handsome oil-cloth. You can help me nail it tomorrow. We'll paint the legs and no one will guess it's just a kitchen table. Then there are two armchairs I've bought; they'll have to be patched a bit. They're red and triangular, you'll like them."

From under the table he told Kyra to drag out the tool box he had built for himself. It was a heavy wooden box with little compartments in which every tool lay neatly.

While the grown-ups were busy settling down, Kyra, Tassia, and Sonia spent most of the day on the porch staring at the other children at play in the yard. Sonia was the first one to venture down. At first she just stood about uncertainly, biting her thumb and frowning. Then, still with a very serious expression in her blue eyes, she started to run with the others. When someone caught her, she gave a little shriek of delight and her face grew rosy and dimpled. Not long after, Tassia too joined in the games when Shamira, a tall, thin, freckled girl with a piercing voice and abrupt movements, called out to ask her if she could skip rope. Tassia had good reason to be flattered, for Shamira was the undisputed leader of the yard.

Kyra hung back from joining the children. Her very first encounter with one of them, a boy who lived across the hall, had been unfortunate. He had come onto the porch with a top which he spun with a piece of string. Till he called out to her, Kyra had paid no attention to him.

"What's your name? Mine's Nika," the boy volunteered. "I might let you play with my top. You haven't any toys, have you?"

"No, thank you," Kyra had answered politely.

"Why not? You've no toys of your own, I know that."
The boy had come right up to her, curious and stubborn.

Kyra had turned red with anger. What if she had no
toys now, what of it? But there wasn't any use telling him
what had happened. He would not believe her.

"Fool!" Kyra said in the excess of her bitterness.

Her father's voice called severely from the open window,
ordering her to apologize to Nika.

"Father, he thinks it's always been like this," Kyra had
tried to explain as she ran to the window, but her father would
not relent. He was bent over a half-finished shoe he held
between his knees, tugging at the heavy twine. He had surprised everyone by becoming a shoemaker's apprentice. Their
mother had once taken the children to see him at work in the
cobbler's shop. They had climbed up rickety steps to a darkish
room which smelled of glue and leather, and there, under a
kerosene lamp, sat their father next to two ragged boys. Uncomfortably, the children had herded in the doorway, not
liking to stare at their father, not knowing how to treat him in
such surroundings. They had never wanted to go back.

By far the most disagreeable were her encounters with
Tenghis. He, together with his whole family, had returned to
town for the start of the school year. He pulled her hair and
twisted her arms, and though Kyra fought back like a wild
beast, being the younger, she got the worse of it. He teased
her relentlessly.

"Sissy, Baby, you don't dare disobey Miss Jenkins!"

"Kyra is a stupid fool. Kyra believes that storks bring
babies!"

"Donkey, Donkey, how do babies get born?"

"I know everything, but I won't tell you. What will you
give me if I tell you?"

But Kyra had nothing to give.

One day he suggested a game to which Kyra agreed
unsuspectingly. They would have a food exchange. Kyra,

Tassia, and even Sonia would have to save the small lump of sugar which they got once a day with their tea and sell it to him for paper money. In their turn they could buy from him all kinds of stuff which was sent down from the country: nuts, dried apricots, raisins, churchhelli,* gouzenaki,† anything the next arba brought.

Even though sugar was a treat nowadays, this was a tempting proposal. When the last arba had arrived in the late autumn after harvest, the girls had watched it being unloaded with rapt anticipation. But afterward no one had offered them any of the marvelous things it had brought. After every meal Tenghis had nibbled something sweet, and all day long old Keto had sat knitting and picking shelled nuts from a round tin box. Whenever his grandmother was not watching, Tenghis grabbed a whole handful. The girls had ached with envy and desire.

The next arba was due before Christmas. For one long month, Kyra and Tassia gave up their sugar, which Tenghis hoarded on top of the bathroom stove and ate at his leisure. Under their mattresses a whole pile of paper money gradually accumulated.

At last, one rainy afternoon, the arba arrived. The gates were flung wide open, and amid much shouting and commotion the clumsy water buffaloes were driven into the yard. Immediately all the children clustered around, Kyra and Tassia among them, skipping about with joy, feeling as if every sack and basket which Levan and Illarion helped to unload and carry upstairs partly belonged to them. Already chewing something, Tenghis stood proudly on the cart and made faces at his less fortunate companions. But what did Kyra and Tassia care! They laughed at Tenghis knowingly, made secret little signs, and Tassia even pushed Shamira when her friend tried to grab Tenghis' leg. They helped Tenghis lead the unhitched buffaloes to where hay was prepared for them, glori-

---

* Churchhelli: a sausage-shaped sweet made of walnuts which are strung and repeatedly dipped in grape juice before the fermentation of the juice.
† Gouzenaki: a sweetmeat of nuts and honey, solidified through cooking.

ously aware every moment that they were not just outsiders this time.

A week went by. Tenghis had given the little girls nothing but a piece of sour khlapi.* Miserably they trailed Tenghis, but he stopped coming into the yard and kept within safe reach of his mother or grandmother. There was nothing left to do but corner him unawares. Kyra and Tassia hid behind the banisters of the front stairs, and when Tenghis came down, whistling and jumping two steps at a time, they confronted him, trying to seem unafraid and casual, Kyra addressing him in a businesslike way.

"Tenghis, you see it's like this. We are going to give Mother some of your gouzenaki for a Christmas present. We have no other present, and it's only three days before Christmas. She loves honey and nuts cooked together. So when are you going to get it for us? Please get it soon."

Sticking his tongue out, Tenghis tried to push Kyra aside but she held fast to the banister.

"Let go, stupid; How can I get into the storeroom when it's always locked. Let go or I'll crack you on the head."

Recklessly Kyra hung on to Tenghis' sleeve.

"You ate our sugar, didn't you? You took it away from us every single day. Now you've got to get the gouzenaki. You promised. You can't break your promise. That's dishonest."

"Oh, Tenghis, don't be so mean." Tassia was almost sobbing.

Pushing Tassia aside and giving Kyra a hard punch which sent her sprawling against the wall, Tenghis escaped out the front door.

All the rest of the day Kyra wandered about senselessly, wrapped in a queer, burning daze of bitterness and hatred. She passed old Keto's room. The door was open and there was no one inside. By the knitting on the table she saw the round tin of shelled nuts. Without thinking, without meaning to, suddenly feeling tingling and hot, Kyra dashed into the

---

* Khlapi: thin sheets of sun-dried tomato paste.

room and grabbed the tin. Her clammy hands slipped, the
nails scratching horridly against the smooth metal lid as she
tried to pull it off. Helpless, furious tears were running down
her cheeks.

"What are you doing in my room?" came old Keto's voice
from the door.

At that moment the lid slipped off and fell to the floor
with a tinkle.

"Stealing nuts, sneaking into my room to steal, you little
thief!"

The old woman's fingers forced Kyra's fists open. They
were empty. Kyra trembled all over, feeling weak and wet and
sick. Gripping her shoulder, Keto pushed her out. Kyra could
not hear Keto's angry words for the hissing in her ears: stealing, sneaking, thief, thief! Holding tightly to the railing, she
groped her way downstairs and into the children's room.
Miss Jenkins, Tassia, and Sonia were sitting around the table
making chains of silver paper for the Christmas tree. In the
next room her father was hammering boards together for a
stand for the tree, and her mother was wrapping parcels in
bright tissue paper. Kyra stopped in the doorway between the
two rooms. The scattered furniture, the bare walls, the busy
voices were both in front and back of her. There was no place
for her to escape to, to hide herself in her shame and misery.

"Oh, dear kind God," Kyra prayed, "help me somehow,
please, God. You know I did not mean to steal. I'm not
really that bad, I really am not. I would never have done it
at home, never. I'll always be good when we go back home,
I promise that. You can do terrible things to me, God, if I
don't keep my word. Only, God, kind, kind God, please let
us go home soon, very soon, I pray you."

7. The Epidemics

"Father, did people get sick in crowds like this when you were young?" Her arms around her knees, Sonia rocked herself sideways, her face very small and white above the crumpled nightgown.

"Not when I was your age, but people always do during an epidemic. Typhus epidemics have happened before, but Spanish influenza is a new phenomenon, at least in Russia. But stop rocking, child, you might upset yourself just when you and Kyra are about to get up."

"Is Russudanna Georgievna going to die from typhus like Shamira's mother?"

"Be quiet, Sonia," Kyra interrupted roughly, seeing her father's face twitch, "you always ask the wrong questions."

"Why are they wrong? Three people are already dead in our house, aren't they? And Misha's brother and Tania's aunt next door. Nyanya told me, so there."

Bent over the shoe he was working on, their father said nothing. Kyra thought she heard crying drifting from the wing of the house where Shamira lived—probably Shamira and Nimrod and their small brothers and sisters crying for the mother who had died yesterday. They had cried all night while a voice had chanted prayers in Assyrian. Down the street an organ was beginning to grind out a tune: "In Petrograd there stood a mansion which had rooms to let . . ." The shrill music grew louder, it was approaching their yard. Now it was at the gate. There was a brief pause, then in the yard the organ resumed its screeching: "When I turned toward the doorway there a sailor stood . . ." A voice was calling down to the organ grinder, admonishing him, "Someone's just died in the house." With a last squeal the organ stopped playing. In the sudden silence Kyra heard the heavy thud of her father's twine.

"Father, before I got this influenza and we used to go walking with Miss Jenkins and we'd meet someone and stop," Kyra began earnestly, "I never knew what to say. I mean if one asked, 'How are your sick?' you know, the way everyone asks. It's only all right really if the sick are getting better, but it's not all right if—because some people then began to cry or they looked so awful that it made me want to run away. Miss Jenkins always asked, 'How are your sick?' "

"Let's hope it won't be necessary to ask that question much longer. I'm almost finishing your shoes, Kyra. They'll be ready for you to try on when you get up. Then I'll start on some for Tassia, then for Sonia." Her father held out the shoe on its wooden frame. "Not bad for a beginner, is it? Just this peculiar protuberance on the right side. Can't imagine how it happened."

Kyra pressed her chin hard against her arm, lifted her feet a little, toes tense, curled back.

"Father, don't you mind at all making shoes?" She did not dare look at her father's face but she could not turn away either, so her eyes attached themselves to his hands, narrow agile hands which were moving neatly, intently about the formless shoe.

"I mean, Father, are you really going to be a shoemaker?" She squeezed her feet together, brought them down stiffly, then lay motionless.

"I'm learning just in case, just in case—whatever happens, I presume people will go on wearing shoes. You, my daughters, must think me old but thirty-seven is not too old to learn something useful." Her father looked up, smiling, and Kyra knew he had ignored on purpose the meaning of her question. She wanted to cry out, she wanted to ask to be forgiven.

"Father, tell us some more about when you were young and had Norka," Sonia was pleading.

One day their mother simply told them that now their father was ill and must have quiet; but they'd overheard nyanya talking, and knew he had typhus like Russudanna Georgievna. They spent whole days playing in the Old Georgian Cemetery because they were being kept as much as possible away from the house. They played with Tenghis and his cousins Maro and Anya and in the evening they had their supper at Maro's and Anya's house, Miss Jenkins bringing along their own bread and milk. One day they were playing Cossacks and Robbers on the high bluff overlooking the muddy Koura River, hiding behind shrubs and rocks and the old monuments. Kyra crawled through the tall grass and joined Maro in a thicket where they lay in wait for the robbers.

"Do you know about your father?" Maro suddenly whispered. "You're my best friend, so I'll tell you, though of course I'm not supposed to. I heard my mother talking about it. About your father, I mean. Your father is raving. That's when people say things that don't mean anything. Your father keeps talking about the Czar and white birches, and he keeps calling some dog. You understand, he doesn't even know he is talking."

Maro pressed her elbow into Kyra's side. "You won't tell anyone I told you, will you?"

"Father is simply calling Norka." Kyra stared bravely back into Maro's inquisitive eyes.

"Was that his dog? Well, he hasn't got it any more, so it doesn't make sense anyway," Maro said resolutely.

When they returned home, Kyra kept close to the door of her father's room till Miss Jenkins told her to get into bed. She heard no sound from beyond the door other than her mother's low voice and nyanya's felt slippers shuffling around. There was the usual strong smell of medicine but the children had grown accustomed to that. It was useless to question

Miss Jenkins, and nyanya hardly left their father's room. In bed and the light out, Kyra lay imagining what it was that her father had raved about. He was remembering Slavnoe, she thought, and the birch grove there and how he went shooting for rabbits and quail. There was nothing to be afraid of, her father was just remembering, the way she sometimes remembered things and pretended they were still true. Maro's mother just did not know about Slavnoe. That was all.

In the morning her mother sent her out to buy ice. She simply put some money in her hand and told her to hurry. It was as if she had suddenly forgotten that Kyra, although aged ten, had never been out in the streets alone, had never entered a shop alone. Disconcerted, Kyra was about to remind her, then swallowed hard and said nothing. At the front door she crossed herself, then dashed down the two streets to the ice yard, blindly and breathlessly, hugging the bag for the ice to her chest. While the stout Armenian counted her money and chopped the ice, she stood shifting from foot to foot and squeezing her clammy hands. But once safely on the way home, she began to calm down. She walked slowly, looking curiously around at the people. They seemed altogether different now that she was in the street alone. That peasant woman in the faded kerchief and man's high boots who walked crookedly under the weight of a bundle on her left shoulder, that woman was unlike any she had seen with Miss Jenkins, she thought.

"Help a stupid old woman, brother," she begged the passersby. "What do I want with this million roubles here, if they can't buy a little box of matches. How can this be, dear folk?"

The ice in the bag had started to melt and drip on Kyra's hands and dress. She crossed to the shady side of the street, then reluctantly quickened her steps. After all, it was wiser not to stay out too long just this first time—there would be many other times to come.

Kyra and Tassia were writing English compositions, describing an imaginary visit to their grandmother who had a big house on a stately street, and who served chocolate tarts with the afternoon tea. Kyra had come to the end of her copybook and her pen scratched against the blue rough cover. Paper was scarce and one had to use up every available inch. Painstakingly, Sonia was reading aloud from the red Primary Reader, the same one that Kyra had had when she was small and which somehow Miss Jenkins had managed to salvage. Someone opened the door and beckoned to Miss Jenkins. Miss Jenkins went out. She hurried back again with a frightened face. They were to go upstairs immediately, immediately, leaving their lessons and the book.

They sat in Russudanna Georgievna's dining room on tall stiff-backed chairs. From the adjoining room a sweetish medicine smell trickled in and sometimes they heard Russudanna Georgievna's delirious voice. People crossed through the dining room, glancing at the children but no one spoke to them. The children did not speak to each other or ask Miss Jenkins any questions. They sat motionless, in a fog, frightened out of any understanding. Sonia's sandal slid off her foot and fell to the floor with a soft little thud. They just stared at it and after a while Sonia climbed down after it with an ashamed smile. Then they went on staring at the wallpaper and the carpet.

Nyanya opened the door. She came in, her face swollen and red and wet, her arms open wide to the children. Suddenly sobbing wildly, they ran to her and clutched at her apron and her hands.

"You poor litle orphans, you unfortunate ones, what's to become of you now?"

Someone said they should be taken to their mother. They ran downstairs and into the room where their mother was. She tried to come forward toward them, away from the people who were holding her, but she could not stand up and she slipped to the floor and the children threw themselves down against her.

PART III

8. Hunger

When the queue moved up and Kyra reached the doorway of the store, she shut *A History of the Ancient World* in mid-page, stuck it under her arm, and raising herself on tiptoe, leaned out to see around the people in front of her. On the shelf behind the counter there were still several huge loaves of bread. Reassured, she fell back into line. The day before Tassia had returned with only five shriveled, soggy potatoes. Step by step she was nearing the counter. Now she could watch every gesture of the man behind it, his eyes judging the size of the hunk in his hands, the rapid fall of the knife, the meticulous weighing, the adding of a sliver or the slicing off of a corner. Which would it be in her case? Anxiously she counted the times that an extra bit had to be added as against those when the bread was handed over in one piece. She was lucky—the man's judgment seemed definitely to be erring on the side of underweight. She would probably get the extra "dovessok." When the moment came at last to show her bread card, Kyra invariably turned warm with suspense. But there was the man already weighing her ration, then adding a slice, the kind Kyra liked best of all, a little triangle of crust.

Though her bites were mere mouse nibbles, and though she had tried to count till thirty between every nibble, Kyra had finished up the dovessok before she left Golovinsky Prospect and turned uphill toward the house. Since her mother's bread ration had been reduced to half a pound a day, the dovessoks too had become disappointingly small. For a while Kyra trudged on resolutely. Then she slowed down. Carefully she unwrapped the towel in which she carried the bread. She stared at the bread. With her fingertips she followed the bumps on its crust, tentatively pressing, pinching, scraping with her nail. It felt good and smelled good. It was still warm. A little piece would break off so easily, almost unnoticeably. Not so unnoticeably though that Tassia and Sonia wouldn't see. Oh, but how she wanted a big fat mouthful of bread. That's what she'd do when her turn came to fetch it next. She would put the whole dovessok at once in her mouth and chew. She'd chew hard and thoroughly, she'd push it around with her tongue, she'd swallow it down all in one lump. Quickly Kyra folded back the towel around the bread, straightened the book under her arm, and started trotting uphill. And to think that tattletale Tassia had almost kept her from taking her turn. Well, she got punished, for now she had to walk to school and back with Kyra instead of her own classmates. The other day Tassia had come upon Kyra slouched on a doorstep, and when she had called and then tugged at her, Kyra wasn't able to answer or to get up. Alarmed, Tassia had told their mother. Yet Kyra felt faint only in the afternoon when there was a twirling in her stomach and a ringing in her head and the lentils or potatoes she had eaten seemed to lump in her chest. In the morning she felt fine for at school they were given tea with brown sugar and a piece of cornbread. Even Sonia went to school for that.

Every Thursday they got plenty to eat, just as much as they could possibly hold. That was when they went to tea at the British Headquarters. When the Germans had been in Tiflis, before the British came, only Nika and Tenghis had profited. They had hung around the barracks and had been given things out of cans to eat, and buttons as souvenirs. Now it was Kyra's, Tassia's, and Sonia's turn, due to Miss Jenkins who had got a job in the canteen and who had told Colonel Smith and Captain Phelps about her pupils. On tall, shiny-coated horses, tall and heavy and shiny themselves, the British officers had come calling unexpectedly one afternoon. They tied their horses to the tree in front of the house and strolled into the yard, talking loudly, spurs jingling. Everyone in the house had run out onto the balconies. Saluting, one of the Englishmen called out a question. Kyra and Tassia came down into the yard and, from a distance, said they spoke English. The officers asked for their mother. Kyra dashed inside while Tassia proudly led them around to the front door entrance. They stayed a long time, and as they left they pulled forth from their pockets chocolate bars and little cans of sweetened milk, then extended the invitation for Thursday afternoons.

By Thursday nyanya had stockings carefully darned, dresses washed and pressed, and the children tried hard to look nice. Eleven-year-old Kyra had grown so much that she had to wear her dress as a tunic over a skirt made over from her mother's. It looked silly and clumsy, and she felt ashamed. To tie her braids she had only pieces of string. Still, there were her shoes, the ones her father had made and of which her sisters were terribly envious. It was splendid to kick aside the homemade rope-soled slippers and to see her feet neat and trim in real shoes with hard soles and heels. Every week Tassia asked her hopefully whether the shoes weren't begin-ning to pinch her toes, but for nothing in the wide world would Kyra have admitted it.

It was a long way across the river to the British Head-quarters, so they started out early, taking turns walking at their mother's side. Since their father's death they did not often get a chance to be together. Now that their mother was teaching at school and giving private lessons in French and German, she usually worked late into the night, correcting copybooks and preparing for the next day's classes. Each time Kyra glanced up sideways as they walked along, she felt a squeezing in her throat; her mother looked so tired and thin in the straight black dress she always wore now. When she smiled at Sonia's chatter, it was only with her mouth, her eyes never changing. It was the eyes that bothered Kyra especially, for they were blue no longer, but a dull gray. Yet she was not more than thirty-five.

At the gate of the British Headquarters, while their mother pulled the heavy clanking bell, the children smoothed their hair, straightened their stockings, and looked each other up and down. The soldier, Frank, grinning in welcome, came to the gate and said, "Nice to see you again," then locked the gate behind them and led the way across the yard. They entered the building through a dark empty hall, went through a room full of crates, then entered the huge center room where stood the table all ready for tea. A square of yellow butter, strawberry jam, a hunk of bright cheese, two plates overflowing with biscuits, a loaf of white bread, sliced and ready to eat were there right in front of them, within sniffing distance, almost within reach. Colonel Smith and Captain Phelps smiled and shook hands and told them how very hot the weather was, not much better than Palestine.

"Let's sit down to tea right away, please Captain Phelps, please, please," Kyra implored silently, fervently.

When nothing happened, fingers squeezed into fists, body rigid, Kyra continued as an incantation, "Please, Captain Phelps, we so want to eat, it makes no difference to you, but we so want to eat."

Tassia's face was puckered and beseeching. As for Sonia, their mother never let go of her hand. Their mother frowned reproachfully, and Kyra tried to keep her eyes on Colonel Smith's moving lips, and tried to smile at the right time during the story he was telling. At last, slowly, they moved toward the table. Kyra moved as in the kind of dream in which legs are numb and, try as one might, one never gets where one wants to. They stopped and stood around the table, Captain Phelps deciding on their places. They sat down and waited. Huge cups of dark tea were placed in front of them by Frank. Cans of condensed milk were passed around. Kyra stared at the slim arched stream of milk as it flowed into her cup, filling it. She drank a little bit off to make place for the sugar. It was real white sugar in lumps. Tassia was watching to see how many lumps she would take. She did not dare take more than one. Then Colonel Smith told them to help themselves to anything they wanted. Just at first it made no difference to Kyra what it was she was eating. Plain bread was really best for it could be swallowed the quickest. It was perfect bread with no straws to catch in one's teeth or gritty sand. It was the softest, smoothest bread imaginable. Colonel Smith handed over the cheese and the butter and the jam. The children took of everything, smiling gratefully, swallowing fast to say "thank you." It seemed unbelievable that here they were eating and eating and there was always more in front of them as if the food would never run out.

With her third cup of tea, Kyra paused between mouthfuls and glanced around. It was truly unfortunate, she thought, that her mother had to talk to the Englishmen and could not concentrate properly upon eating. The Englishmen were shocking; they actually put butter and jam on the very same biscuit. How they would regret it when the supply ran out. Still, if they were that unreasonable, one did not have to feel badly about consuming so much of their good food. Under the table she nudged Tassia who looked up immediately with a smile. Afterward they went on nibbling half-heartedly, feeling stuffed, heavy, rather sick. The Englishmen had straddled their chairs and pulled out their pipes, the sweetish smoke enveloping the children in a drowsiness-laden cloud.

Their mother had told them to obey the Englishmen, and the Englishmen had suggested that they play in the yard after tea. So instead of resting in some cool corner, they wandered out into the hot sunlight. They squatted with their backs against the wall and tried hard not to feel sick. After he was through with the dishes, Frank, who was also the cook, joined them in the yard. It was a peculiar looking yard, with white lines chalked across it. Frank told them that those chalked lines were for games. The idea of the big Englishmen playing in the yard like any small boys made the children giggle. Frank grinned back at them with his long yellow teeth, the furrows in his sunburned face deepening. He kept wagging his head till they grew grave once again. He had two little daughters back in England, he told them.

Going home, they walked slowly and not talking much. Heat rose from the pavement, flies buzzed incessantly and tried to settle on their faces, the streets seemed steeper, more winding than usual. Their mother carried a bundle prepared by Frank and though he had been careful to make it look as little as possible like food, people stopped and turned to stare after them. From every street corner beggar children surged forward, snarling and cursing or pleading humbly, then trailed along tugging at their clothes, claw-like fingers snatching out for the parcel. On either side of their mother, the little girls held tight to its corners, slapping at their pursuers with their free arms.

9. Escape

Hard yellow sunshine filled every space to overflowing: the yard, the steep narrow side street, Golovinsky Prospekt beyond. The mountains looked bare and burned. In the far distance Kazbek glittered like a white jewel. Turning her head from the window, Kyra slipped back into her usual position in the red armchair, cheek pressed against its back, her feet curled under her. Her eyes strayed back to the open book on her lap, Tolstoy's *War and Peace*. She did not want to emerge from its spell. She was reliving Natasha Rostova's rapture as that golden girl waltzed with Prince Andrei at her debut at the glamorous ball. Wonderingly, she reread the sentence: "Na-

tasha was happier than she had ever been in her life. She was
at that height of bliss when one becomes completely kind and
good and does not believe in the possibility of evil, unhappiness and sorrow." How splendid!

She did not want to hear what her sisters were talking
about. She did not want to see them squatting there, side by
side, on the floor. She tried not to heed their repeated re-
minder, "Kyra, Mother told you long ago to go and try to
borrow a little kerosene for tonight," and the reproach in their
voices. She pressed her face farther into the bend of the armchair, tightened her body into a stiff lump, shoulders hunched
up, damp fists clenched. How she hated to get up, it was such
an effort, such torture. Hot waves would begin ebbing in her
head, and things clicked in her knees the moment she stood up.
It was queer how one's body could feel so heavy and foreign
on the outside, and at the same time, sharp and empty inside.
Like a lot of dough with a kitchen knife buried in it. When
they quarreled Tassia would call her "Dough" or "Jello," and
she looked that way too, just the opposite from Tassia and
Sonia who were all skinny except for their swollen stomachs.
How ugly her little sisters were, crouching there with their
shaved heads. Her own hair was to have been shaved off too,
for it fell out and got matted just as badly as theirs, but she
had cried so much that her mother had only cut it short to the
tips of her ears.

Tassia and Sonia in the middle of the floor were breaking
up dog biscuits with a hammer and putting the pieces in a
pan of water to soak. First, carefully so as not to waste anything edible, they scraped off the green and gray mold with
a penknife onto a piece of newspaper. The smallest biscuit
splinters they put into their mouths to suck.

Really and truly, in one more minute she would get up,
Kyra decided. But, oh, why could not they leave her alone?
Just to stay like this in the red armchair forever and ever. She
had placed the armchair right under the window between her
bed and her end of the table so that, without getting up, she
could reach to open the window and her drawer in the table,

and in the evening when the tiny wick lamp left her corner in darkness she could pull herself around into its dim circle of light. It was only that her mother used every pretext to get her to walk about. That sounded like nyanya now, shuffling along the porch. She would sit just a few minutes longer, just long enough to ask nyanya how her bones were getting along.

Nyanya was no longer squat and comfortably soft, but all sharp angles, and she complained that as she walked her bones rubbed against each other—small wonder for whenever Sonia began to whimper and fret, nyanya slipped her some of what little she herself had to eat. Nyanya continually cried and prayed over Sonia, as though, just because she was little, she deserved more food than anyone else. By the way nyanya sighed as she pushed open the door, it was clear that her bones were very much in her way. She stood leaning against the door, her face cupped in her right hand, her left slowly rubbing her hip through the knitted skirt which was hitched up by some string round the waist.

"Sonia, my little angel, will you knead my old bones for me?" Nyanya's eyes were red and watering and she spoke in a whisper.

"Just a second. One more to break up." In a businesslike way Sonia scraped the biscuit, then tossed it over to Tassia to hack. "Hope they give us bread soon instead of those horrid things."

Slowly nyanya lowered herself and lay on the floor, face down. With a conspiratorial wink at Sonia, Tassia pulled off her shoes and, approaching nyanya from the rear so as not to be seen, clambered upon the small of nyanya's back while Sonia stepped up onto nyanya's shoulders. They slid off and climbed on again, struggled to remain upright, then tottered and ducked, knocking into each other, clinging to nyanya's clothes, finally tumbling off, shrieking with laughter.

"Sonechka, Tassenka, just press in with your little feet; don't tumble so."

Conscientiously, Tassia squatted, holding on to the string

at nyanya's waist, then getting her balance, reared herself up and minced away with her feet.

Watching the spindly legs of her sisters in their much-patched drawers and Sonia's eager face as she tried to imitate the mincing, Kyra laughed till she almost wriggled off her chair. Then suddenly, resolutely, she got up. She held on to the edge of the table for a second, wagged her head, and proceeded with dignity to skirt the group on the floor.

"Just like monkeys," she dropped witheringly, to repay Tassia for her earlier taunts, "two skinny monkeys in torn drawers. I'm going for the kerosene now that I'm ready to go."

She tiptoed through the room where her mother sat with a pupil, crossed the front hall, then stopped at the bottom of the staircase. There really wasn't much chance of borrowing from Russudanna Georgievna. Maybe she should try Shamira's family first? In the dazzling sunshine which splashed through the front door panes she stood blinking, weary already. With a guilty little shrug, she turned about, recrossed the hall and slipped into the dark storeroom under the staircase. She felt for matches, struck one, and lit the lamp made of an ink bottle with a wick stuck through the cork. Unwieldy shadows sprang up the walls, fat darting shadows which paused abruptly and fluttered and then lay still. Kyra made her way among piled up boxes and baskets to a green oblong trunk in the corner where the ceiling sloped sharply under the stairs. With hands and knees and head, she uplifted the heavy lid and tugged out an old leather case. She crouched on the trunk, the case between her knees, opening it. Inside were two rows of bottles with tiny round sugar-coated homeopathic pills. Slowly, cherishingly, Kyra pulled out a bottle at a time and ate just two pills out of each one. The day she had first discovered the old medicine chest, in her joy and greed she had chewed up a whole bottle of pills, but afterward she was more cautious. It was piggish of her, of course, eating them up by herself like this. Still if she confided her find to Tassia and Sonia, the bottles would be emptied in no time.

With her back pressed against the wall, Kyra relaxed and sniffed reminiscently. The small storeroom still held a faint smell of chocolate, though the Huntley and Palmer's tin had long been empty and was now used as a stand for the lamp. Those were good days when they had the side of bacon hanging here from a hook in the ceiling and when a little sack of flour had stood in the farthest corner carefully hidden under a blanket. That was when the British contingent had left Tiflis, taking Miss Jenkins with them and discarding perishable foodstuff. Miss Jenkins had cried a lot at the parting, and Kyra was ashamed to remember that she, Tassia, and Sonia had hardly listened to her farewells in their eagerness to get at the food. Well, now Miss Jenkins was probably feasting every day on white bread and butter and sweet condensed milk and corned beef, and all the other wonderful things the Englishmen had had at their Thursday teas. She wished Miss Jenkins well for through their years together she had done her best for them—but that was not what she wished to think about now.

A dreamlike numbness gradually took possession of Kyra. Eyes tightly closed now, she was floating gropingly toward a happy memory, any single happy memory on which she could feast without reservation. Back through the years she glided. She had it! It was the day of her sixth birthday and the proudest day of her life. She might be able to reconstruct every detail if she truly blocked out the present . . .

The afternoon had been snow-darkened, with purple-blue shadows and early blinking lanterns, but in the ballroom, after the heavy curtains had been drawn and the chandeliers lit, it was bright and warm. Kyra sat waiting for her guests in a dress which was all lace over a soft creamy slip with a petaled bow on one side. Her grandmother had sent it to her from Paris. Tentatively, Kyra had scraped a foot against the floor. The ballroom had been prepared for her in just the same way as for a grown-up ball: parquet polishers that morning, thick felt pads attached to their feet, had slid and glided over the great expanse of floor till it shone like a samovar.

Sleigh after sleigh drew up, their runners humming. Solemn, cheeks still pink from the frost, each clutching a birthday present for her, her guests advanced to where Kyra stood at Miss Jenkins' side. To open the presents more easily, Kyra sat down on the floor but Miss Jenkins immediately made her get up. Giggling delightedly, Tassia, unnoticed, hid under the piano with a whole armful of packages Kyra had not managed to reach. Kyra glared down at her sister, made little signs with her hand, but Tassia would not look up. Fortunately, their new baby sister Sonia was too young to attend.

In a small adjoining sitting room an orchestra was playing. Miss Jenkins chose Kyra's first partner for her, a boy in brown velvet with damp curls and damp palms. They danced the pas-de-quatre, the pas-de-grâce, and the polka and the boy in brown velvet stepped on Kyra's toes. A grinning freckled boy in a sailor suit took her by the hand. Kyra noticed his governess had pushed him in her direction. Whenever he got a chance he spun her around, whirling faster and faster, till the floor seemed to be standing on end. "You're not a crybaby," he told her when the music stopped. They played musical chairs and blindman's buff, and all the other games Kyra suggested. Nine-year-old Tania, the daughter of Aunt Lydia, kept running up to her and swinging her by the arms. She had never paid any attention to Kyra before. They played follow the leader, and Kyra was chosen to lead. Sitting in the row of governesses along the wall, Miss Jenkins smiled and nodded approvingly whenever she caught Kyra's eye, and every so often she beckoned her over to straighten the bow in her hair and the bow on her dress. "Isn't she pretty?" one of the governesses exclaimed too loudly. "She's a nice child," Miss Jenkins murmured. Then to the playing of a march, they trooped into the dining room. The candelabras were lit. Instead of the children's table in the bay window, the long table in the center was laid for them. In her mother's place at the head of the table Kyra cut her birthday cake, pink-frosted, round, rising in tiers.

When the children had all gone home, Kyra was called into the library. Coffee was being served. Her father let her have the half-melted sugar lump from his demitasse. Her mother kissed her, asking if she was satisfied with her party. Then she sat in a deep armchair. She sat quite still, wanting neither to chatter or laugh or move. She was acutely conscious of herself sitting there and of all that was around her— of her father who was listening to a hoarse-voiced, white-bearded general and smoothing his own dark moustache, and of her mother in a deep blue velvet dress laughing at something one of Kyra's young aunts was saying, of the dark paneled library with its row of portraits, and even of the clock on the mantelpiece, and the tall silver bucket which was a racing trophy. Blue smoke curled upward and smelled beautiful. She could also smell the black coffee and her mother's perfume. Each thing was distinct, yet they seemed to blend together, they seemed to belong to each other. In some peculiar way she, Kyra, belonged with them too, belonged with the portraits on the wall, with her mother's perfume, with the heavy silver bucket. It wasn't very clear how that could be, yet that was the way she felt deep inside.

A few rooms away the orchestra was still playing. The music had been slow and subdued, then suddenly it paused and broke into the loud challenging chords of a mazurka. Kyra's eldest cousin approached her armchair. He was at the Corps des Pages and wore a uniform embroidered with gold. Bending one knee in front of her armchair, he kissed Kyra's hand as one kisses the hand of a grown-up lady. Solemnly, he said, "I beg the honor of dancing the first mazurka with you at your White Ball."

Smiling dazedly, hesitantly, as though in a dream, Kyra stared at the gold on the uniform, at the bent head, at her own hand which her cousin still held.

Her mother came to her rescue. "You must not forget Dmitri's request, Kyrochka, even though you have long to wait till your sixteenth birthday and your first ball."

Then the spell was broken and Kyra bounced herself in the armchair, laughing and clapping her hands in her joy. She promised Dmitri that she would not forget.

10. The Fall of Tiflis

Sitting on the windowsill in their mother's bedroom, Kyra and Tassia stared out toward the low eastern hills. Sonia knelt between them, her nose squashed against the windowpane, but every time the booming came, she glanced back at her sisters, round-eyed, startled anew. In the dining room their mother's voice was saying good-bye to a pupil, then she opened the door and came in and joined them at the window.

"I'm afraid I will be losing my pupils. Well, we'll get along somehow. Anyway, one can't expect people to study diligently when their minds are on other things. I would be taking money for nothing."

Then their mother stood silently for a while, very close to all three of them, leaning against them with her arms and hands and shoulders. Kyra knew she wanted to speak of important things and was preparing herself, but Tassia could not wait. "Mother, it isn't true, is it, that the Bolsheviks are coming here? Tenghis says that the Georgians won't let them, that they'll fight and fight and chase them away."

"I don't know, Tassenka, and Tenghis does not know. It is natural for the Georgians to want to defend their Republic, for you know how proud they are of their new independence from Russia. But there are others who think differently. No one can foretell what will happen. But whatever happens, I don't want you to be afraid. No one wants to harm little girls like you. I don't like to see you frightened."

"But we're not, of course not!" And at the next cannon thud Sonia stuck out her tongue, while Kyra and Tassia scornfully shrugged their shoulders.

There was a knock at the front door, and kissing them, their mother hurried out to her next pupil.

Everyone in the house was upset and frightened. Old Keto murmured prayers; her hands could scarcely hold her amber beads, so frail and wax-like had her fingers become. Russudanna Georgievna was forever running downstairs to Nika's mother, talking of nothing but her young brothers, Illarion and Levan, who were fighting just beyond the mountains. Nika's mother talked of Nika's father, who was a general and also away fighting. So was the father of Anya and Maro, and every day the girls would be sent over to ask if there had been any news. Russudanna Georgievna became nasty to Kyra's mother because Russians, all Russians were enemies. Russudanna Georgievna's eyelids twitched queerly and her fingers did unnecessary things with bits of paper or the ends of a tablecloth.

Kyra began spending most of the day in the streets. People were talking, arguing, crying. No one noticed her or cared what she was doing, and it made her feel very alone and separate, yet at the same time mixed together with hundreds of other lives.

Each day the mountains echoed with the sounds of guns, the pavements trembled perceptibly, and one could distinguish the dry relentless staccato of rifle fire. At night the red glow of burning villages could be seen beyond the mountains. Regiments of soldiers marched through town. Wounded, clay-smeared men were brought back from the trenches just outside the summer resorts on the road to Tiflis. Tales were told and repeated of what took place after the occupation of a town by the Reds.

Kyra was forbidden to leave the house. But she was no longer content to sit reading in her armchair. She squirmed and fidgeted on the windowsill, jumped out into the yard every moment or so, and stamped about in a fury of restlessness. Finally she sneaked out. The street as usual was flooded with sun. The air was fittingly gentle and scented for an afternoon in early spring. With the gay, fresh sky overhead and this wealth of sunshine, it was difficult to believe that anything was really wrong despite the ceaseless dull thundering. She strolled leisurely up and down the narrow streets, stopping to sniff the fragrance of the bright new buds, watching the patchwork of light and shade thrown down onto the cobblestones by grilled gates and fences and balconies. She hung about the steps of a house in which a classmate lived and shouted her name up a couple of times. Behind a closed window a woman appeared shaking her head, and Kyra wandered on again.

After a while she descended to Golovinsky Prospekt and turned slowly homeward. All of a sudden she became conscious of the glaring emptiness of the wide street. All the streets, in fact, were deserted. There was nothing but the cobblestones and the sidewalk and the straight row of trees and white walls of houses and closed doors. And the quiet. The firing had stopped. Kyra tried to shrug her shoulders, whistle jauntily, but before she could help it, before she had time to reason with herself, terror seeped into her. It clutched at her knees, her stomach, her chest; it held her from head to feet in a sticky grip; it throbbed in her ears. Past blank house after house, across purple shadows cast by the trees, across dazzling spaces of sunlight, she walked on rigidly, not daring to waver her glance. Her heelless soft shoes thudded incredibly, as if they too were in league against her, maliciously trying to attract attention to her unfortunate self. Kyra wanted to kick them off, to creep on barefoot, but she could not bring herself to make the bold motion.

Then she heard other steps, steps which had come from nowhere at all, steps just behind her, close, close to her back. She lurched forward, but her legs would not run. She walked and walked and the steps followed, and it seemed a century that she was walking. Kyra waited to fall and die. Instead, unexpectedly, she stopped abruptly, and in wild despair swung around to face her pursuer. She screamed as the person ran headlong into her. Then, instantly her scream petered out, and weak from relief and shame, still faintly trembling, she tried to grin at the small, shriveled old woman whose eyes stared dazedly into hers. The toothless mouth began moving but no words came. For a moment Kyra felt she was slipping into a bad dream. She shook herself away from it and began to stammer something.

A deafening detonation rocked the street. It made Kyra hop like a sparrow, the old woman's face bobbing in front of her, a crooked white blotch dripping tears. The roar echoed, rolling away. The old woman crossed herself, then again and again in little hurrying crosses as if only their number mattered in keeping evil away. At last she managed to speak.

"Barishnia, dear little Barishnia, don't refuse an old woman, in the goodness of your heart don't refuse your protection. I said to myself, the barishnia won't mind my hiding behind her, in the goodness of her heart she'd shield an old woman. The young have no fear of the devil himself, but an old woman like me is frightened to near death, is frightened out of her wits by those goings on."

Kyra smiled magnanimously and gave her consent to be followed. In a muttering of blessings, they started off again along the dead street. Kyra stalked unconcernedly, swinging her arms and, head high, giving a little devil-may-care whistle every time a volley of shots splintered the stillness, and all the time throwing encouraging, kindly, yet high-spirited glances back over her shoulder.

That night a sudden pealing of church bells woke them. The blackness in the room was like the blackness outside but for the red-orange light over the mountains. The bells went on tolling loudly and urgently, the sound ever swelling as new ones joined in. Then Kyra became aware of a great commotion all around her and also outside in the street. There were shouts and sobbing and men's hoarse voices giving orders, the clanging of hooves against cobblestones, the slamming of doors, the jingle of spurs. Wildly Kyra began calling her mother, and her mother ran in, half-dressed, her hair still in a braid down her back. She told the children that the Georgian troops were retreating, that they had entered the city, the men rushing to their homes to bid their families farewell before retreating farther toward the Black Sea. Illarion and Nika's father were there, and Levan had been brought in, wounded. The children were to dress, but on no account were they to leave the room for they would get hurt in the reigning panic. They were to stay quietly with nyanya.

Nyanya, carrying a candle, had come in behind their mother, and stood weeping in the middle of the room. Sonia was impatient.

"Why do you always have to cry, Nyanya? Look at me, I'm not crying."

Hurriedly Kyra pulled on her skirt, blouse, and shoes and tiptoed through the dining room to squat in front of the keyhole of the door which led to the front hall. She could not see much of anything, but to judge from the sounds, everyone was gathered in the hall. There was Russudanna Georgievna's voice, high-pitched and crazily pleading, and Kyra's mother's voice calmly and patiently repeating some words, and Tenghis was screaming fitfully, now straining his scream to the utmost, now abruptly checking himself only to begin an instant later all over again, and someone seemed to be moaning, and a man's voice was husky and hurried. Then the front door was held open for Kyra could feel the draft, and after a while it was closed and there was the jingling of its keys and chains and the thumping of heavy things pushed against it. The women's voices had become a mere whisper and their footsteps cautious and secret. The staircase creaked weakly, and suddenly there were no more noises either in the house or in the street except for the tolling of bells. Kyra was creeping away from the door when her mother opened it and came in.

Silently, she passed from room to room, stopping nowhere

and she seemed not to hear the children's questions. Then she began to open drawers hurriedly and pulled things out, only to let them fall again. She called to nyanya and Kyra and Tassia. She placed in Kyra's cupped hands the rings off her fingers and the platinum cigarette case which had been their father's, and handed Tassia the case containing the pearl collar which she had not been able to sell. She told nyanya to see if there was coal left in the samovar and, if so, to empty it in the stove to start a small fire. Then she and Kyra and Tassia went down to the yard. In the dark yard women were moving stealthily, carrying things wrapped in handkerchiefs and firearms, digging holes in hidden corners, groping along the pillars and beams which supported the wings of the house, waiting for each other at the cellar entrance. Kyra and Tassia started down the slope to the circus ruins. The Bolsheviks would never find their things buried under the old bricks and boards. But how frightening it was, slipping and skidding in the dark, how much deeper and farther and lonelier than they had imagined it possible.

Afterward they sat in the dining room for it was but a tiny room with one window and that one faced the wall of the neighboring house. Their mother threw papers in the stove and watched every scrap till it was burned. First, she had let Kyra see them, their father's will, the copy of the deed which made Kyra, as eldest, the mistress of Slavnoe, the birth certificates, photographs of her father in different uniforms, letters. The thick cardboard of the photographs would not burn till kerosene had been sprinkled on them.

At last their mother rose from in front of the stove, her face spotted from the fire, and pulled a chair into the far corner. Her eyes turned away, hands pressed together, she sat utterly motionless. No one spoke. Sonia fell asleep against nyanya's shoulder. The small lamp had been placed under the dinner table. The hall door had been bolted and a chest was standing against it, the window shutters were closed. They knew that all about them in the house and in the town people were hiding in the darkest, farthest corners and waiting. The church bells had stopped tolling and the silence was immense.

Dawn came. Through cracks in the shutters one discerned the outlines of the hills. Then against the paling grayness of the sky and the mountain slopes, shapeless gray masses came sliding down. As the sun rose those masses grew more precise, fell apart into figures on foot and on horseback. The men marched briskly, almost at a run; horses dragging machine guns skidded down the steep descent.

Before noon Tiflis was completely occupied by the Red Army.

The searches and arrests took place mostly at night. So did the executions. The children would wake up with a terrified start, instantly sweaty, their hearts thumping, when around midnight came the rumble of heavy wheels over cobblestones in the distance and long, moaning wailing. For a few minutes they would lie very quietly, trying to believe that they were dreaming those sounds, that when the thumping died down in their bodies there would be nothing to hear but the ticking of the clock . . . There was the ticking, hasty, monotonous, safe. Maybe the other was truly a dream this time.

But now the rumble was unmistakable. They thrashed about on their beds, pulling the covers over their heads, postponing the listening. After a while it was no use.

They crept from their beds across the room to the window and pulled the shutters a tiny bit apart. The noise reached them unevenly, breaking off when muffled by buildings, but ever growing in volume.

"It's passed the Cathedral. It's always loud past the Cathedral square."

"And now by Anya's and Maro's house."

"At the bend by the Opera."

They whispered. They knew that others in the house were stirring and listening just as they were. Old Keto would be lying more dead than alive, and Russudanna Georgievna, too —that's what they said about themselves. It was because they feared the night might come when Levan would be driven to the execution field. His wound had kept him from escaping. He stayed hidden in the cellar behind piles of firewood and charcoal. Undoubtedly he, too, was listening. Sooner or later he would be discovered in the cellar with his wounded shoulder. That's what everyone said.

It was so quiet in the house when people were listening. There was nothing but the dry ticking of the clock on the chest and the darkness behind them in the room with the blurred outlines of furniture nearest the window and the narrow stripe of gray moonlight slanting through the shutters left ajar.

As the clanging and thundering of the great motor lorry approached along Golovinsky, the wailing broke up into hoarse shouts, shrill screams, sobbing, and howling. The children stood motionless against each other, the skin of their napes tightening, their eyes unblinkingly fixed on the stretch of avenue visible from the window. It still looked peaceful and familiar. There was still the single dim street light, the row of houses with the jutting balconies, the huge cypress black against a more luminous black, the starry, rounded sky resting on the hills. Then suddenly the roar was upon them. Their window rattled.

First the huge square hood came into view, then soldiers in the driver's seat, then dark figures standing packed tightly, their outstretched arms and bare heads outlined above the chain of soldiers perched on the sides of the truck. The truck advanced heavily, jerkily, swinging round the tramcar rails, blotting out the lantern light for a second. The dark mass of prisoners swayed with every jerk. The soldiers' bayonets glistened. The truck went by. It disappeared from view, headed for a field outside of the town. Only the horrible howling remained hanging in the air.

The children closed the shutter and moved away from the window. They moved slowly and stiffly in the dark, feeling with outstretched hands for the table, the chairs, their beds. They did not speak, each struggling to swallow down the sobs lumped in her throat.

Crouching on her bed, her nails digging into her neck, Kyra prayed frenziedly, "God, all-powerful God, don't let it happen. Save them, save them. Do a miracle." Then again she started to listen. It was just possible that something might happen to save them, just possible that they might escape, that there would not be any shots. God, let them escape this very moment, right at this instant before it's too late. God, do it, do it. Maybe it's happening, maybe they're escaping. Oh God, are you helping them just this once? She listened unmoving, trying to still her trembling.

At the first volley, she threw herself face down, grabbing at the pillow and pressing it over her head. She sobbed till she fell asleep from utter exhaustion.

Perched side by side on the porch railing, Kyra and Tassia stared gloomily into the yard. It was empty except for a crazily scuttling rat who sniffed and poked, then dashed about in circles, reckless with hunger. Half-heartedly Kyra flung a stick in its direction, but the animal only paused for a moment, sitting up on its haunches, its sharp nose still sniffing. Beyond the yard, Golovinsky Prospect also lay deserted. Earlier in the day processions had advanced along it: soldiers and men and women with red banners, marching briskly, beating drums, singing. Tanks had rumbled by and armored cars and shiny clanging field guns. Shouts and cheering had drifted from somewhere. Now that dusk was falling, all was very quiet again.

Through the open window came the sound of Sonia's tearful, exasperated voice. Wearily hunching her shoulders, Kyra frowned and kept still. Tassia called reproachfully, "Sonia, aren't you ashamed of yourself? Such a big girl always whimpering."

"Oh, don't bother with her," Kyra's own voice was exasperated. "What's the use? As if possessed of a devil. Milk,

milk. What next? It's all the fault of that woman yesterday, gloating over what she'd brought back from the country. Hope the old fool chokes on those eggs and milk, chokes and dies! And if Sonia does not stop sniveling, I'll give her a good beating. Do you hear me, Sonia?"

"Just imagine, Kyra," Tassia rocked herself to and fro dreamily, "imagine if we all of a sudden had lots of bread, lots, lots, and also herring and potatoes, just stacks of them. And also a cup of milk for Sonia. But we'd have a whole houseful of bread, so we could eat ourselves as much as we could eat and there would still be enough for everybody in the whole of Tiflis!"

"Well, who wouldn't like that? What I wish we had is heaps of old clothes. People like that woman yesterday, and Russudanna Georgievna—they have trunks of stuff, drapes and tablecloths, and extra skirts and coats. Of course they can wrangle good things from the peasants."

A ragged beggar woman came stumbling into the yard. Kyra glanced at her idly.

"Mother's considering trading her blanket, but it's still chilly at night. Soon it will be warm."

Kyra's glance went back to the beggar woman. Instead of calling out in the usual singsong way of beggars, she just sagged against one of the house pillars. The shawl about her head was slipping. In the gathering dusk Kyra could make out the very white face, the dark eyes turned toward them. Suddenly Kyra screamed. She tumbled down from her perch and screamed as she ran across the yard. It was Tamara.

Doors slammed and people came stamping down the wooden stairs their screams mingling with Kyra's. Tamara was surrounded. Kyra slunk away the moment someone caught hold of Tamara. From the far side of the yard she turned to watch. She still felt the heavy numbness of Tamara's body against her shoulder as she strove to hold it up till her screams brought help. Avoiding another glimpse of that body, she followed the movements of the hustling group. In the deep of her stomach something rolled nastily and the roof of her mouth felt dry and unsmooth. Tassia came to stand beside her, turning her head as if about to say something, but remaining silent after all. Tamara was carried past them up the stairs.

Presently they too crept upstairs to Russudanna Georgievna's apartment. They came across Tenghis. The three of them stood by a closed door and listened to the sobbing inside. Old Keto was crying with a thin whistling sound; she was the most dreadful to hear. Levan's voice, still weak from his wound, was stubbornly insistent. At first they did not hear Tamara.

Tenghis whispered, "I think Uncle Nikolai has been shot."

Standing taut and motionless, the children began to tremble and then, one after another, they slipped to the floor and lay flat on their stomachs. It had become dark in the room but for the sliver of light under the door and the vague beams of a moon which hung somewhere high in the sky. Kyra pressed her hot cheek against the floor. Oh, Tamara, her beautiful fairy-tale Tamara, what had they done to her? It was unbearable that this wretched woman was the lovely, tender, softly smiling Tamara whom she had so worshipped.

Tamara's voice came without warning, hoarse and loud. "They came for us at night, and at dawn he was shot. They drove us on all night, walking and walking. Why couldn't they kill right away? They said they were taking us to Tiflis, that they had orders to take us to Tiflis, but then they finally led us down into this ravine and said this was as far as they'd go and it would be all the same in the end where one was shot. Georgi started to reason, so they shot him first. They had taken Georgi and his old father, and David Amilahvari, the priest from Kaspi, and two peasants from the mill, and still somebody else, I can't remember." Tamara's voice died away for a minute. "Their hands tied behind their backs all the time . . . couldn't do anything . . . strung in a row and then fired upon . . . fell on the rocks and writhed so . . . shot some more to kill. Nikolai fell on his face but he moved, his shoulders moved, and then he lifted his face. I tried to crawl, they hadn't shot at me, thrust me aside . . . couldn't get to him, but he looked my way and he was all twisted. They shot him again at close range . . . they came at me . . ."

Fists against her ears, Kyra rolled on the floor, sobbing weakly. Tenghis sprang up and dashed at the door. It swung open, then closed behind him. Kyra's outflung leg hit against a sharp edge and the shock brought her back to her senses. She tugged at Tassia. They got up together and felt their way downstairs and back to the porch. The moon now hung brightly over the yard, over Golovinsky Prospect beyond. Both the yard and the avenue lay empty.

11. Easter, Holy Easter

Sprawled on her bed, Kyra waited till it was time to go to church. In the next room nyanya was laying the table, the familiar small sounds succeeding each other as she swished open a clean tablecloth, patted it down, arranged the cups and saucers and plates, pulled open a drawer, knocked the bread knife against the wooden bread board. There would be a baba * when they came back from church; a baba of black bread flour to be sure, but tall and round and decorated with a paper nosegay nonetheless, and a brightly colored egg for every one of them. It was nyanya's secret how she got hold of the eggs—her present for Easter. When they came home from midnight service, happy and hungry, they would feast and drink tea and sing "Jesus has risen," and it would be a real Easter despite everything.

* Baba: a traditional Easter cake, decorated and cylinder-shaped.

Kyra's mother stopped in the doorway of the children's room, peering into the semidarkness, then silently went away again. Kyra was careful not to stir, warding off the possibility of a last appeal. Her mother did not want to take the children to church; she had given in only after Kyra had violently pleaded and threatened to run off alone. Now evidently she was still hesitating.

From the street rose ever louder a hubbub of screeching and whistling and catcalls, and from time to time a shot cracked dully. Did she really want to go to church very much? Kyra suddenly wondered. Yes, of course she wanted to go. Nothing would stop her. Shame on those who were frightened. Only a coward would stay home on Easter night.

"Tassia, you do want to go to church, don't you?" Kyra called out challengingly.

"Of course I do." Tassia's voice was sleepy.

A joyous exaltation seized Kyra. She straightened out on the bed, chest high, arms outflung. A minute later she jumped up. She ran to the chest and pulled open her drawer, ransacking it for clean underwear and her least-darned socks. She would mend every little hole before she changed; she would sponge and wash herself all over even though the samovar had gone out and there was no hot water; she would wear only white and be spotless and pure. It was Easter night and she would make herself look as holiday-like as she could.

She lit the lamp, stacking books around it to keep the light from Tassia and Sonia, then cross-legged in her red armchair, she bent low over the needle, trying to darn neatly and evenly, feeling with every stitch more deserving and good. She contemplated hemming the piece of cloth she used for a handkerchief, but decided instead to do without blowing her nose. Lamp in hand, she tiptoed through the dining room, glancing apprehensively at her mother's door. In the storeroom under the stairs which served them as washroom since the pipes froze that winter in the unheated house, she stripped resolutely and crouched in the basin, pouring tumblerfuls down her back and ladling again and again from the big earthen jug. Gooseflesh puckered her skin, a pool was spreading around the basin, but Kyra kept doggedly on till she emptied the jug. She rubbed her knees and elbows till they were as red as an Easter egg. Carefully, so as not to rip them anew, she slipped on the clean bodice and knickers. Then she had an inspiration. In place of a white dress, she would wear her mother's dressing jacket and keep it wrapped around her with the help of pins and a wide belt. There it was, hanging from a hook, so soft and pretty, the very thing for Easter. Kyra reached for it, stepping back to a dry corner of the floor. Clearly her goodness was being rewarded already, otherwise she wouldn't have had such a brilliant idea. It seemed fine on her, it made a splendid dress—maybe a little too short and rather lumpy under the arms, but who'd ever notice that.

Proudly Kyra emerged from the storeroom, certain that her mother couldn't possibly refuse to take her to church now.

"Mother, look at me! I can wear it, can't I? I was washing and it was hanging, and suddenly, just like that, it occurred to me—"

Smiling, her mother made Kyra turn about near the lamp. Tassia, from the door of the children's room, grunted appreciatively and enviously, even nyanya coming up from the kitchen, all ready for church and grave-faced, nodded approvingly. Trying to imitate nyanya's gravity, proper for the occasion, but still elated inside, Kyra began hurrying Tassia and Sonia.

Without descending to Golovinsky where the militant godless paraded noisily with banners and effigies, they followed little dark streets in a roundabout way. At times the shouting and whooping reached them full force, then muffled by buildings, the voices would sink to a confused babble. But it was a beautiful Easter night, full of fragrance and shimmering stars, with a radiant sliver of moon floating over the roof tops. Kyra breathed hard, sniffed, expanded her chest, listened to the cheerful ring of their steps. They caught up with other people hurrying in the same direction. There were whispers, reassuring exclamations. They walked on in a group. Excitedly Kyra smiled up at the earnest faces about her. Then quickly reproving herself, she too began to feel solemn.

From the far end of the street they caught sight of the church. Its steeples rose light and calm above a black tossing, eddying mass through which yellow torches zigzagged and darted. A clamorous din surrounded the church. At first it seemed like a nightmare unexpectedly conjured up, incongruous and unseemly; then its brutality gave it significance—an attack on God was on.

In front of them knots of people had stopped, hesitating. Others were turning back. Kyra was afraid to glance up at her mother. They were walking very slowly now in the middle of the street on the cobblestones, all in a row. Kyra wanted to hurry, to run toward the church, to close her eyes and run through the shouting throng. It was dreadful to be moving slowly to this mob with the torches. They would be late. They wouldn't hear the "Jesus has risen" amid this howling and screeching and drunken snatches of song. They wouldn't see the procession of priests and choirboys going round the church three times bearing the icons and banners and lighted tapers. They would miss everything if her mother did not hurry.

In the glare of the torches she could now see individual figures. She could see those who stood lined up on either side of the gate to the churchyard, the gate through which they would have to pass. In a little while they would go past that man with the outstretched waving arms, and the one who seemed to be stamping about as he jeered and bellowed, and the skinny young boy yelling over and over "Down with your God," and the tall man who was reeling and swinging something over his head. If she could only close her eyes and dash through, dash straight through without once glancing up.

Perhaps if she kept her head bent and never glanced up from the cobblestones right under her feet, she could pretend that all was as it should be and this was really like any other Easter. She could pretend it was like last year, when she was ten, and the very first Easter she was taken to midnight service.

Then she had walked between her father and mother. As they had come down this street her father had called to her, "Kitten, are you walking in your sleep? Better give me your hand." No one called her Kitten any more, but she was the very same as she had been then. If only this very moment someone would call to her "Kitten." Then it would be as if she were walking in her sleep, in the same sleep her father had mentioned.

Glass crashing, glass grinding and ringing as it fell to the pavement jerked Kyra violently back into reality. A stone had hit the heavy panes of a tall window. Her mother had stopped abruptly, pulling the children to her. For a while they stood very still, staring ahead, Sonia frightened and clinging to her mother's dress, Tassia quietly crying, Kyra rigid, fists clenched. Everyone else in the street had paused, too. The dark street, the two blank rows of low houses, the silent people, all seemed to be patiently waiting. It was midnight.

A bell boomed. Joyously every bell in the bell tower tolled and pealed. Jesus had risen from the dead. Voices singing the triumphant words drifted toward them. In the street the knots of people began to sing too, not loudly but with an eager solemnity and the warmth of tears restrained. There was a tickling in Kyra's throat and for a while, when she tried to join in, she could but whisper the words.

Suddenly a shot banged loudly. Others followed, and again there was the crash of glass. They were shooting up at the belfry. For a moment the bells became quiet, then they tolled on, softly at first, then swelling together like a tide. Nyanya came up to their mother, saying through her tears, "Jesus has risen, Barinia, may He bless you and keep you. If I'm not to see you again in this world, pray for me, Barinia, and burn a candle for my sinful soul."

She kissed Kyra, Tassia, and Sonia three times on their cheeks, and also their mother, then, weeping with fear, she went on alone toward the church.

"Mother, I'm going with nyanya, I want to go, please

don't hold me." Kyra was trying to wriggle out of her mother's grasp.

"Let me go, too, let me go." Tassia's voice was equally desperate.

They saw nyanya in her white kerchief approaching the mob at the gate.

"Mother, please, Mother—"

Without letting go of the children, their mother turned and began walking back up the street. She did not speak. At the corner she paused for another glimpse back. But they could not see nyanya anymore. At last their mother said, "Don't cry, Tassenka, and you, Kyra, don't rage so. I know it's hard to bear but you have to bear it. They're just young hooligans, they don't know what they're doing. It's Easter now, you shouldn't be miserable."

Feeling the terrible sadness in her mother, Kyra gave up pleading and, pulling her hand away, walked on obediently. But to herself furiously, senselessly, she kept repeating over and over, "I curse them, I curse them, I curse them," and with every step it seemed she wallowed deeper in her wretchedness and rage. It was a great sin she was committing, she knew it, cursing in hatred and anger on such a holy night, yet she could not stop herself. With her free hand she crumpled and crumpled the white dress she had invented for Easter.

Toward morning nyanya came home unhurt.

Outbursts of shooting continued in the streets. The front door was kept locked and barricaded, and the children were told to stay away from the windows.

In the afternoon Kyra and Tassia were sent upstairs to say good-bye to Tamara who was about to try to escape across the Turkish border and join her parents in Constantinople. They did not want to face Tamara. She had become worse than a stranger, someone of whom they preferred not to think. They lingered on the stairs, sliding down the banisters a couple of times, then crouched listening at the keyhole. From behind Tamara's door no sound came at all. Before knocking, the children argued at length as to which one should enter first, but in the last moment Kyra managed to push Tassia ahead. Already halfway through the door, Tassia pinched her hard in revenge.

Stiffly, eyes glued to their feet, they crossed the room to where Tamara sat, and curtsied without uttering a word. In her confusion Kyra finally whispered, "I hope you have a good trip," but as soon as she'd said it, she began to blush, so utterly embarrassed that she could but shift from foot to foot, and swallow hard. There was nothing she wouldn't give Tassia if only Tassia now would say a few words. Sideways she squinted in her sister's direction, and immediately saw that she could expect no help. Eyes still cast down, Tassia stood as rigid as a stick.

"Shaliko, maybe some chairs." It was Tamara who finally spoke, and though her voice was queerly hollow, Kyra started in relief. They were not after all alone with Tamara. Quickly murmuring, "How do you do?" to the man whom she had not noticed in the semidarkness, she hurried to a chair at the far end of the room. The man, apparently a distant relative, was now speaking in a slow, drawling way about his own worries, and from her corner Kyra could watch and listen safely, and perhaps later sneak away unnoticed. It really wasn't so awful to look at Tamara as long as she avoided catching her glance. Tamara's hands were very white and still against the black dress she was wearing, and though it was warm, she had a heavy shawl around her. Gradually the sharp ache in Kyra began to subside. Her swelling self-assurance made her generous.

"Come and sit with me," she called to Tassia who had remained miserably at Tamara's side. As Shaliko continued his monologue, Kyra nudged Tassia to suggest they leave unobtrusively, but she was stopped short by sudden savage yelling under the window. Then there was a shot and more shots and a another yell, long and agonizing. The sound of it froze Kyra in her half-turned position. The next moment she was scrambling past Tassia and bolting toward the window.

Kyra saw four soldiers standing by the neighboring house, drunkenly swaying and shooting again and again. At first Kyra thought that they were shooting for the mere fun of it. Then, to the right, down the street, she saw a man running.

The running man leaped sideways and thrust his body against a door, then against a yard gate. Then he darted back across the sidewalk. He began zigzagging round the slim trees along its edge. Suddenly he was stumbling. He was down on the pavement, lying all crumpled up. His arms moved, stretched. He started dragging himself forward. Without lifting his head, he dragged himself on to a tree. He sunk behind it. A dark streak remained along the pavement where he had crawled. Now he was trying to rise to his feet, holding on to the tree. He was running. After a few steps he seemed to be almost shuffling along. A little farther, he fell again and Kyra heard a succession of short cracked howls.

Once more the man was lurching forward.

Too frightened to cry out or even to stir, Kyra leaned against the window. Then she became conscious of movement beside her. It was Shaliko hunching and straightening his shoulders, fidgeting with his hands, and muttering. "If I tried to run out and pick him up . . . kill us both. Drunken wretches . . . shoot us both . . ."

Kyra felt sick. She had to close her eyes for a second. When she opened them, she glanced quickly at Shaliko. He had turned toward Tamara and his jaw was moving soundlessly. Tamara was still in her chair, only her hands had changed their position, now tightly clasping each other. Shaliko's voice came again, hoarse and rough.

"The front door is locked and bolted. I wonder where they keep the keys. Where would you keep the key? I'm a stranger in this house, you know."

Kyra was about to shout to him, but before she could she saw his glance fall furtively on the spot by the door where the key was hanging. Instantly he turned aside, his eyes met Kyra's, and she knew by their awful stare that he guessed she had followed his glance. Then his eyes ran on searchingly,

searchingly, and his hands opened box after box on the table.

"It's there, look, it's there," Tassia's voice was thin and squealing.

Kyra caught hold of Tassia's shoulder, pressing her fingers in tightly, then as Tassia went on shrieking and pointing, unheeding the grip, she let her hand fall. She flattened herself against the windowpanes, the sick feeling in her making her see the street as through a thin flowing mist. A little to the left the four soldiers stood as before, not firing, shouting drunkenly as if uncertain what to do next. She shifted her glance down the street where the man had been running and found him sprawled on the sidewalk, half hidden by a tree.

Suddenly there was a violent clanging directly beneath her. The gate of their yard had swung open. Straining to see downward, Kyra caught a glimpse of a dark head and a shoulder stiffly bandaged, and the next instant Levan was dashing down the street.

"Tamara, Tamara, it's our Levan," Kyra screeched. Fists at her throat, she held herself from turning to the soldiers, from seeing them shouldering their rifles again. Levan ran swerving from sidewalk to the cobblestones and back to the sidewalk, and Kyra knew he, too, was expecting shots. Levan was brandishing a cane as he ran, and he never once glanced back.

Shaliko had pushed open the window, leaning out and yelling. Kyra, too, leaned out as far as she could. The man on the sidewalk lay strangely twisted, his head and neck bent far back as if they had been the first to fall while the body was still straining onward. Levan had almost reached the man when the first shot came, and though Kyra had been waiting for it, she started back and screamed in terror. Partly shielded by the tree, Levan bent over the man, raising him a little from the pavement. More shots crashed. A moment longer Levan remained bending, then he put the body down, straightened up and started running back up the street, zigzagging as before.

Kyra dashed out of the room and through other rooms,

knocking blindly into furniture, and down the back stairs into the yard. Levan was standing in the middle of the yard talking to the people who had gathered around him. Levan was talking calmly and he was buttoning his shirt at the neck. Kyra rushed up and stopped, and did not know what to do. She had wanted to kneel in front of him, throw her arms about his legs and thank him, if only wordlessly. But now she felt too shy. Noticing her dash toward him, Levan said, "Don't cry. He's better off dead. Those bullets made a sieve of his body."

Kyra wiped her eyes with the back of her hand. She stood on one leg, then on the other, still wanting to do something and not knowing in the least what to do. As from another world, she heard her mother's voice anxiously calling her name and Tassia's, and then Tassia shouting an answer. At last Kyra, too, shouted back, "I'm here!" impatient to be left in peace. She had stopped thinking of the dead man since Levan said he was better off that way. It was Levan himself standing there talking and half squinting his eyes every time he smiled who had become terribly, terribly important. It was amazing, incredible, that she had not noticed before how important and wonderful he was. She must have been extraordinarily stupid. It was as though she were seeing him for the first time.

Guardedly now, Kyra continued to stare at Levan. She studied him from feet to head, the soft knee-high boots, the dark riding breeches, the white shirt of coarse linen buttoned high at the neck and belted tightly with a narrow strip of leather studded with silver, the very broad shoulders held high and the left one bandaged, the dark face with the broad mouth and the even white teeth, and all the funny little lines around the eyes when he smiled. Levan was so tall that she had to throw her head back to watch his face and the longer she watched it, the more bewildered she grew. Something altogether unusual was happening.

The little knot of people began to break up, but Kyra was quite incapable of taking a step from Levan. As he, too, turned to go his eyes fell again on Kyra. He paused for a second, then laughed, put his good arm around Kyra and lifting her off the ground, ran a few steps with her. He put her down just as suddenly and ran on, up the stairs, three steps at a time. Blushing, Kyra stood where he had left her.

PART IV

12. An Anachronism

Grave events had given birth to the tiny French Lycée in Tiflis. After the revolution, Monsieur Renant, until then an obscure teacher in one of Petrograd's schools, had thought it wise to flee the bloody insanity of a foreign people. Carried by the panic-stricken crowds of refugees which preceded the retreat of the White Army across the whole of Russia, he found himself finally deposited in Tiflis. It did not seem plausible at the time that the Bolsheviks would ever advance as far as Georgia. Moreover, the small country had proudly announced her independence in 1918 and seemed ready to defend it at any cost. Monsieur and Madame Renant stayed on in Tiflis, glad to see the sun once more after the endless grayness of the northern sky, pleased to take part in the edu- cational life of the new republic by opening their Lycée in an old private house with numerous balconies and verandahs and a splendid view of the mountain of St. David.

By the very fact that it was French, Monsieur Renant's Lycée was exclusive. It was attended by upper-class children and those of such foreign merchants and consuls as happened to be in town. For a year Monsieur Renant congratulated himself on the brilliant success of his venture, and then it became apparent that the Bolsheviks were not to be deterred by Georgia's proclaimed sovereignty. The Lycée closed during the short-lived resistance and the bloody months that followed the occupation. But the following fall it reopened discreetly and, occupied with more important matters, the Bolsheviks paid no heed to it for a time.

Kyra leaned against the tail of the grand piano in the corner of the large hall where she had been told the fifth form pupils gathered. It was her first morning at the Lycée Français and she felt timid and lost standing there all by herself amidst chattering, bustling children. A group of tall girls had stopped close by, but they were showing something to one another and talking excitedly, never glancing at her. Another girl ran up to them, curly hair disheveled, black eyes snapping, hands tugging impatiently. Kyra recognized her immediately. It was Princess Lilly Argadze, with whose English governess Miss Jenkins used to be very friendly. Several times Miss Jenkins had taken Kyra and Tassia to have tea with Lilly and her brothers. After a while Lilly caught sight of Kyra and went over to her smiling. She asked about Miss Jenkins and how they had all been during these last years.

Someone was drumming a waltz on the piano, and after Kyra had told how Miss Jenkins had left with the British troops and then become silent, not knowing what more to say, Lilly put an arm on her shoulder and asked if she wanted to dance. Kyra took a step forward; they began turning. Sweat-drenched, Kyra was suddenly aware that she could but fumble with her feet and skid and step on her partner. She had utterly forgotten how to waltz. She tried to mumble this to Lilly, but the others had moved aside for them, the piano was loud, and Lilly kept laboriously turning her round and round. Then Lilly stopped and said something gaily. What it was she said Kyra failed to hear. Face burning, looking at no one, she was making her way back to the piano when she noticed a door opened onto a balcony and ran to take refuge against its iron railing, her back to the hall.

A flock of dainty clouds floated above the roof tops,

rested against the rough dark mass of St. David's mountain. Longingly, Kyra stared at the mountain. How many times on mornings as still and bright as this one nyanya and Tassia and she had climbed the rock-strewn path to the church half-way up the mountain, carrying bottles in which to bring home holy water from its miracle-working spring. Kyra was brought back to reality by the sharp ringing of a bell in the hall. She darted from the balcony. In the hall she saw that everyone was moving, falling into groups, and that each of those, in turn, was straightening itself into a double line. Kyra did not know where she belonged. A side door was thrown open and a round little person with flaming hair and the eyes of a bird appeared, calling in a precise metallic voice, *"Silence, mes enfants!"*

Silence reigned immediately.

"Mettez-vous en pairs."

There was shuffling as the children formed a long double line, every form a little distance away from the next. Kyra found herself pushed into line next to a girl her own height, and though the girl looked pleasant, she pinched her hard when Kyra turned to ask a question. Then the queue stiffened, chanting, *"Bonjour, Monsieur le Directeur,"* as Monsieur Renant entered.

"Bonjour, mes enfants."

To the tune of a march on the piano, the children filed three times around the hall before turning to their respective classrooms.

Kyra sat through the morning in a daze. Her head ached from her efforts to understand what the teachers said. A slim young Frenchman talked loudly and drew incomprehensible diagrams on the blackboard; an elderly bearded one mumbled, rubbing his spectacles, and Kyra realized that she had for-gotten her French just as thoroughly as her dancing. How everyone would despise her when they found that out. She had chosen a bench in the farthest corner and sat hunched up, hoping to go unnoticed and unquestioned. She did not even dare blow her nose, and just sniffled quickly whenever a voice rose loudly enough or chalk screeched against the blackboard.

During recess, when everyone else, laughing and shouting, hustled out of the classroom, Kyra remained in her corner. She could hear incessant stamping of feet, cries of "*à bas les hommes,*" "*à bas les femmes,*" and occasionally a disheveled panting figure rushed momentarily back into the classroom. The strange game progressed all along the wide porch which ran the length of the building. When a noisy group paused in front of the open door Kyra slid forward just in time to see Lilly swinging a textbook at someone, and a thin agile boy darting up, grabbing and holding on to a tall girl's shoulders while she twisted and tugged to set herself free. Suddenly there were rapid warning shouts, "*Attention!*" and as the hubbub subsided immediately, Kyra recognized Madame Renant's metallic voice raised in disapproval.

The girl who had pinched Kyra while they stood in pairs in the hall strolled into the classroom, smiled at Kyra and came up to her desk. Shaking her head, she pointed toward the porch.

"They're always getting in trouble," she said.

"Weren't you playing?" Kyra asked, noticing that the girl's straight hair lay neatly down her back.

"No, I don't like games like that."

"What kind of a game is it?" Kyra asked curiously.

"Oh, girls fighting boys, and forfeits and—you know. Do you like games like that?"

"I don't think so," Kyra murmured, though the game had seemed lots of fun.

"Lisette is the one who punches and kicks the most, and she simply shrieks when she swears. She's half Turkish, half Hungarian, but she swears in French. Eva, Lilly, and Data always start everything, though. Data is that good looking boy who sits just behind Lilly. He's frightfully lazy—he's so lazy that he hits his nose with his fist till it bleeds, and then gets permission to go home. I think that's simply awful, don't you? Someday Monsieur Renant will surely catch him."

"Is he terribly strict, Monsieur Renant?"

"He is, but he's a good man. You know what he did, don't you?"

Kyra shook her head, but the girl hadn't really waited for an answer.

"He sent for food from abroad! Oh, we'd heard about it being on its way, and then that it was detained by the government, but of course no one believed it, and then suddenly it came! Oh, you should have been here. Some of us were called into the hall after classes, and there were bags and boxes and cans all over the floor. I got flour and chocolate and soap. I'm sure you would have been given something. Oh, it's too bad you weren't here. What's your name? Mine's Nina Nandelli. How are you getting along? Tell me if I can help you, won't you?"

Kyra confessed that she hadn't gone to school very much and that she seemed to have forgotten most of what she had known. Well, then she would lend her some notebooks, Nina suggested, and help her with lessons till she got caught up. Would Kyra like to share a desk with her? In her gratitude Kyra could only nod her head vigorously and smile up into the girl's funny round eyes.

When her mother decided to send her to the French Lycée where discipline was strict and scholastic requirements stiffer than in the free Soviet schools, Kyra had not argued. If she had to go to school at all, it made little difference, it seemed to her, where she went. From her mother's point of view, Kyra knew, she was growing up a "solitary little barbarian" and, at thirteen, badly needed supervision and the healthy influence of her peers. Above all, it was Levan from whom her mother was determined to keep her away. But even that did not matter much now that Olga Ivanovna was always snooping about, opening the door of the children's room whenever she knew Levan was there. Once Tassia had even caught her listening at the keyhole. It was dreadful that people could not have an apartment to themselves any longer, shortage of living quarters dumping strangers like Olga Ivanovna amidst you.

One day a man in a military tunic came to measure their rooms. Then they got a notice that they were occupying too much living space, so many cubic feet too many. The very next morning Olga Ivanovna had made her appearance. They learned later she had a nephew in the Housing Commission. A corner of the dining room had been screened off for Olga Ivanovna's bed and trunk, but she seldom remained for long behind her partition. Not that Kyra cared what the woman saw or heard, but Olga Ivanovna seemed to take great delight in hinting afterward to her mother.

It had been the first unpleasant thing between them. Her mother had said that she did not wish Kyra to see Levan alone; that due to shock he was irresponsible and thoughtless, even unbalanced. Shamefacedly and in silence Kyra had listened, remembering that first afternoon when Levan had suddenly entered her room when no one else was around. He had seemed to her in an unusual, strangely gay mood. Laughing and teasing, he had picked her up and bounced her in his arms, then suddenly he had begun to kiss her. He kissed her mouth hard, and she was very frightened. With fists and knees she pushed away from him and he put her down, but forced her to stand in front of him while he said he was a beast and would she forgive him. Wriggling free, Kyra had dashed to hide under the stairs.

For two whole weeks she hid whenever she heard his steps or voice. Then one evening she was playing "Meridians and Parallels" with Tenghis, Tassia, and Shamira on the terrace upstairs. It was a game of Kyra's own invention and she was so engrossed in making Tenghis stay on his meridian and not run out in loops, that at first she did not notice Levan who had pulled a chair into the corner of the terrace. Even though he was staring over the terrace wall and the circus ruins to Golovinsky Prospect beyond, Kyra could not go on playing. She pretended to the others that it was getting too dark to see the lines they had chalked on the floor. Someone suggested hide-and-seek, and Kyra agreed for it meant she could hide any place off the long porch and in the empty kitchen and pantry. It became completely dark and from her hiding place Kyra could see nothing of Levan but the burning end of his cigarette. All at once she could not stand it any longer. Scrambling out, she went quietly back onto the terrace and stopped a little way from Levan.

"Who's that? You, Kyra? Tired of playing?"

"Yes," Kyra muttered stupidly.

Levan began talking of the twinkling lights of the city, and that now that his shoulder had healed he would begin to risk venturing out. Kyra stood saying nothing, even in the dark not daring to turn her head toward him. Then his hand reached out for her.

"Come and sit down; there's room."

Without letting go of the terrace balustrade, she moved in his direction. He made room for her on the chair and she sat leaning against him, his arm about her, his face stroking her hair.

Afterward she was never frightened of him. If he was irresponsible and unbalanced, what difference did it make to her? Her mother said he might do her harm. Thoughtlessly, she had been about to ask, what harm, but stopped herself in time. Bending her hot face even lower, she wished her mother would say nothing more, would stop talking. Grown-ups just did not understand about Levan, didn't know how wonderful he was. That beast of an Olga Ivanovna! If it weren't for her, her mother would never have known, never have been so upset. Though she had wanted terribly to explain, Kyra in her embarrassment had been unable to utter a single word. When her mother, later, broached the subject of the Lycée and the hard work expected of her if she was to get a scholarship, Kyra did not demur. It was the least she could do to make up for Levan.

To arrive at the Lycée Kyra descended to Golovinsky, walked its whole length and then took streets running upward again, for the street which formed a shortcut between her

house and the Lycée was the one on which the Cheka * stood.
And unless she happened to be late for classes, she avoided
going that way because one was apt to hear the screams of
the tortured. From the great Erivansky Square, Kyra turned
and walked along uphill streets, seeing above the houses the
bald brown summit of St. David against the gay morning sky.
Now she could tell if she need run the rest of the way or keep
on strolling leisurely, for groups of school children surged
from around street corners, either dashing breathlessly or
lingering to play or fight. The daily consideration, as far as
Kyra was concerned, was to reach the Lycée hall just as
Madame Renant entered and the column formed to march to
class—not a moment sooner. For once in the presence of
Lilly and her friends, she could not fight off a heavy oppression, a feeling of hopeless inadequacy.

From her place at Nina's side, Kyra observed her classmates diligently, cautiously, her mother's remark that she'd
been growing up like a young barbarian coming back to her
mind again and again. Theirs—currently the senior grade—
was a small class, twelve in all, four of whom were boys.
There were a few with faces pinched and resigned, and shabby
clothes, especially a refugee boy from the north, whose hands
were purplish with chilblains, and a girl as thin and uncertain
in her movements as a toy clown, who would burst into tears
without apparent reason. Madame Renant often sent for her,
evidently out of pity. But the rest seemed light-hearted and
at ease, chattering in groups between classes, staring confidently up into Monsieur Renant's face, answering questions,
laughing at witticisms the teachers occasionally permitted
themselves. Even her new friend Nina, earnest-minded though
she was, giggled when ink got spilled or someone tripped,
though immediately after, she'd shake her head as if in wonder
at her own silliness.

Lilly sat on a front bench and the group around her

* Cheka: abbreviation for Extraordinary Commission (the dreaded secret
police who abused their power through arbitrary arrest, torture, and con-
demnation to death).

was the most difficult to watch, for they wriggled in their seats
and turned around to whisper, and for nothing in the world
would Kyra be caught staring at them. Yet her eyes turned
again and again in their direction. What made them so attractive, she wondered. Their clothes were very different from
hers or even her new friend Nina's—shoes with heels, and
dresses which must have been ordered especially for them!
Kyra studied her own person in her clumsy rope-soled sandals
and gray flannel dress made over from a bathrobe; her mother
had spent several evenings cross-stitching in red around the
neck and cuffs. Still, little velvet-eyed Gayané, daughter of a
Persian consul, wore silk shirtwaists and thin silk stockings,
yet Kyra's gaze seldom turned to her.

Next to Lilly sat Eva; behind them Lisette and the boy
Data. Sprawling carelessly, a mischievous glitter in her black
eyes, Lilly scribbled notes, turned to slip them over to Data,
made faces at Lisette, coaxed Eva to sit forward so that she
could whisper in her ear. Compared with Eva, she certainly
was not pretty with a mouth too large, a nose too broad, but
her sparkling eyes and smile made her disturbingly alluring.
Eva, almost fifteen, was beautiful—tall and self-confident. No
higher form than the fifth existed at the Lycée at the time, so
Eva had to be placed with her juniors. She sat calmly, smiling
occasionally at Lilly's whispered remarks, answering in exquisite French any question that stumped the rest of the class.
Eva's opinion seemed to carry weight with everyone at the
Lycée, from her classmates to Monsieur and Madame Renant.
To Kyra she seemed a being immeasurably wonderful, in-
finitely enticing. Data had large gray eyes in a slender, delicately featured face, and a slow, bored way of talking. Kyra
noticed he seldom bothered to say a word to anyone apart
from Lilly and Eva. Bent over, hands shading his eyes, he sat
through most of the classes, engrossed in a novel. Evidently
Lisette wasn't a fully privileged member of the little group,
for often she raged at being left out of the plans that were
being discussed by Lilly and Eva in Russian. She was a large-
muscled, heavy girl, with frizzled yellow hair over her fore-

head and ears, and a loud voice which she could not control. Whenever she was called upon to recite in class, she stammered and rolled her blue eyes in despair, and invariably sat down in an angry stream of tears. Nina explained to Kyra that Lisette's only claim to the fifth form was her father's threat to take her from the Lycée if she were placed in a lower grade, and that because her father was a rich Turkish merchant, he was one of the few who could pay the whole tuition fee. Lisette's sobs never lasted longer than a few minutes; soon she broke into smiles and gleefully punched a neighbor's back.

It dawned on Kyra that she herself never laughed, that she held her mouth tightly closed, only stretching her lips a bit when she knew that something was supposed to be funny. Neither could she chatter the way most of the others did, just saying anything that came into their heads. But why can't I, she kept asking herself, why can't I? What is so wrong with me?

13. The World Opens Up

At Nina's side, Kyra was busily pasting together links for a paper chain. Though the sale of Christmas trees was forbidden, Monsieur Renant had been promised one from the country in exchange for a skirt of Madame Renant's. They sat at the long table of the Lycée's conference room, a bright lamp overhead, heavy window drapes shutting out the dusk, the clamor of voices and the rustle of paper all around them. Multicolored baskets, brightly painted nuts, stars, and tissue roses lay heaped in the center of the table. Kyra worked diligently, happily, comparing her chain with Nina's, trying to be neat and avoid glue smudges.

The door opened and Eva came in, late as usual. As Eva started to pull off her coat, Kyra noticed that she was burying her nose in its collar to hide a peculiar triumphant smile. Glancing over to where Lilly sat, Kyra saw that she too was aware of that smile. Eva pulled up a chair next to Lilly's and asked in a carefully casual way, *"Et bien, ma gosse, quoi de nouveau?"*

Immediately a chorus of voices rose.

"Eva, have you done *l'exercice de grammaire* for tomorrow? I'm the first to copy it!"

"No, Eva, don't forget you promised I could copy it during Neval's class."

"Eva, how about those cursed trigonometry problems? That was a real inspiration you had, writing the formulas on the back of Maranovsky's chair."

Eva raised her hands to her head.

"Not all at once, my dears, you're swamping me. Why doesn't someone borrow from Alek or Nina, they're just as good."

Gay voices continued to call out all around Kyra.

Eva was bending toward Lilly, and Kyra made out her whisper: "Lilly, *j'ai à te parler, viens.*"

Eva picked up her coat and Lilly followed her out into the corridor. Strain as she might, Kyra could hear nothing but a few stifled exclamations. After a while, Lilly returned alone.

Eyes glued to Lilly's face, humbly, mutely, Kyra implored. Though Lilly took part in the general conversation as before, her cheeks glowed and she fidgeted restlessly. Kyra kept on staring. She could not help herself. She had to know, she had to know. Then, unbelievably, Lilly leaned over in her direction.

"Would you like to walk home with me, Kyra?"

Without another word, they rose from the table, found their coats. Kyra muttered a hasty good-night to Nina. They hurried down the stairs and into the street. The night was warm for Christmas, the air heavy and sweet-smelling. As they turned into a small street, Lilly said abruptly, "Eva has a *rendezvous* with Rezo Garidzé tonight."

Her fingers pinched Kyra's elbow.

"You see, he met her on Golovinsky this afternoon and followed her. She was with Nonna, her elder sister. Nonna stopped to talk to someone, and Rezo went up to Eva and told her she had become very beautiful and grown-up, and that he wanted to see her alone. Then he begged her to meet him at the old cathedral."

"Yes, yes," whispered Kyra.

"Rezo Garidzé himself! You know, he's the most interesting and attractive man left in Tiflis. And he admires our Eva! Maybe he's in love with her. Just think, from now on, when he meets her on Golovinsky—"

Kyra was not listening any longer. Instead, something strange and strong grew in her, expanded, overflowed.

"Oh, Lilly, there are marvelous things in the world! And I want it, I want it so. Oh, just anything!" She pulled herself up, half afraid that Lilly would snicker, herself not at all sure what she had meant.

"Yes, there is everything in the world. Only things are so against us . . . what with our social origin and our mothers' expectations. But I'm going to fight, fight!" Lilly had understood and Kyra's exaltation enveloped her as in a whirlpool.

"Me, too, me too; I'll fight for something too."

They walked a little way in silence. Under a street lamp Kyra saw Lilly's face was grave and tense.

"You know, Kyra, it's like this. I've thought about it a lot. Most things around us are beastly—people shot and exiled and tortured, bread with straw to eat. But those things I cannot help. Well, if I want other things, it's up to me to get them for myself. Nobody else will give them to me, that's clear. Nobody but myself even cares if I get them. Do you understand? I can't prevent the things that happen, but I can make other things happen too. Oh, I've thought so much about it. I've even written poems about taking from life all that one is able. Eva has read my poems, of course, and she agrees. Do you?"

"It's wonderful, wonderful, Lilly. Of course, I agree with you. And I'll do the same thing. How is it that it's never occurred to me before? You know, Lilly, I knew you had a secret. And this is it, I'm sure, it's it."

"Well, good-bye, Kyra, I turn home here. See you to-morrow."

"Good-bye, Lilly."

All next morning Kyra had turned expectantly to Lilly, waiting to be called over, waiting for something to happen. But it was as if the tremendous conversation of the night before had never taken place. Lilly and Eva whispered to-gether and paid no heed to anyone else. When they gathered again in the evening, Lilly and Eva, Lisette and Data sat on the opposite end of the table from her, and in the clamor of voices, Kyra could not even hear what they were talking about. She was so utterly disappointed that she decided that she might as well go home. She began to put away the paper roses she had been working on.

"Do you want to do something with us?" Lilly had ap-proached her from behind and was bending to her ear. "Put on your coat and pretend you're going home, then sneak down the balcony to the third form classroom—it's the very last one down—and be very quiet."

Kyra, filled with joy, could not find a word to whisper back, so she nodded her head and kept on nodding it vigor-ously even after Lilly had slipped out of the room. She pushed her chair back slowly and picked up her coat. Nina got up, too, for they had planned to walk home together. Kyra tried to sound casual.

"I'll meet you downstairs, Nina, I'm hot in my coat," and she dashed out before Nina could stop her. She crept through the dark hall, down the long balcony which almost encircled the building. For a minute, heart thumping, she stood in front of the classroom door, then gently pressed the handle. It was black and silent inside. A whisper came from somewhere.

"Kyra?"

"Yes, yes," Kyra cried out in relief.

"Idiot, Madame Renant will hear."

Kyra crouched in the doorway, listening. Then a match flickered in the classroom, a stump of candle was lit, she was told to come in and close the door.

"Your steps sounded funny, we weren't sure it was you," Lilly explained. "Data, where did you hide that bottle?"

From under a desk Data lifted a bottle, handed it to Lilly who held it to her mouth. Lisette was passing cigarettes around.

"They're Turkish, they're good," she kept repeating in her broken Russian. "They are the best of all that my father has."

Kyra had never smoked before, but she took a cigarette and lit it at the candle just as the others did. Smoke crawled into her nose and eyes and tickled her throat. She tried hard not to cough. It was her turn to drink from the bottle.

Eva and Lilly sprawled on top of a desk, Lilly dangling her legs, hair disheveled, dress unbuttoned too low; Eva casual, amused, talking of her rendezvous with Rezo Garidzé the night before.

"He is not only charming but clever. Meeting at the Cathedral gave him the occasion of recalling an illustrious ancestor, an archbishop who valiantly protested against the uncivil habit of our early feudal princes of selling off unwanted young relatives to the Turks, as well as the young of their vassals of course—the boys for the Sultan's Janissary guard corps, the girls for harems. You see, the Church objected to losing Christian souls to Mahomet."

Then Lilly began telling jokes she had recently heard, most of them incomprehensible to Kyra. Squeezing herself onto the bench that Lisette leaned against, Kyra could still hardly believe in her good fortune—that she was among them, listening, being given wine, joining in their laughter, being hushed together with the rest. There was Eva actually saying to her, "Kyra, bang Data on the head next time he laughs so loud."

Recklessly snatching a copybook from the desk, Kyra waved it about Data's head.

"Stop it, you mosquito, or there'll be a fight."

Kyra blushed and threw the copybook quickly back into the desk.

Moving over, Data leaned against Eva's knees, and Eva played with his hair and stroked his forehead. Lilly and Lisette paid no attention to this, Kyra noticed. With the candlelight full upon it, Data's face was beautiful, and when he lifted his long lashes to look up at Eva, it was a shock to see how gray and immense his eyes were. Still, Kyra wished that Lilly and Eva would stop bothering with such a rude, conceited boy.

"Well, children, it's time to go home." Eva put out her cigarette, lifted Data's head off her knees.

One by one they sneaked out of the classroom, along the balcony, down the stairs.

After the others had turned homeward, Kyra fairly skipped down Golovinsky, chanting to herself in time to her skips.

"Now it's begun, now it's begun, and that's how it's to be and I'm so happy, so very happy, and it'll always be like this."

She laughed and would not allow herself to think—that she would do later in bed. Meanwhile she just wanted to keep on feeling the way she did, all expanded and unreal, like a bright balloon. As she went through the yard and up the steps to her room, she heard the soft tinkling of guitar strings and Levan's voice humming on the terrace above. For a moment she stood still, head back, staring into the round glittering sky. Then softly, lest she wake her sisters, Kyra crept into her room and undressed in the dark, for the first time omitting to go to kiss her mother good night.

Since Christmas was over, and with it the evening gatherings at the Lycée, it had become difficult for Kyra to leave the house after dark. The few times that Eva and Lilly had called for her, she had waited by the window, all ready and anxious, yet pretending to be busily occupied. When she heard their voices at the yard gate, she almost prayed that they would not laugh so loudly and cross the porch with such a clatter of high heels. They would burst into the room as if blown in by the wind, and Kyra would dash to her mother to explain that she had been asked to Lilly's for evening tea. By her mother's look one night, Kyra knew that she had begun to have doubts but could not bring herself to question the truthfulness of her daughter. Even nyanya, sitting on the porch steps, muttered as they passed her on their way out, "Can't that child ever stay home? Running around with those short-skirted and fidgety ones—"

Now dashing along the street toward the prearranged meeting place, Kyra remonstrated briefly with her conscience: what truth can I tell Mother? If I told her we may just wander about the streets or sit on some wall, she surely would not let me go. Well, what am I to do? We have no place to go. Her thoughts leaped to the evening ahead. What would it be this time? The last time they were together it was during recess and they had been playing *"à bas les hommes, à bas les femmes,"* as usual. Kyra had fought at Eva's side, a volume of Victor Hugo in her hands. The boys had been victorious, and while forfeits had been discussed, Kyra, panting, had leaned against the blackboard. When Lilly's laugh rang out defiantly, she moved forward, curious to see whom Data would choose to kiss—Lilly who looked as if she wanted to be kissed, or Eva, lovelier than ever with hair disheveled and sparkling eyes. Data blushed, grinned, then suddenly half swinging around, brushed his mouth against Kyra's cheek.

Stepping back, Kyra had hurled her Victor Hugo straight at him. Would Data still be angry? And, more important, had Eva truly forgiven her? Eva had said, "That was so childish of you, Kyra."

Here she was. There was the single lantern; there was the wall curving into a narrow cobblestoned alleyway.

"Friend or foe?" Lilly called out gaily. "Now that Kyra's here, only Data and Sandro are missing, but they are the most important because they're bringing the wine. Kyra, have you met Ahmet? Lisette, don't push so."

Squeezed in between Dolly and Lisette, Kyra was breathless from happy excitement.

"Data? Sandro?"

"Wait till you see what we bring!"

"I've got good news too, *mes amis!*" Lilly almost squealed in her triumph. "I've made a definite arrangement for tonight. We're expected at Ekka Vashvili's."

"Who is that?"

"Her grandmother is our seamstress; she's always worked for us, and I've always known Ekka. But that's beside the point. The point is Ekka has only a grandmother who will not be home tonight—Ekka will see to that. There're no brothers or sisters snooping around. We'll have the room to ourselves!"

"How about this Ekka herself?"

"She's only too flattered to have us."

"Let's keep to the dark streets. Don't forget we are supposed to be having tea at Data's parents at the other end of town."

Lilly led the way, Ahmet at her side. Sandro's tall figure was always just behind Eva on the narrow sidewalk. Data, his arms laden, walked whistling. Kyra followed Lisette, even though Lisette was shouting some long explanation to Eva and could pay no attention to her. Why don't *I* shout something to Lilly or Data? Why can't *I* think of something to say to them? Kyra prodded herself. I could ask Data if the book had hurt him. As a matter of fact, I really ought to ask. But he's so conceited, he may not even answer me. Still, if he kissed me—of course, that was only because he could not decide between Eva and Lilly. I can't just go on walking like this behind everyone and not saying a word. She ventured. "Lilly, Lilly, did your mother suspect anything about to-night?"

"Oh, Mother always suspects me. Ahmet, do you know how lucky you are to be a boy? I'm sure you don't have to be always inventing stories the way we have to."

Kyra fell back to Lisette's side.

"Here we are. That's her window all lit up."

Lilly rapped on the window. It opened, and a fat girl leaned out over the sill.

"You just wait and I'll bring a candle to the door right away or you might stumble in the hall." Ekka led them along a smelly corridor, cluttered with boxes and cupboards, into a long, low-ceilinged room with a broad couch smothered with embroidered cushions, and a table under a gaudy hanging lamp.

"Ekka, we've brought along wine and other good things. Data, we'll unload you now. You look like a wet-nurse with twins."

Kyra made a gesture of helping Ekka with the glasses but Ekka did not want her to bother. Sandro's brown strong hands were busy with corkscrew and bottles, but he was turned toward Eva. Although he was fifteen, he was almost as tall and broad-shouldered as a grown man, good looking, eyes aglitter with intelligence. Ahmet, on the contrary, sat idly tilted astride a chair. He had limpid, slanting eyes in a lovely olive-skinned face, and spoke softly, lazily, and as purringly as a cat. Lisette, trying to snatch something away from Data, darted about the room with shrieks and giggles until they both tumbled down upon the sofa.

"Is there anything I can do?" Resolutely Kyra walked toward Eva, Lilly, and Sandro.

"Oh, there's nothing; just enjoy yourself. Sandro has taken full charge."

There was nothing left for Kyra to do but to go and sit on the edge of the sofa.

"Has everyone a glass? I'm going to propose the first toast of the evening. To charming inspired Lilly who turned our gathering into a soirée." Glass in hand, Sandro towered over the rest of them.

"I'm suggesting playing Winks to begin with," Eva decreed, adding in French, "We really should go carefully until we are more sure of the discretion of our hostess."

"Kyra, I'm choosing you. All right?" Kyra had not noticed Data at her side. She started, glanced up at him to make sure she had heard correctly, blushed, nodded, and began draining her glass in big quick gulps. They pushed the big table aside.

Data had led her to a chair and stood behind it. When Lilly winked at her and later Sandro, Data's hands grabbed her shoulders and pulled her back in time. When once she had managed to wriggle forward, as the game demanded, and escape Data, he got her back immediately without bothering to wink at anyone else. After that his hands were just above her shoulders, their grasp always in time. But Kyra had no longer any wish to escape.

Incredulous, she heard Lilly exclaim, "Enough of this childish game. Eva, I tell you, it's all right to go on with our party. Ekka is dependable."

They sat around the table and on the wide sofa. Data perched on the arm of Kyra's armchair, but they did not talk or even glance at one another, both listening instead to the banter that went on between Lilly, Eva, and Sandro. Data joined in sometimes, and even Kyra occasionally made a retort. Ekka passed the wine around, filling a glass as soon as it was half empty. She had been asked to sit down with them, but she only beamed and shook her head.

"No, I want a man who'll hurt when he makes love, a man who might tear me to pieces," Lilly's bold cheerful voice proclaimed. "What can be more disgusting than a pink, angelic-looking young man who drops a kiss clumsily somewhere on your eye and leaves a wet spot."

"I think kissing on the mouth with the tongue is disgusting," Data said, and Kyra saw him blush immediately.

"Silly baby. Perhaps Kyra will teach you to think differently."

Kyra went hot all over. Turning her face aside and shielding it with her hands, she gave up all pretense at composure. How could they say things like that? Please, please, let them say nothing more and spoil everything. There was Data, right above her, watching her, maybe smiling. Parting her fingers a little, Kyra squinted up and saw Data sitting straight and motionless, his eyes fixed on some object far away on the opposite wall.

"To Eva, our Circe!" Sandro stood up, raised his glass. "To Eva, the most beautiful, the most intelligent, the most wonderful—" Everyone hurried to touch glasses with Eva.

"To Lisette, blonde Lisette, whom fate brought from afar as a gift to us!" Sandro bowed exaggeratedly low and repeated his toast in French to the accompaniment of Lisette's delighted giggles.

"To Lisette who believes all, understands nothing," Lilly whispered mischievously.

"Que dis-tu là, Lilly?"

"I'm toasting your innocence, *ma petite*."

"Je n'ai rien compris et je m'en fiche."

"To wide-eyed little Kyra!"

"In still waters devils abound." Lilly leaned over and pulled Kyra's hair.

"I hadn't noticed what pretty hair you have," Data whispered.

"To our amiable hostess and her absent grandmother!"

"To Ahmet, whose ancestors refused the joy of wine!"

"To my cousin Data, known as the handsomest schoolboy in town!"

"Sandro, I'll hit you, you swine!"

When later they were playing forfeits and it was Kyra's

turn to go out and wait in the hall, she snatched up the candle Ekka had left burning there and tiptoed to a mirror set in one of the cupboards. He really likes me, Data really likes me. It's too improbable to believe. Kyra had never thought of herself as pretty—on the contrary, as rather plain, taking comfort in the belief that there was "something" about her face that made it look "interesting." Staring in the mirror now, she was overcome by surprise. Instead of the pale pinched little face she was accustomed to with its deep-set, almost sunken eyes and tight mouth, she was gazing at a flushed beaming countenance and eyes that were as shiny as wet pebbles. Wild with delight, she got her face as near as she could to the mirror. Yes, it was her face, and it was pretty! She had never seen herself smiling before!

"Kyra, we called you three times and here—" Data had come to fetch her.

Kyra turned from the mirror with such a happy expectant face that Data stopped short. He stood in front of her staring, smiling, his lips moving without saying anything.

"So, so," Kyra was saying in herself, "let him do it, let him."

Taking a step forward, Data grabbed her shoulders and pressed his mouth against hers.

14. A Grim Sequence

Kyra had just climbed through the window into her room and was beginning to unbutton her blouse in the dark when she heard banging on the front door. She jumped into bed as she was—in skirt and shoes—and pulled the blankets over her face. There were sleepy voices, steps, the noise of the front door chains being removed, then a shrill, unfamiliar boy's voice came from the dining room which was now Olga Ivanovna's room. Letting the blanket drop, Kyra sat up.

". . . And so the soldiers wouldn't let him say good-bye to anyone and they kept rushing him, and one of them pulled all his papers out of the desk and put them in a suitcase to take away. And the doctor was as white as death itself, and his hands shook—I could see from the doorway—and he kept wanting to say something, but he couldn't. It was then they found a picture of you, Olga Ivanovna, in the desk, and the soldiers asked the doctor whose picture it was. When he said he'd forgotten, why, then one soldier hit him on the head with a rifle. It was frightful. After they took him off, my father right away sent me here to tell you." Olga Ivanovna's liaison with the doctor was hardly a secret for he continued his visits after she had installed herself in their dining room.

Olga Ivanovna's loud sobs interrupted the boy and Kyra heard her mother's voice asking questions, calming Olga Ivanovna. Tassia and Sonia had begun to stir in their beds.

"Kyra, are you awake? Is it a search?"

Hurriedly Kyra threw down her shoes and pulled off her skirt.

"Don't call Mother, Sonia; wait a minute, will you? It's not a search. It's only that the doctor has been arrested."

"I want to call Mother, why shouldn't I?" whimpered Sonia.

Olga Ivanovna was making too much noise, however. Olga Ivanovna sounded like a peasant woman at a funeral, exclaiming and lamenting for the whole world to hear.

"Oh Lord, have pity on me," Olga Ivanovna wailed. "What am I, poor unfortunate, to do now? What did they take him for? Gentle as a lamb he was and he meddled in nothing. What could they have invented against him? Nothing wrong did he ever do, I know it, no wrong to anyone. And where did they take him to, where am I to search for him?"

"Oh, I wish she wouldn't scream so," Tassia's own voice had begun to quiver. "He used to be an army doctor, so she really shouldn't be surprised. Kyra, may I come and sit on your bed?"

"All right."

"Will they shoot him?" Sonia shouted from her corner of the room.

"Shut up, Sonia, you mustn't shout such things so loud," Kyra protested.

"But she can't hear me, she's shouting much louder, and I only asked anyway."

"Sonia, you're so—" Tassia stopped, not finding the right word.

"So what? Why can't I ask a simple question?"

"Oh Sonia, keep still!"

"Tassia, stop shivering and shaking the bed. You may stick your feet under the blanket if you want to."

Tassia's cold feet touched Kyra's, drew guiltily away.

"I wish she'd stop that wailing."

"The last time he was over—that was yesterday afternoon," Kyra whispered reminiscently, "he asked me if I'd like a ribbon, a ribbon I could use in my hair. He said he had found a blue ribbon tied around some box and it still looked pretty strong."

"He always asked me how I was getting along in school. Kyra, he had so many gold teeth. Do you think they'll pull his teeth out if they shoot him?"

"They might. Don't think about it."

"I know, but it just keeps going through my mind."

"I hope he had time to find his hat. Funny, how he was always losing his hat. And he's so bald, he's sure to catch cold without it in the middle of the night like this."

Olga Ivanovna was quieting down. Their mother's voice gently and patiently repeated over and over that she should lie down and rest till morning when she could start out on her round of the prisons.

It seemed to Kyra that no sooner had she closed her eyes than voices rose again all around her. Head under the pillow, she tried to tell herself that she was dreaming of frightened voices calling and weeping, but the sound grew and now footsteps were running down the outside staircase. Side by side Tassia and Sonia crept to the windowsill and leaned far out, calling for nyanya.

"Oh, what's happened now?"

"Don't know. Nyanya and everyone's in the yard."

"But, who?"

"It may be the Gossinsky's. There are lights on that floor in the wing. Wait, I'll call again."

After a while nyanya came up on the porch.

"An evil night this is, God protect us! Go to bed, my dear ones, you'll be catching cold. Make the sign of the cross and go back to bed."

"But what happened?"

"It's Pavel Andreevitch Gossinsky," nyanya whispered. "I saw him. As they were carrying him upstairs I got a glimpse of him, all covered with blood he was, torn and bleeding all over."

"But what happened?"

"Well, I don't quite know. It seems he heard someone screaming, some woman screaming, and he ran to help. He's not a strong man, Pavel Andreevitch, the more glory to him. Just down the street it happened, otherwise he'd never have crawled home. It seems a whole band fell upon him."

"Oh!"

"Did his sisters weep! Maria Andreevna, the one who's the schoolteacher, ran down the steps, and when she saw him, down like a rock she went in a dead faint."

"Don't tell any more," Kyra whispered.

After nyanya had got Tassia and Sonia back into bed and had gone away, Kyra lay on her back without moving, without closing her eyes. The house was now silent. With the shutters closed it was pitch black in the room. Kyra stared into this relentless blackness, her hands and feet growing colder, stiffer, stranger to her. It seemed any moment she would stop breathing, she wouldn't dare go on breathing. She felt the way she used to, sometimes, long ago, in Slavnoe, when she was a little girl and afraid of the ghost who walked about at midnight clanking his chains. But then it had been possible to scream, to wake nyanya up, to have nyanya light a candle in front of the icons. A candle could not help now in this horrible dreaded night which contained everything, hid everything, in which every kind of evil thing happened.

Again, terror was holding Kyra's body as in an iron mold.

Then either Tassia or Sonia turned over, sighing and muttering. That helped. Kyra breathed deeply, moved, sat up. She felt for the matches on the chair by her bed. Holding a lighted match, she got out of bed, crept to the table and lit the lamp. Then she went round, locking the shutters of the windows, trying the door to see if it was properly bolted.

Before starting for work their mother asked the children to be particularly considerate of Olga Ivanovna when she came back from her round of the prisons. It was most unlikely that she would obtain any information about the whereabouts of the doctor. Earlier, bringing in the samovar, nyanya had said that Pavel Andreevich was not expected to live through the day.

Outdoors it was gloomy too. It had been raining. Without bothering to wash or replait her hair properly, Kyra took a few gulps of tea, snatched up her schoolbooks, and left the house. Deep mud covered the sidewalks, torrents raced down the steeper streets. In her torn outsize rubbers, Kyra had a hard time picking her way around the biggest puddles and balancing herself precariously on the more prominent cobblestones. When she dropped her volume of Lafontaine's fables into the slush, the last thread of her endurance snapped. To the devil with everything, to the devil with the Lycée. It had started to rain again and she was getting drenched through. No, she wasn't going to the Lycée that morning. She turned homeward.

As she passed by the kitchen basement window, nyanya called to her and she stopped and went in. It was warm in the kitchen for nyanya was roasting acorns on the stove and grinding them for coffee. Drinking tea at the kitchen table sat nyanya's crony, one of "God's folk." Teasingly, Kyra referred to these protégés as "God's little cows" (the Russian for ladybugs) for they did resemble those insects, so humble were they, so pious and self-effacing. At Kyra's entrance the ragged old woman hurriedly put down the saucer from which she had been sipping tea and, sliding from the bench, bowed low.

"Good morning, Barishnia, God be with you, but how wet you are! And I was just having a cup of tea with Ekaterina Vassilievna here; nothing like a cup of hot tea on a day like this."

"Yes, yes, of course, do sit down please, and go on with your tea." Kyra turned away irresolutely.

"Oh, I can stand a bit, it'll do me no harm. Here, you sit down, Barishnia, and warm yourself up a little. You look as if you needed it, if you'll forgive me for saying so. And I'll be on my way in just a minute, I won't get in your way."

Not heeding Kyra's protests, the little old woman hastily pushed aside her cup and saucer. Kyra let herself be led to the bench and let nyanya pull off her wet coat, rubbers, and shoes.

"The Lord be merciful, Kyra, what have you been doing? The state you're in!" Nyanya grumbled anxiously.

"I got drenched on my way to school and I've got such a headache from all that happened last night." Kyra knew nyanya needed no further explanation.

Leaning her cheek against her clasped hands, the "ladybug" stared at Kyra dolefully.

"Those schools and the goings on today are enough to give any poor child a headache and worse. Now, what good can come out of all that learning? And the cruel deeds! In our grandfathers' days they did not bother their heads with such matters, and how much better they lived—in a quiet, seemly, Christianlike manner. They said their prayers morning and night, asking the Lord for guidance, and all was well

with them. And what's the world come to today? The Anti-
Christ himself could not ask for better!"

Nodding her head, nyanya settled down to grinding the
roasted acorns, while the old woman, perching herself at the
far end of the table, upon Kyra's repeated invitation, resumed her tea-drinking.

"Yes, wicked things are going on in the white world.
Wicked, sinful things. The merciful Lord himself can't put
up with our sins any longer."

Glancing cautiously about her, the old woman leaned
toward Kyra and continued in a low, meaningful voice, "I'll
tell you, Barishnia, what I've heard said—I was telling Ekaterina Vassilievna just before you came in. In my pilgrimage
to monasteries and holy places I hear whispers here and there
of what's about to happen. There are signs a-plenty for anyone who has eyes to see. The earthquakes now that are rocking the earth—they say whole villages are destroyed by them.
And in one village, after the earthquake, what do you think
appeared? Red wolves, just as the Bible says. They devoured
the dead and the living, and there was no killing those red
wolves. That's just what the Bible prophesies before the coming of the Anti-Christ, but that's not all. A peasant woman
told me that in their village a calf was born with two heads;
a monster against all God's laws. And people are killing each
other, brother against brother, son against father. It's a certain sign that the Anti-Christ is walking among us and that
the white world will be coming to an end."

"But there've always been bad earthquakes in the Caucasus," Kyra began sensibly, but nyanya interrupted her.

"It's not for you to teach one of God's folk, Kyra. It's
given to them to see more than you do."

"Well, where is the Anti-Christ, then?" In spite of herself, Kyra was impressed.

"There can't be much doubt as to who he is."

Kyra guessed they meant Lenin.

Obviously thinking it wise to change the conversation,
nyanya started talking about Olga Ivanovna and the happen-

ings of the night. She did not like Olga Ivanovna for moving into their apartment.

"I'm sorry for her doctor, all right. He was a polite, well-meaning man. As for her, anything that happens serves her right. The old witch, carrying on like that in front of innocent children. Pushing herself into the home of good people and behaving as though she had no shame."

Snorting scornfully, nyanya got up to have a look at the stove and fetch more hot water for tea.

Head resting on her folded arms, Kyra listened and smiled vaguely, as one half-asleep. It was peaceful and pleasant in the kitchen, and the roasting acorns smelled bittersweet. The crackling and squeaking of the coffee grinder in nyanya's hands was pleasant too. A boy on a donkey trotted into the yard, shouting *"Matzoni* for old clothes," and presently his dark face appeared at the kitchen door and two grimy hands held out an earthen jar of sour milk. Nyanya shook her head at him and the boy disappeared. They could hear the quick patter of donkey's hooves over the cobblestones and the boy's voice chanting *"Matzoni"* growing steadily fainter.

Heavy, leisurely steps were descending from the terrace. Kyra sat up straight, listening. Then she jumped off the bench, snatched up her shoes in front of the stove, jammed her feet into their warm damp stiffness. Nyanya was scolding her, but she paid no attention. She stood by the kitchen door, slowly went up the balcony steps, stood again, as if engrossed in deep thought, before going inside. Once in her red armchair, back turned to the window, she bent over a book and waited. She heard Levan crossing the balcony, approaching her window. Only when he leaned over the windowsill, reaching out for her braids, did she start up in surprise.

"Oh, it's you, Levan!"

"What are you doing home at this hour?" He leaped over the windowsill and took the book from her hands. "And what have you become so engrossed in? Maupassant. You're too young for it. I don't want you to read stuff like that." Flinging the volume under the table, he caught hold of her arms and lifted her out of the armchair.

"Well, tell me, why aren't you in school?" He sat down in her armchair, pulling her onto his knees.

"Oh, I decided it was silly to go to school every day, so I just stayed home to read and to think."

"To think about me?"

"Of course not. Why should I? I did not even know you were home."

"All right. Why should you? Why should you think about me?"

"Is anything—what's the matter, Levan?"

"Nothing. I did not mean anything, little girl." But he looked away from her, and his face was heavy and unsmiling.

"Please, Levan, tell me," Kyra pleaded.

"There's nothing to tell. It's simply—well, it's not very easy——this continual uncertainty, this continual threat. I can be arrested any day or night, at best to be sent off to rot in a Siberian mine. I'm always expecting it, without warning, without even a chance to say good-bye. It's surprising they haven't bothered with me till now. Nikolai is dead, Illarion has disappeared somewhere, I'm the only one left. In the meanwhile there is nothing I can do, absolutely nothing. I should be finishing the University—I only had a semester to go. That's out of the question. I want to work, I should be working, taking care of my mother, and that of course is impossible. There's just not a thing I can do."

Lifting Kyra off his knees, Levan got up, walked the length of the room, came back. He lit a cigarette, leaned against the table, staring at Kyra, but not really talking to her any longer.

"Not a thing to be done. I'm like a hare running in circles with the dogs closing in. And there seems to be no way out. That's the worst of it, not even hope of any way out."

"No, no, Levan, they'll never do anything to you, I know it, I'm sure of it."

Kyra threw herself on Levan, her arms trying to reach

around his neck, her face squeezed against the rough stuff of his shirt.

"Levan, Levan, don't think like that, please think of other things."

"What is there?"

"Of course there are other things. Listen, there's a very beautiful girl I've seen you with on Golovinsky. Her name, I think, is Zina. You were walking arm-in-arm. And you can't help anything by thinking about it."

"Yes, Zina's lovely. She's like her brother. You remember her brother who was killed? We used to be friends in school."

"Well, you see?" Kyra's voice sounded hoarse even to her own ears. To cover it up, she coughed a little.

There were voices on the porch. Kyra moved away from Levan.

"Good-bye, little one." Leaning across the table, he took her hand and kissed it, then walked out of the room.

Back in her armchair she must have been half dozing, for only when books were slammed on the table did she become aware of Tassia and her classmate, Galia. Galia and Tassia were almost inseparable, and people usually remarked on how nice they looked together, Tassia with blonde short pigtails, dimples, long legs, and a boyish smile; Galia dark-curled, feminine, with golden eyes and a soft mouth. Just now they certainly did not look at their best, both very upset, and Tassia red-eyed.

"What's the new trouble at your school, Tassia?" Kyra asked, not really wanting to hear more woes, but concerned despite herself.

"It isn't her fault at all. It's only because Tassia's class president."

Tassia interrupted Galia. "It's not really new, Kyra, it's just another injustice. As you know, ever since the Manual School has been merged with our high school, it's been beastly.

The whole bunch is badly behaved and couldn't care less about learning. But, as class president, I'm expected to keep some order, at least to see to attendance at classes, but how can I? They pay no attention to me or to anyone else, for that matter, but because the grown-ups are helpless, it's always I who get blamed. Today I suppose it was a different matter, and those beastly Manual School children have triumphed now. During recess, to keep our spirits up, we often sang the old song with the refrain:

> "And for our Czar
> Our Faith and Holy Russia
> We give a loud great cheer.

To taunt us, the Manual School children took it up, changing the last line to:

> "We give a loud great sneer.

So then we made up another refrain to sing at them:

> "For the Soviet
> Of commissars and workers
> We give a loud wet sneeze.

No one seemed to take it seriously, not even they themselves. But suddenly today the principal sent for me. And you know what? She forbade us to sing. She said it would get reported to the authorities, and not only would we be expelled, but we'd get our parents into trouble too. Oh, she said it sadly enough and then she added, 'You are only children. It's normal youthful competitiveness,' or something like that. She was upset, but she was firm."

"The mangy dogs." Kyra swore, suddenly seized by a great compassion for her sister.

Nyanya's voice was calling from the porch, "Are you all home? Dinner's ready."

"Sonia's not back. Let us eat anyway, we're hungry."

Though it was Tassia's turn to lay out the plates and

forks and serving spoon, Kyra took it upon herself and went into Olga Ivanovna's room, where the small dinner table still stood. "Galia, if you haven't anything better than beans at home, sit down with us."

The three of them had begun to eat when Sonia ran in, threw her books on the floor and dashed to the table just as she was in her coat. "Oh, it's beans again, and I so want to eat."

"Then why are you so late?"

"We had a lecture about God after classes, that's why I'm late."

"Sonia, did you have to go?"

"They made everyone go. That man told us there is no God and it's all priests' lies, and the Virgin Mary is not the Virgin Mary, but she's something else—bad."

"Sonia, aren't you ashamed of yourself! Why did you listen?"

"We're supposed to listen, or what do we go to school for?"

"Sonia, don't be stubborn, please," Tassia pleaded. "You must get to understand that not all that you're taught is true."

Seeing Galia's disapproval, as well as the distress of her sisters, Sonia relented somewhat. "Well, one girl from the upper form raised her hand and said what he was teaching was wrong, that God was good and above us all, and mockery and insults would change nothing. You should have seen the man's face. And he banged his fist on the table and went on banging until the inkpot and pencils and ledger all fell to the floor. The girl who stuck up for God wanted to leave the room because he was calling her horrid names. He would not let her; he shouted he would break her yet. Brave as she'd been, she was trembling all over. Our class teacher was there, but she didn't interfere and just sat there getting pinker and pinker. Then she burst into tears. It was such a—so now you can see why I was late home." Sonia had begun gulping down the beans, and it seemed that there was nothing more left to be said.

15. Data

When Data called for her that evening, he summoned her out onto the balcony with a new important air. Curious, Kyra hurried out to hear him explain in a whisper that he had brought a friend along who was now sitting waiting on the front doorstep and that this friend of his wanted to meet Eva.

"You'll like Irakli a lot, and so will Eva and Lilly," Data assured her. "You'll probably fight over him. Not that he'll care. You see, he's extraordinarily clever, and older than we are. Don't make him wait. Hurry and ask your mother if you can come with us."

Annoyed, Kyra made Data plead with her quite a long time. As they crossed the yard, she talked loudly and vivaciously and laughed challengingly, the way Lilly did, just to show this Irakli that she, for one, was perfectly satisfied with her present friends. At their approach the boy on the doorstep turned his head, looked Kyra over from head to foot, and started to rise slowly.

"Kyra, please meet my friend, Prince Irakli Georgiani."

"Why were you so long?" the boy asked Kyra, instead of any greeting.

"Because I did not want to come," Kyra answered as offhandedly as she could.

Smiling in a calm, irritating kind of way, the boy looked at Kyra more closely. Kyra stared back. He certainly is not handsome, she thought, that aquiline nose in such a thin face, and those narrow strange eyes.

"Well, let's go," Irakli commanded.

"I don't like your friend at all," Kyra whispered angrily to Data.

Irakli overheard her. "So you dislike me already, and what for?"

"You're rude," Kyra managed to answer haughtily.

Data was tugging at her sleeve. "Kyra, please don't quarrel with him; and Irakli, she's right, you were rather rude. Do be nice, both of you. What's the matter, anyway?"

"We'll be good, Data, don't worry. At least, I'll be nice and I'll overlook Kyra's horridness. Come on, Kyra, let's be friends—Data wants us to."

Still laughing to himself, Irakli took her arm, and afterward, all the way to Eva's house, he was charming and attentive and amiable, teasing Kyra about herself and making her feel important and desirable. When Kyra ran in to persuade Eva to put her hat on and come out for a walk, she described Irakli so enthusiastically that Eva made fun of her.

"Now, Kyra, you're imagining things. He can't be cynical and sarcastic and cruel, and at the same time warm, kind, deep and all the other things you say. And as for his 'beautiful sad soul,' you couldn't have seen much of it walking down Golovinsky. To me he sounds like an arrogant and unpleasant boy."

They went to sit on the balustrade of the old Cathedral, Irakli at Eva's side talking about religious festivals up in the mountains, peasant superstitions, and sacrificial rites and pagan ceremonies inherited from the distant past. Though he was talking only to Eva, Kyra could not even pretend that she was not listening. It started to rain. Eva suggested that they go to Gilda Goldberg's, a new girl at the Lycée that fall.

Kyra had disliked Gilda from the first day she appeared at school, especially her pointedly superior manner, which her looks did not in the least justify. Gilda Goldberg had black locks falling to her shoulders, greasy eyes, the whites of which looked yellow, a bad complexion, and damp hands which she was continually rubbing. Her dress was of silk, though too short and tight for her. By mysterious hints, she immediately gave everyone to understand that her father was not the kind of homemade speculator everybody was more or less these days, but a big man who was in the habit of making big money. She had invited Eva and Lilly and Kyra to stop in at her flat whenever they wished to, and had asked them to be sure to bring some boys along.

Gilda greeted them and then, as Eva and Irakli went to sit on a stiff-backed little sofa apart, she went on with her conversation, turning to Data and Kyra.

"Father and I are looking for a nicer apartment, of course. That is, if we decide to stay in Tiflis. Father's business affairs may call us away any moment. It's only been a month since we left Moscow, and I miss it already. Of course, we really live in Berlin. I'm half German, you know. So please overlook the state our apartment is in: Father is so busy and I'm rather impractical, just artistic, my Berlin friends used to tease me." Gilda gave a self-deprecatory gurgling laugh, pointing to the walls of which every available inch was covered by crookedly hung watercolor sketches.

"My poor efforts," she sighed softly.

Heavily mascaraed women, their faces swept by mauve and blue shadows, their fingers pale and indefinitely long, balancing indefinitely long cigarette holders, alternated with mincing youths, equally pale and blue-lashed, attired in tight black clothes with vicious looking flowers in their button-holes.

"Do they look like that in Germany?" grinned Data.

Without deigning to answer, Gilda turned languorously to Eva and Irakli. "Do tell me, what does one do here for amusement? I've seen no cabarets, no dance halls such as we have in Berlin. Father has been worried that life's rather dull for me in your little town, with all my men friends left behind."

Irakli gave her a vicious squint.

"Well, we arrange parties among ourselves," Eva answered guardedly, "that's the only way there is to get amusement. Just a few persons gather together, for as you've probably learned, there is not much room in which to give parties."

Data was pulling at Kyra. "Let's go in that back room," he whispered. "I've got something for you, something you'll like."

Unwillingly Kyra followed him, but insisted that the door be left open. She was anxious to watch Irakli; she did not want to miss anything he might be talking about.

"Look, Kyra, I've got some apricot brandy for you. It's sweet. Let's have it here alone." And Data put a small bottle into her hands.

"Data, you've stolen it again!"

"No, Kyra. My word of honor. I'll tell you how I got it if you don't believe me. Father was playing cards as usual, and he was winning, so I borrowed some money from the pile in front of him."

"But that's stealing," Kyra insisted. "You just like to steal." Kyra herself had swiped things from the cooperative store—bits of bread, potatoes and apples—but only when she'd been hungry. This was different.

"I did not steal the brandy. I bought that." Data turned such hurt, innocent eyes toward her, that Kyra softened immediately.

"I love sweet brandy."

Suddenly Data threw his arms around her. "But I'd steal anything for you."

Whatever brought this incredibly lucky, indulged, handsome boy to me? Kyra mused, contentedly, feeling almost maternal. Gently she freed herself and skipped laughing around the room. As she skipped past the open door, she glanced into the other room. Eva was listening patiently to Gilda, while Irakli sat back smiling sardonically, his narrow eyes almost closed. All of a sudden he sprang forward, saying loudly and sharply, "As for me, I would not even see another person as long as I live, if I could manage it. I'd have a vineyard and build a hut in the middle of it, and there I would sit."

"Wouldn't you like to have someone with you? Wouldn't it be horrible to be all alone like that?" Eva asked him.

"If anyone came near my hut or my vineyard, I'd shoot

him." Then he got up and pretended to be searching for matches. Kyra went back to Data.

"Irakli is so strange," she said slowly.

Catching her hand, Data pulled her down onto the couch beside him.

"I love you," Data said and blushed, but went on looking at Kyra with shiny embarrassed eyes.

"No, you're in love with me," Kyra corrected firmly.

"Yes, everything. Let me kiss you."

In the semidarkness, Data's face was soft and childish, little shadows slipping back and forth over it. A wave of new tenderness made Kyra shiver. He's mine, he's mine now, she repeated to herself proudly and contentedly. He's in love with me and he promised to do anything for me.

"I like you so much, Data, when you look like this."

"Like what?"

"Sort of warm and nice, not the way you usually are. You know, I did not like you at all at first, so aloof and conceited."

That she had been afraid of him and his arrogance, Kyra would not admit even now. Data smiled reminiscently.

By turn they took sips of the apricot brandy. In the next room some discussion or argument was going on, Eva's calm voice and Gilda's excited exclamations interrupting something which Irakli was trying to prove. Irakli's voice had become polite and matter-of-fact, but there was a ring to it that worried Kyra for some reason.

"Data, how is it we've never met Irakli before and that you've never even mentioned his name?"

"In the last year or more I have not seen him much. But Sandro and I have know him ever since we were children. Now he mostly avoids people. He has been through hell, black hell, and things are still very bad for him."

"Tell me."

"Well, he's the only one left, all the grown-up men in his family were killed. He's living with his mother and sisters in the cellar of their former house. I've been there; it's always

completely dark. And they have nothing. They were robbed of
every little thing. There's never any food either. I don't know
how Irakli gets by. He's devilishly proud, he'll never say anything. They must always be on the point of starving to death,
all of them. I don't even know what Irakli does."

Data was silent for a long while, his face frowning,
turned away. When he spoke again his voice was unrecogniz-
able. "The old prince, his father, and his two grown-up brothers
were shot right in front of him, right in the same room where
his mother and he and his sisters were hiding. Alla—that's his
younger sister—ran out of her corner and ran toward the
soldiers, so one of them hit her with his rifle across the face
and now she's almost blind."

They stared into opposite corners of the room. Somewhere a clock struck. The voices in the outer room had
quietened too. Data picked the bottle from the floor, but only
looked at it and put it down again. Then Eva appeared in the
doorway.

"It's time we left; you two have certainly not been much
help this evening," she murmured reproachfully.

Irakli went with Eva; Data saw Kyra home.

16. Irakli

Curled up in her red armchair, Kyra was daydreaming. At the
opposite end of the table, thumbs in her ears, Sonia leaned
over a book, from time to time muttering to herself and casting
angry glances at Tassia's friends by the piano. (The upright had been left to them by a family which fled the Bolsheviks.) Earlier in the evening she had had a quarrel with
Tassia about the noise and the piano playing, and Tassia had

told her to go off to their mother's room if she wanted to study. Now, stubbornly and proudly, Sonia was demonstrating how her sisters "ruined" her life. Elza, Tassia's classmate, was playing soulfully, tenderly, a perfect background for Kyra's thoughts.

Kyra and Eva and Lilly had seen Irakli once again. Instead of going to the Lycée they had gone walking in the Botanical Gardens and the Moslem cemetery beyond. Irakli had taken them there. The cemetery, mostly in ruins, was white and beautiful hiding on the hillside. Yet it was a strange place for them as was the whole eastern sector of Tiflis with its tiny yellow streets and stone steps running precipitously in all directions, low flat-roofed dwellings, walled yards, and precariously jutting balconies. Some streets seemed deserted but for the occasional dark figure of a veiled woman; others seemed a bright bedlam of merchants and donkeys and buffalo carts. From the high rocky bank of the Koura, the old fortress Metekhi—now a prison—faced them, with its forbidding blank walls and its squat, crenellated turrets.

Irakli had seemed gay, and Lilly had never left his side. Afterward Lilly said to Eva, "I don't know how it happened, Eva, but I'm in love with Irakli. I'm desperately, overwhelmingly in love. What am I to do?"

"You can have him then, my poor girl," Eva answered.

Kyra, too, had fallen in love with Irakli, though no one knew about it.

Now Elza began playing an étude of Scriabin and Kyra closed her eyes. If Irakli were here listening to the music . . . Irakli had a way of looking at you as if he understood everything there was to understand. But when he smiled, it was so bitterly that it hurt to watch him. If only there was something she could do for him. If he had that hut in the middle of a vineyard, she would creep to his doorstep in the darkest hour of the night and leave him a basket of food. She would slave all day long in the fields and buy him the food. He would never know where it came from till one moonlit night he would see a shadow moving among the vines and then he would shoot, for hadn't he promised to shoot anyone who entered his vineyard? He would wound her, and when next morning he walked in his vineyard, he'd come across her, dying.

Nyanya threw open the door and thumped through the room with the samovar in preparation for tea. A few moments later Kyra's mother looked in. She made a sign to Elza not to interrupt her playing, and sat down in Sonia's chair. Smiling blissfully, Sonia climbed onto her knees. As usual, their mother looked tired, but Kyra saw that she was happy in finding all her three daughters at home and occupied so peacefully.

"Just so long as Sonia doesn't start complaining about her quarrel with Tassia." Kyra was full of sudden concern for her mother.

When Elza stopped playing, and they all went into the other room to have tea, Kyra lingered behind. Hearing a knock on the window, she turned, blinked and, unable to believe her eyes, saw Irakli leaning against the windowsill. She dashed out of the room and around to the porch. Irakli came forward toward her.

"You seem upset at seeing me. I thought we decided to be friends."

"Yes, yes. I just did not expect you."

"Of course not. And I'm sorry if I interrupted. As a matter of fact, I heard music a moment ago, so I waited."

"No, really, it's all right. And everyone is having tea now. Will you come in and have some tea?"

"I came with a request. Sandro and I want to commemorate an anniversary. But I won't mention that again, nor should you. Anyway, Sandro has gone ahead to that exotic classmate of yours, Gilda by name, if I am right, to arrange about gathering there. Will you come? We'll stop on the way for Eva and Lilly, and of course Data."

Of course she would come. Breathlessly, she ran back to tell her mother that she was being invited to a classmate's for tea, and then to the nook under the stairs to change into her velvet-paneled green dress.

Never had Golovinsky Prospect seemed so enchanting nor the walk so short. To add to Kyra's bliss, they passed Levan standing with a group of men in front of the Georgian Club. Levan saluted and Kyra nodded negligently and gracefully, just the way Eva nodded, and then she overheard one of Levan's friends ask, "Who is that with Irakli Georgiani?"

Never before had Levan's friends noticed her. She had been just a schoolgirl with hair still in braids. She would have dearly liked to turn and walk once more past the Georgian Club. But instead she tried hard to keep an aloof, disinterested air.

Leaving Irakli to wait, she dashed to Lilly's and was met by her mother who explained that Lilly had just run upstairs to borrow some sugar, and asked Kyra to make herself at home.

"But I'm not staying," Kyra murmured. "I've come to get Lilly to—"

"Now listen, child," Princess Argadze interrupted. "Lilly must have told you that I have forbidden her to go out. I found some poems which she left lying around, and I won't have her doing the crazy things she seems intent on. I'm not questioning your plans for this evening, they're probably harmless. That's quite beside the point, so there is no use pleading with me. Now, if you want to change your plans and spend the evening here, I'll be delighted to have you. Otherwise, you better run along without seeing Lilly. It will only make her more unhappy."

Lilly had, in fact, told them that very morning about her misfortune, but in her joy at Irakli's coming, Kyra had forgotten all about it. Head bowed, she moved toward the door.

"I'm sorry, Kyra. It's not your fault of course. Come again soon and spend the evening here with Lilly."

Upset and indignant, Kyra hurried on to Eva's, but a

few streets away. Eva would surely find a way to get around Lilly's mother: she always managed things. She found Eva lying on her bed reading, her two sisters and her brother playing cards in the same room.

"Eva, Eva, an awful thing has happened!"

"What is it, Kyra? Mother and Father are in the other room, so you'll have to whisper it here."

Eva's brother shrugged his shoulders contemptuously. "Don't imagine we're interested. She can shout her woes for all we care."

Nestling close to Eva, Kyra breathlessly related all about Irakli and the proposed gathering at Gilda's, and her encounter with Princess Argadze. But Eva shook her head.

"Nothing can be done. When Princess Argadze gets into that state about Lilly, it's hopeless. She always gets over it pretty quickly, but in the meanwhile it's best not to irritate her."

"You're coming, Eva? You must, anyway, you must."

"I can't, Kyra, how would Lilly feel? She's frightfully in love with Irakli and I'll do everything in my power to help her. As yet he's not particularly interested in her, but give her time."

Kyra was not listening. "Oh Eva, please, please."

"It's no use, darling. Be reasonable. Tell the boys it's off for tonight. You can tell Irakli I'm in bed, or that we have guests, or anything you like, except the truth."

Doing her best to hide her bitterness, Kyra kissed Eva, and ran out. They were letting Irakli down just when he needed them, when he needed companionship in order to overcome some great pain. They did not deserve his bothering with any of them again.

Irakli took the news calmly, suggesting that they stop at Gilda's to let Sandro know of the failure of the plan.

In the reddish semidarkness of her flat, they found Gilda reclining on a couch, Sandro at her side. There were flowers in a black vase, and an array of high-stemmed goblets on a mauve tablecloth, as well as some bottles already uncorked. After all the preparations she'd made, Gilda declared, she would not stand for their leaving immediately. It would be too unspeakably dreary for her to be left alone just now. Overruling Irakli's protests, she slid to the front door, locked it and hid the key in her garter. Then she made her way back to the couch and Sandro, and all one could hear were gurgling laughs and sighs.

Shrugging his shoulders, Irakli sat down and poured himself some vodka while Kyra wandered up and down the room like an unhappy animal.

"Stop looking so put upon." Irakli spoke to her crossly. "I won't fish for that key in her garter, so resign yourself to your captivity. Come over here and stop running around."

Without looking at Irakli, she sat down on the very edge of the hard-backed little sofa, lit a cigarette, and drank some wine. She knew Irakli was watching her. She put out her cigarette, locked her fingers together and tried to fight this thing off which was engulfing her. But when Irakli stretched his arm and put it on her shoulder, she leaned against it, eyes closed, smothering a moan. He pulled her over closer and took her in his arms.

How she loved him, God, how she loved him! If he'd only let her, she'd do anything for him. She'd give her whole life up to him. She'd tell him how much she loved him, even more, that she felt like kneeling in front of him, worshiping him for his suffering. Let him do anything he wanted with her if it would make him just a little happier.

All Irakli did was to kiss her eyes, whispering to himself in Georgian, and smiling sometimes in a gentle lonely way. Kyra lay in his arms without word or movement.

Without any warning he suddenly pushed her away, and jumping up, stalked over to Gilda.

"Enough of this nonsense. Give me that key. We are going."

His tone was such that Gilda sat up immediately and pulled the key from her garter.

Utterly bewildered, Kyra followed Irakli out. At first

she did not dare break the silence, but when she could stand it no longer, she slipped her hand timidly under his arm, looking up at him with a hesitant smile.

"Irakli, I wanted to tell you before, I love you." She whispered it so softly under her breath that she was not sure he had heard her.

Abruptly stopping, he faced her with anger. "Why are you looking at me like that? There's absolutely nothing for you or anyone else to be happy about. Your head is full of nonsense. You should be ashamed instead of smiling at me like a lamb."

"What have I done wrong, Irakli?"

"Wrong, wrong—you and your friends have not even learned the meaning of right and wrong. You don't know what you're doing. Just a herd of little lambs skipping thoughtlessly this way and that. Into men's arms, into drunkenness, toward anything that is easy and pleasant. What have I done wrong? What have you ever done that is not wrong? If you had an iota of intelligence you'd understand."

As if defending herself, Kyra lifted her hands to her face.

"You and your wonderful friends." Irakli's voice rose to a shout. "I could murder all of you, cut your soft throats. Useless, uncomprehending, full of your own little importance, your little ideas, your insipid little desires and vices—you're despicable."

Irakli's mouth twitched; his face was fierce with loathing. As Kyra stood and trembled, it semed to her that the whole earth was turning in circles about her. The boy's voice, furious and desperate, hit at her head like a mallet. Then the voice broke off, and she heard his heavy breathing. Neither of them moved.

"Don't stand there. Come on," Irakli shouted again.

They walked on. Trees rustled and threw black shadows on the sidewalk, shiny and wet from a recent brief shower. All was as before.

"What are you good for? What are you going to grow

up into? Why, you're a child, you're only half-formed. Your thin arms and shoulders, your childish breasts. Sooner or later some cad will take advantage of you. What do you expect? Just to go on painlessly flitting around? You're so foolishly vulnerable and trusting. In our life it's madness to be like that. I could have done anything I wanted with you. Isn't that true? Answer me."

He waited, but Kyra did not answer.

"Now you're ashamed, you're probably ready to cry. So much the better. You're not really rotten, I know. You're only living up to other people's ideas. Be proud; be yourself; be strict with yourself, won't you?"

"I don't want to, and I won't," Kyra managed to whisper.

"Why won't you, you poor silly girl?" Irakli spoke unexpectedly softly.

"What's the good of being strict with oneself? What for? Who cares?"

"You, yourself, should care. And I, for one, don't like to watch you twisting yourself out of shape like this."

They reached Kyra's front door and stood on the step, Irakli talking in a lowered voice.

"It's all so unnecessary and stupid. How old are you? Fifteen? Tell me, for example, how many men have kissed you in the last six months? I suppose you'll have to begin counting on your fingers."

"Oh, what difference does it make whether it's six or five—and now you."

"And now, me." He took her hand. "Kyra, I know you care for me, so for my sake, if not for yours, give up all this nonsense. Don't have anything to do with anyone till you're more grown-up. Promise me."

He now bent over her hand and kissed it several times.

"And you?" Kyra whispered.

"I'll never even try to see you again."

For a long while Kyra stared at Irakli, at his thin face with its tight mouth and its expression of sadness and resolution. She touched his hair, then immediately let her hand drop.

"No, I won't promise anything to you. I can't, do you see, I can't."

She turned away to hide her distorted face and then, knowing she would begin sobbing in a moment, ran indoors without saying good-bye.

When next morning, weary and miserable, Kyra made her way through the crowd of children in the Lycée hall, she heard Gilda's voice cheerfully relating something. A nauseating wave rolled through her body, yet she could do nothing but approach steadily. Already Lilly's and Eva's eyes were upon her. She could make out Gilda's words.

"Oh, you really should have been with us. Both Kyra and I had a thrilling time, a perfectly thrilling time. There she is now. Kyra, how did you enjoy yourself with Irakli last night?" Eva's and Lilly's eyes never left her face. She stopped, her legs suddenly stiff and heavier than stone, while her head felt as if breezes were blowing through it.

"Why did you do this, Kyra?" Eva asked quietly.

Kyra moved her head helplessly, but did not speak.

"What you did is unfair and dishonorable. I see we were mistaken in you."

Eva turned her back and walked away with Lilly.

The continued existence of the Lycée Français was miraculous. Its exclusiveness, its formal, old-fashioned methods and polite ways were an anachronism under the Soviets. There had long been apprehension and rumors among teachers and pupils alike, and yet when the blow came, it was without warning. One morning a large notice was posted on the front door announcing the closing of the school for its catering to "the offspring of the enemies of the people." Most of the children gathered in the great hall, nevertheless. As usual, at a quarter to nine, the doors of the Chancellery were thrown open and Madame Renant appeared, saying in her precise voice, *Bonjour, mes enfants.*

"*Mettez-vous en pairs,*" came the familiar command, and the boys and girls ranged themselves two by two, each form a little distance from the others.

Then Monsieur le Directeur 'came in to the pupils' chanting of good morning. Instead of the music and marching, however, Monsieur Renant began to speak. His voice was steady, but the children noticed that his hands shook and that somehow he had grown slighter and grayer overnight. He said only a few words—how sorry he was that he was forced to close the Lycée, and that he hoped his pupils would be happy in other schools. His eyes moved along the column of children, then, going up to the upperclassmen, he shook hands with each of them, made a bow to the rest, and walked very quickly out of the hall.

The Renants had been ordered to leave the country within twenty-four hours. That evening a small group of the older students gathered at the station to see them off for Batoum, the port on the Black Sea. Police officials were shouting orders and rummaging in the luggage. Then the couple was led off to be searched. Monsieur Renant was only allowed to wave to his pupils from a distance.

Glumly they walked away from the station, Eva and Lilly as usual ahead of the others. Kyra trailed far behind with Nina and Lisette. Lisette was doubly unhappy. Her father's store had been requisitioned, and he and Mrs. Najaf-Sedik had received orders to be ready for deportation at a moment's notice. Neither Eva nor Lilly nor Data had said a word to her since the episode with Irakli.

They crossed the bridge over the Koura and, as they trudged up the steep hill toward the center of town, Eva and Lilly paused. When Kyra reached them, they unexpectedly linked arms with her from either side.

"Let's be good friends again, Kyra, and hold on to one another. We want you, we miss you." Kyra could only nod and stare tremulously into their faces, not risking uttering a word. They understood, as she knew they would. Eva sighed, "If only we had been allowed to finish our schooling together, but now each one of us must enroll in a different neighborhood high school. I dread it."

"You know, this is the utter end of something for us, or at least a shifting of emphasis," Eva said presently. "Up to now there's been an awful lot of make-believe in our lives. From now on there may be no escape from facing a pretty painful reality."

They pressed each other's arms tightly as if offering comfort in advance.

PART V

17. Her Sixteenth Birthday

Kyra got through reciting the battle scene of Pushkin's "Poltava" and, remembering no further, launched herself into Lermontov's "Demon." She lay on her back, her pillow squeezed in her arms, her eyes closed. Well, here I am, Kyra said to herself, pretty near two hours of poetry, and here I am where I started. Awake. Earlier that night she had written in her diary: "Tomorrow, January 12, 1923, is my sixteenth birthday, the day I was to have my White Ball." Sensibly she had decided to stop at the bare statement and go to bed. Her attempt at good sense had not been rewarded, she was unable to sleep. Now she lay still, waiting, and almost immediately the horrid sense of unreality which she had been fighting off took possession of her again. Tomorrow is my sixteenth birthday. It would have been the day of my White Ball. Am I the same Kyra or am I not? The question came back. Am I still the same Kyra as that child before the Revolution whom everyone so confidently expected to see dancing in her first long grown-up dress in a glittering ballroom? Is it still me? Where did I stop being the earlier Kyra? How did it happen? Kyra moved her head slightly, set her teeth into her knuckles. If I have to think, I must think clearly, she admonished herself. Then she had a revelation. It happened when I forgot to think I was that Kyra and began to accept this—this of the new life. When? Not when we first came to Tiflis, not even when we first came to this house, not even when Father died. I was still that Kyra then. It must have happened unnoticeably. But how could it have happened without my raging and struggling, fighting, or, for that matter, crying? Just as if it had never occurred to me that things might have been otherwise. God, it was peculiar how things happened and went on happening, and one could do nothing about it. Or, could I have done something? Could I have done anything to change anything from how it is now with me? I never thought about that. If I had any choice to make, I just did not know it. Is this, then, my life? Can it be mine and meant for me, or is it somehow a mistake? Kyra scowled and squeezed her fists tighter. Now I must not get muddled up—I seem to be muddled up. Is it possible that this is my life and not a—a what? Oh, some kind of a loop or knot or semicircle, before returning to my own real life? That's what I've been counting on—I did not know it because I never thought about it—but of course that is what I've been counting on. I'd then be the same as that first Kyra. I'd be her. But where is my real life? God, what is happening to me, what is happening? Here I am, and tomorrow is my sixteenth birthday. It's as if I'm walking along a road, on the road and way as it went in nyanya's story: "Ivan Czarevitch went on the road and way, going whither his eyes gazed; it may be far, it may be near, it may be high, it may be low. The tale is soon told, but the deed is not soon done. He came at last to an open field where three roads crossed, and as he stood at the crossroad considering which road to take—" God, there it is, that's what it is. I'm on a road with no crossroads.

Kyra turned over, lay for a moment on her back, arms outflung, then sat up in bed. Pulling up her knees, she hugged them tightly, rocked herself a little. Suddenly she threw back the bedclothes and swung herself out of bed. She felt her way around the red armchair, climbed onto the windowsill, pulled open the shutter and the window. It had rained for days, but it had stopped now, and there was a dim moon. The cool damp night struck Kyra's face and body, making her shiver. She tightened herself into a ball, warming her toes with her hands. Wavy, wispy clouds were gliding by monotonously, covering and uncovering the moon. Below the streets were wrapped in dreary mist with but a few watery lights visible. Just back of the nearest street lantern a black silhouette of a cypress tree projected itself sadly. As Kyra gazed, her mind gradually gave up its whirling and struggling. I am I, she said to herself wearily, and whatever is happening to me is happening to me in my life, and if that's not true—she dismissed further thought. Instead she began composing a poem about a silly young girl. It began and ended with the refrain:

> That we are born for happiness
> Who could have told you that?

When she got back into bed and finally fell asleep, she had a short, terrible dream. She sat at one end of a crowded room, on a chair, all by herself. People kept passing her but avoided glancing in her direction, ignoring her on purpose. Still she had to stay on in the room. Suddenly she knew something was about to happen. People had stopped moving and talking. The room itself seemed to have lengthened and become peculiarly light with a white light which came from nowhere at all. A very wide door on the opposite end of the room started to open. Now, everyone except Kyra was pressing back against the walls, watching, fearful. Without surprise, aware suddenly that she had expected him all along, Kyra saw her cousin in his uniform of the Corps des Pages coming in through the door, then gliding gracefully across the floor toward her. He looked completely unchanged since the evening of her sixth birthday; the gold on his uniform glittered as it had then, and he smiled at her in the old way. As he reached her, he said reproachfully, "You promised to dance the mazurka with me tonight, don't you remember?" Music was floating in the air, now it became thunderingly loud and challenging, and Kyra recognized the mazurka which had been played when her cousin had first asked for the dance. Joy, sudden and intense, filled her. "Of course, I remember, I was waiting for you," she said and gave him her hand. As he bent over to kiss it, she saw a wide bleeding wound behind his left ear.

In freezing terror, Kyra woke up.

The following morning was like any other day except that nyanya went to church at sunrise and brought back a slice of holy bread wrapped in a clean handkerchief. Crossing herself Kyra ate it the proper way, palm open to catch any crumbs and before she had sullied her mouth with other food. Tassia and Sonia wished her happy birthday. Her mother's present to her was a cameo pendant which a pupil had given in payment for lessons. Also they were to have fresh butter and ham for dinner. Unfortunately a compulsory political lecture followed by a meeting were scheduled at the school where her mother now taught, making it impossible for her to be present at Kyra's birthday dinner.

It had rained all day and it was still raining when Kyra left the house in the late afternoon. She had no special place to go and thought vaguely that she might stop in at Lilly's or Eva's or call on Nina Nandelli. But she did not really feel like seeing them. Aimlessly she wandered in the gray streets, glad of the wind and the rain which she had to battle. It grew dark and she still trudged on, tired by now but unable to decide what to do with herself. Turning a corner, she ran straight into someone and was about to hurry on without lifting her eyes, when she was grabbed by the arm. It was Masha, a girl in her class at the Soviet school which Kyra had recently begun to attend. Masha was a member of the Comsomol,* energetic and cheerful, and her speech still resembled a peasant's. Something about Kyra's face must have made her curious for, peering down and without loosening her grip, she started to ask questions. Where was Kyra going on a rainy night like this? What weighty problem was on her mind

* Comsomol: Young Communist League.

that she bumped into people and failed to recognize a class-mate? When instead of answering Kyra smiled helplessly, Masha gave her arm a tug.

"Just as I thought, well now, it's just as I thought." She laughed good-naturedly. "You're in a state about something or other, aren't you? I can see for myself, darkness or no darkness. Listen here, you know I rather like you. Maybe I shouldn't say so, your being a bourgeois offspring, maybe I shouldn't bother with you. But look, why don't you come along with me? We'll cheer you up. I'm on my way to a gathering. Now don't shake your head. We won't hurt you. Maybe you'll like us when you get acquainted. Come on, let's hurry before we turn into drowned rats."

Kyra felt so bleak and sorrowful that she allowed her-self to be led. Masha hurried her down the street, through a yard, up a flight of rickety stairs. As they mounted the stairs a hubbub of voices grew louder. Masha left her waiting on the landing and felt her way down a corridor, pushed open a door. When light spilled out into the corridor, Masha yelled, "Come on, comrade, now you can watch out for the baskets and trash they keep piled up here. Ought to be reported to the house committee before someone breaks his neck. Just lack of social consciousness."

Kyra groped her way to the door and followed Masha in. The narrow room was gray with smoke and so crowded that Masha slapped shoulders right and left in order to gain passage. Kyra clung on to her and as they moved through Masha shouted introductions. In the farthest corner stood a table with bottles and plates. Pulling off her coat, Masha thrust it under the table, and Kyra followed her example. Then they each picked a square of herring off the dish on the table and ate it between slabs of black bread.

"Better give our feet a rest while there's room to sit down." Masha shoved Kyra toward a dilapidated sofa. A man in a leather jacket, his shirt open low at the neck, made room for them and then got up to get them some vodka. Kyra took a gulp and, tears in her eyes, began to choke. She had never drunk vodka before and this was homemade and raw. Masha pounded her back till she could breathe again. She took another swallow the way Masha told her to, just tossing it down the throat. She ate more herring and thick slices of pickled cucumbers and obediently she accepted another glass of vodka. The heavy tobacco smoke singed her eyes, dull insistent drums started beating against her ears. Someone was now singing a Comsomol song, the entire roomful uproariously repeating the refrain. Red faces, red kerchiefs, unbuttoned shirts, the stale acid smell of sweat and herring and vodka surrounded her like an impenetrable wall. The man in the leather jacket was singing too, leaning heavily against Kyra.

Dirty plates piled up on the table in front of her. Fascinated she watched the outline of grease and herringbone on the plates' cracked surfaces. Then she followed the design that dirt and dampness had made on the wall opposite her. She felt the man's arm tighten about her waist, but she had neither the strength to push him away nor even to refuse the vodka which he kept lifting to her mouth.

"Come on, comrade, you don't seem to be gay. I like you. What is your name?"

"Kyra," Kyra whispered miserably.

"Well, Kirusha you'll be to me. Comrade Kirusha, how is it I've never seen you before? Maybe you've been around without my noticing you?"

"This is the first time—"

"What are you so sad about, Kirusha? Don't you like me? What's eating you?"

"It's my birthday," Kyra explained.

"What kind of a reason is that to be sad? That's no reason at all. The more grown-up you are, the more useful you'll be. Here, let's celebrate your birthday, Kirusha. First, I'll kiss you, and then you can kiss me, and then we'll have more vodka."

Masha did not seem to be next to her any longer and Kyra could not see her anywhere. But then all the figures had lost their outline, stamping in front of her in one indistinct mass, sometimes approaching so near that she was forced to lean back on the sofa, sometimes swaying away, almost dissolving into tobacco smoke. But the shouting voices, the singing and laughing never ceased for a moment. Kyra made an immense effort to collect herself, to distinguish Masha's voice among the others, call to her, tell her that she had to get away. She opened her mouth, but somehow could not call. The foggy mass of figures swayed backward and then forward right against her chest. With a groan, Kyra closed her eyes.

"Hey, she's passed out!" Water was sprinkled into Kyra's face.

Masha came up and bent over the sofa, her face as red as the kerchief around her neck, her eyes glistening merrily.

"Well, comrade Kyra, I guess we've both had our fill of vodka. Had a grand time. Hold on to me tight now and I'll take you home."

18. Tassia's Ordeal

Kyra detested her new school, the 19th Labor School which was the result of a merger between the gymnasium Tassia had attended and a Manual Labor Institute. The pupils from the latter were, naturally enough, backward in learning, but it was decreed that they be placed in the various grades according to age rather than knowledge. Matters were further simplified by cutting off approximately two years from the old high school curriculum and, as a result, Kyra found herself in the senior class with only a term between her and graduation.

Seated at a long unpainted table which took the place of desks, Kyra felt angrily exasperated most of the time. She was squeezed in between two girls who idly sprawled against her, making it all but impossible to take notes. Worst of the two was the girl on her right. A sturdy, big-featured, handsome girl with extraordinary red cheeks, she looked as if she had been roughly slapped together of crude and brightly colored clay. Although an ardent Comsomol, she had at first taken a fancy to Kyra, assuming a protective and jocular attitude, tickling Kyra's neck and slapping her on the back. Kyra came to detest her for her attitude toward the few old professors who had remained in the school, especially her hissing when Nicolai Petrovich, who taught Russian literature, so much as mentioned Turgenev, Peter the Great, or any foreign poet. Of course, Kyra could say nothing. But one day, when the girl had unexpectedly approached her from behind and placed her rough clumsy hands over Kyra's eyes, she had struck out in sudden fury, whirling around and crazily pounding with her fists. Grinning foolishly, taken aback, the girl stood stock-still for a moment, then she fell with all her weight upon Kyra, slapping her, strangling her, tearing her clothes. For all her unexpected strength born of despair, for all her kicking and biting, Kyra would have fared very badly had it not been for the interference of some of the other girls.

As soon as the bell rang for recess, Kyra would always hasten out into the narrow darkish hall to rejoin Tassia and Galia. Tassia was a comfort—just fourteen, idealistic and enthusiastic, she was not yet ready to accept defeat, although as class president her word carried weight only with her former classmates, the Manual School children keeping sulkily apart. Whenever possible, Tassia heatedly pointed out to "her side" the wrong and injustice rife in the school. As was Kyra, they were particularly incensed by the indignities inflicted upon their now helpless teachers.

* * *

It was during recess one day that Grigori Alibekoff first made his appearance at school. Kyra was sitting on the windowsill between Tassia and Galia, and all three noticed the boy immediately. He had stalked in whistling, a torn cap pulled way over his eyes, hands in pockets. Scowling, he glanced about him, then turned his back as if in answer to the inquiring eyes focused upon him. He was a tall, strongly built lad, older than most of them, handsome despite a wide scar running across one cheek, and there was such an air of toughness about him that no one ventured to approach him, much less taunt him as was the custom with newcomers; not even the brashest of the Comsomols dared.

The new boy stayed on in school, no one really knowing where he had come from or anything about him other than his name. In the classroom he slouched in the far corner, obstinate and frowning, and the teachers soon refrained from asking him questions. It was between and after classes that he made himself felt. Leaning loosely against a wall, he would start orating ringingly. As listeners gathered around him, he would push his cap to the back of his curly head, his voice growing more and more defiant as he shouted the names of Lenin, Trotsky, and Marx, and called for the throwing off of fetters, advancing in battle, stamping the enemies underfoot. In substance, it in no way differed from what everyone had already heard hundreds of times from the young speakers in military shirts. The difference lay in Grigori Alibekoff's stance: he openly and arrogantly bid for a dominant role. He prompted and, when necessary, bullied the lazy Manual School students into establishing the Atheist Club and Lenin's Corner, with himself as chairman of both.

The Atheist Club in a windowless, stuffy room under the stairs served as headquarters to Alibekoff and his associates. Enormous pictures of Lenin and Trotsky were pinned to the door, and the dingy walls inside were brightened by posters ridiculing Christ and the Virgin Mary and depicting fat priests dangling from gallows. Alibekoff's disciples strutted in and out or squatted on the floor, smoking against school regulations and clumsily rolling reeking cigarettes, sometimes unable to overcome their nausea.

The commotion about the club intrigued even some of the former gymnasium pupils who would hang around the open doors, looking in, tittering somewhat shamefacedly among themselves, yet pressing forward when Grigori Alibekoff opened his mouth to talk. Presently, on several occasions, Kyra saw Galia standing a little way off, raising herself on tiptoe to get a glimpse over the backs and heads of others. Just silly curiosity, Kyra thought, yet she noted Galia's intent gaze and strained mouth. She took a chance at lightheartedly teasing her. "Galia, you seem quite infatuated with the splendid Alibekoff. Too bad for you that you two are in enemy camps."

Tassia began by joking about it too, but once Galia suddenly frowned and Tassia became exasperated. "I refuse to believe, Galia, that you're seriously taken in by that buffoon. Why, he's scarcely able to read and write, and repeats ready-made slogans like a parrot. Just because he's handsome and domineering and can make his eyes flash, you stare at him like a hypnotized rabbit."

Instead of protesting and defending herself, Galia turned her back and walked away. From then on she stayed away from all her old friends. A few days were to pass before the final blow fell.

Kyra and Tassia were passing the open door of a classroom where a Comsomol meeting was being held for the purpose of denouncing the school librarian for her bourgeois ideology and lack of class consciousness. Unbelievingly, they caught sight of Galia inside, and paused. Alibekoff, as usual, was presiding, but it was toward Galia that faces were turned. She must have just finished saying something for some were cheering and others grinning approvingly, while Galia herself stood self-conscious and pink. Grigori Alibekoff banged his fist against the table on which he was perched. "Comrades, I see we're unanimously agreed. We shall not allow ourselves to be poisoned by rotten reactionary ideas, whoever the scribblers of those books might be. Down with the accursed bourgeois notion of culture—we fight for the rights of the proletariat!"

"Galia, Galia, how is it possible—" Tassia whispered in a moaning kind of way.

They went out into the street and stood by the school gate waiting for Galia to come out. They did not speak. Kyra avoided asking Tassia what she was going to say, to do. They both just stood watching sparrows hopping on the cobblestones and heavily laden donkeys trotting by.

When Galia at last appeared, she was with Grigori. Gesticulating and talking excitedly, she was looking up at him with a glowing face. Grigori was humming casually with his usual arrogant, self-satisfied smile. They passed Kyra and Tassia without a glance.

As Kyra tiptoed along the porch so that her mother would not hear her coming in so late, she was dismayed to see a streak of light between the shutters of the children's room. Before opening the door, she tried to peek through the keyhole, but could not catch a glimpse of anything unusual. At intervals, some low queer sound reached her. Making the sign of the cross to protect herself against any possible unpleasantness, Kyra pushed the door ajar. Half-hidden behind a stack of books placed so that they would shade the lamplight, Tassia lay crumpled up in Kyra's armchair.

"Tassia, why aren't you in bed and asleep?" Kyra whispered sternly, resenting the anxiety she had just been through.

Tassia lifted a piteous face with eyes as red as a rabbit's and trembling parched lips. She tried to say something, but the corners of her mouth stretched helplessly and her face puckered up in a new fit of weeping.

Pulling off hat and coat, Kyra perched on the arm of the chair and pushed the damp hair off Tassia's forehead.

"You've talked to Galia, is that it? I saw you sneaking out before classes were over."

Tassia blew her nose and wiped her eyes, then whispered miserably, "Kyra, I did not know people could do such things. People you love and trust, and then suddenly—I don't understand it.

"What happened?"

"After I saw Galia at that meeting yesterday and then coming out with Alibekoff himself, I knew it was too late to try to win her back gradually. So today during recess I went up to her and said right out, 'Listen Galia, in the name of our old friendship, will you come with me now for a minute? Let's slip out through the basement. I have to talk to you.' Galia started to frown and stood there hesitating, and I just kept on repeating, 'Please, please come, Galia.' By the way her eyes looked I could tell she was embarrassed and uncertain whether to go or not, then she tossed her head and said she would for it was just as well to get things over with. So she followed me through the basement, but did not speak, and I didn't say anything either till we got out onto the street. You know, Kyra, last night I kept thinking and thinking just what I would say to Galia if she consented to listen and I had it all prepared in my head. But when we had turned round the corner and stopped, and I looked into her face—well, I knew all arguments and reminders were useless. Kyra, she stared at me as if she really hated me, as if I were her enemy. So all I could do was to just cry out, 'Galia, Galia, this cannot be. I can't believe you've turned traitor.' And she pressed her lips tightly together and answered in an icy way, 'I don't feel and think the way you do any longer. I was young and silly before, but now I've changed. I have changed my ideas about everything and it's none of your business why.' She just said it simply, like that. And then I sort of went crazy."

Sonia stirred restlessly in her cot in the corner of the room. Tassia fell silent while Kyra turned the wick in the lamp still lower. In the dim yellowish semicircle of light,

Tassia's face looked haggard, her brown eyes hot and immense. After a while she went on in a whisper:

"So I sort of went crazy and grabbed her by the shoulders and shook her and screamed right into her face, 'You lie, you're a cowardly liar. It's all because you're in love with that cad, Grigori.' At first she looked scared—you know, I'm really stronger than she is—but when I let go she just straightened out and every inch of her expressed scorn. I'd never seen her look like that. She began to say something, but what was the use of listening? So I turned and began walking away. Then I ran."

Tassia pressed her fists to her face.

"The devil alone knows what's come over Galia," said Kyra. "That Galia of all people should become traitor! Galia, whose father was murdered by the Bolsheviks. Galia, who professed to be such a patriot. Remember how often she spoke about dedicating her whole life to her country's good? And then to sell out like that to that scummy Alibekoff and his disgusting band—so easily, so quickly. How can she not be ashamed?"

"It's as if everything has broken into bits and there is not anything worthwhile left," Tassia said bitterly. "I'll never believe anyone again; I'll never love anyone again; I don't want anything, anything any more. Oh, how could Galia do this? Galia, my Galia, Galia—" and again Tassia started to cry. "And she used to speak of self-sacrificial love, of following her beloved into exile if the Cheka grabbed him, to be worthy of him, share his suffering. I forgot to remind her of all this when she stared at me as she did."

The next morning Tassia told the school director that she resigned as class president. From then on both she and Kyra began cutting classes, but it went unnoticed in the general disorder. Alibekoff's despotism was growing rapidly, especially since he had formed a Comsomol cell in school whose power seemed to be unlimited. He terrorized both his fellow pupils and the teachers by the mere threat of reporting them as "undesirable counter-revolutionary elements." A month dragged by, but a short time remained until the end of the school year and Kyra's graduation.

One day, as Kyra and Tassia sat reading on the classroom windowsill, Galia suddenly walked straight toward them. She looked as if she had been flogged, red spots on her cheeks, hair disheveled, eyes wild.

"Something incredible has happened—I have to talk to you. I have to talk to you immediately!" She clutched at Tassia, pulling her off the windowsill. Helplessly Tassia turned toward Kyra for support.

"Yes, Kyra, come too. I don't care. I need advice and two heads are better than one—I don't count mine." Galia sounded as if in truth she had lost her mind.

Galia hurried them into a narrow lane back of the school and stopped abruptly. "It's the most awful thing. You must tell me what to do, Tassia, you must tell me though I have no right to ask you. But there is no one else I can trust. It's about Grigori—"

For a moment Galia kept still, trying to control herself. Then, eyes fixed on Tassia's face, she started speaking in a high peculiar voice.

"I'll tell you everything just as it happened. It happened this morning. I was alone with Grigori in the Atheist Club. He was at the table and he had pulled out some papers and was examining them. I came up and stood at his side. Then I just idly picked up his membership paper from the League of Young Communists. Maybe for no good reason I even began to read the entries. I don't remember. And suddenly I heard him laughing, you know, gaily and somewhat sarcastically, as if at some joke. So I asked him of course what he was laughing about. And he snatched up the paper with all the signatures and held it up to me. 'Can't even you see what this is? Forgery, the most obvious forgery and nothing else.' He said it and went on laughing. Then he told me everything about himself. He said he was no Comsomol and did not give a damn one way or another, because he had always wanted to be just an adventurer. He said he was determined to get from life all the excitement and all the good things one could get if one was smart. As for all his speeches and clubs, well, it was fun to boss people around and have them scared. He called the Manual Institute pupils imbeciles. He despises them. He said he ran away from home years ago because his father had been killed in the war and his mother was poor and was always complaining and trying to control and reform him. Since then he's wandered from town to town, stealing, forging—he entered our school with a forged certificate."

"Why in hell did the idiot confess it all to you?" Kyra interrupted brutally. Galia looked at her helplessly.

"He wanted to impress me, maybe. He knew I was terribly in love with him and I suppose he thought I would never dare tell on him. Oh, he said it because he felt like saying it. That's how he is."

"Which makes him as much of a fool as all of you whom he fooled. Well, what are you going to do?"

"Wait, Kyra, don't shout at Galia. What's the use now?" Tassia spoke patiently and resignedly as if she had just shouldered a heavy burden.

"Tassia, tell me what to do. I love him. He seemed so wonderful and strong in his beliefs. But how can I conceal a crime like this? I can't keep it to myself—I can't!"

Tassia only moved her head. It was not even a nod. Galia began talking again, just as if Tassia had answered her, giving additional details, trying to remember Grigori's very words, the expression on his face. Large tears slid down her cheeks, her eyes never left Tassia's.

Kyra got up from the crumbling stone wall on which they had been sitting and began to move away. The deep hurt done to Tassia would never be healed, she felt sure. As for Galia, it was clear that she did not need advice, for otherwise she would not have turned to Tassia. So as not to betray her feelings, Kyra waved to them as soon as she had safely turned her back.

Next morning the entire school was summoned into the big hall. The director, a weary, browbeaten old man, made a vague speech about upholding the honor of the school and the need for youthful idealism and honesty. Then Galia, as white as the plaster walls of the hall, came forward onto the platform. For a long moment she stood hesitating and pitiful, unable to meet the hundreds of eyes intent on her. But when at last she spoke, her voice was surprisingly deliberate. Almost word for word she repeated the story of the incident as she had told it to Tassia and Kyra the day before. As she finished, the director formally announced that Grigori Alibekoff was hereby expelled from school and would, furthermore, be handed over to the proper authorities. But where was Alibekoff?

Later that day in the Director's office Galia was questioned by representatives of the Young Communist League. Her report was accepted and additional evidence was soon turned up in a search of the Atheist Club quarters. Either through mismanagement or haste, or plain impudence and negligence, Grigori had left compromising papers in the drawer of his rickety desk. A summons for Alibekoff's detention was issued but the boy himself had vanished, and as far as the school knew, he was never apprehended and called to account.

Returning from Kyra's graduation, walking in step, their arms linked with their mother's from either side, Kyra and Tassia felt both solemn and lighthearted The ceremony had been brief despite the political speeches. To her great relief, Kyra's participation was limited to the recital of two of her own poems chosen by her favorite teacher, old Nicolai Petrovich, and which dealt with a forsaken park from which even the phantoms had fled. The subject was hardly appropriate to the occasion, but the audience of parents and other relatives had applauded.

Kyra rejoiced, "If they had not cut down on the courses I would have had two more years of school in front of me. What luck!"

"I'm far from sure that you should consider it luck. It

would have been much better to have had the extra schooling. You're too young to stop studying altogether and, as to being accepted by an institute of higher learning, let's hope it will prove possible and not worry about it today."

Their mother had recently been threatened with dismissal from teaching on the grounds of undesirable social origin. Others already had been purged. She had been offered temporary work in Armenia in makeshift shelters for Christian refugee children who had fled the invading Turks and been salvaged by the American Near East Relief organization. When the job was offered, she was not in a position to hesitate, for, once purged, one was unlikely to regain a work permit, especially in teaching. Kyra and Tassia were well aware of the grim situation on the Armenian-Turkish border: the once flourishing town of Alexandropol had been burned and lay in ruins; outlying villages were devastated; the dispersed survivors, half-crazed by hunger and fear, jammed the abandoned Russian garrison barracks where they were cared for by the Near East Relief. The girls knew about the Near East Relief because of the soup kitchens which had been established in Tiflis to which they reluctantly went when food was too scarce at home.

"Kyra, Tassia, I did not want to distract your attention from your final days of school but now it is impossible to put off talking any longer. There is no question, of course, that I can't take you children to Alexandropol with me. It is not from gruesome sights that I want to protect you, but from the diseases among those poor people. We shall just have to accept being separated for the next few months. A room must be found for you in some cool and quiet mountain village, well on this side of the Turkish-Armenian border. Kara-Kala and Djalal-Ogly were suggested to me and, Kyra, your strong distaste for Olga Ivanovna notwithstanding, I will have to send for her once I have you settled, for she is the only available adult capable of watching over you. Nyanya could not possibly manage in such an unfamiliar setting. Just now let's not disappoint nyanya by our preoccupied faces as she has been busy preparing something special for lunch to honor your graduation, my Kyra; but as I must leave for work right after lunch I had to speak to you now."

"Yes, yes, nyanya hinted about it to me." For a moment Kyra did not know whether Tassia meant Armenia or the lunch ahead, but Tassia, having skipped a few steps, continued, "She said it was to be a present from Mother and herself to you, Kyra. I hope there will be lots of it because I'm ever so hungry." Kyra pressed her face to her mother's arm.

PART VI

19. Djalal-Ogly

The geese always came first. Honking crazily, beating their outstretched wings, they swept down the village street in a brown cloud of dust. Little barefoot boys dove into their midst, waving their arms and crowding the birds into their proper yards. Then the sheep were driven in, trotting in a thick bleating mass, pushing and knocking into one another and getting tangled up among themselves. The sheep were mild and easy to control except for their silly habit of following each other into the wrong yard. By far the funniest was the onrush of the pigs who galloped at full speed, squealing and grunting, sliding in the dust and tumbling down screeching desperately. The village children laughed so hard at the pigs' antics that they often forgot to open the yard gates in time. But the older pigs knew their way, and even if they rushed blindly past in their excitement, they would soon turn back, all out of breath, grunting solemnly and heavily. The little pink and black piglets followed obediently and the sows always kept an eye on them, turning fiercely on anyone who so much as tried to stroke their offspring.

Heralded by the tinkling of their bells, walking in dig- nified, leisurely fashion, the cows were the last to turn into the street. Everyone stretched his neck to see the one that came first, for if it was a black cow, rain would surely fall

183

on the morrow; a light-colored animal meant fine weather to come. Without any guidance the cows stopped to drink from the trough at the corner, then proceeded straight toward their sheds.

As soon as the livestock was turned in, the village street became silent and empty, the thick soft dust slowly settling down once more. Only from the yards came occasional tinkling and bleating and the clatter of milk pails; dim, veiled sounds compared with the earlier cacophony. The sun slid back of the round western hills and the Armenian night came instantly without lengthening shadows or twilight.

Tassia and Sonia had followed Kekele, their landlady, into the yard, hoping to get milk warm from the cows, and Kyra remained alone in front of the house. Now that no one could see her in the dark, she got up from the bench where she had sat decorously with some of the village women, and climbed up onto the back of a stone sphynx-like beast which stood a little way up the street. Sitting astride the monument, swinging her legs, Kyra began to feel so good that she leaned forward and tenderly, gratefully kissed the broad cold head of her mount. Ever since her arrival in Djalal-Ogly, Kyra had loved the stone beast, but at sixteen she could not allow herself to be seen on its back.

Over Kyra towered a huge walnut tree. Between its branches, far beyond and above, the sky was richly speckled with stars. Arms crossed, Kyra stared into the sky, then softly began to chant to herself. She chanted that the sky would have been exactly the same at this moment regardless of anything that happened to her. This sky full of white stars could have been seen by her over the birch grove in Slavnoe. Only she would not have been the same, she would never have known this far-off village in Armenia, she would have been a different Kyra. Yet the cows and the sheep and the pigs would have come in from their pastures in exactly the same way. They would have bleated and grunted and dashed down the street as they always had, as they always would. Here in the village it did not matter if one man died or if another was born; it did not matter if someone was lonely and despairing and another triumphant—only that which went on forever really mattered.

Kyra knew that some tremendous secret was being revealed to her, a secret still out of reach, but which she was just, just on the verge of grasping. Only two weeks in Djalal-Ogly had made her think and feel differently from the way she had in Tiflis. She would never forget Djalal-Ogly and the things she thought here. She would never forget the peace of nights like this, the exaltation of groping toward great revelations. And yet how restless and angry she had been at first. How she had complained to her mother about being left in such a dreary, sleepy place.

They had first gone to the village of Kara-Kala but there they had met Gasim, the youthful head horse-breeder, who promptly fell in love with Kyra. She had liked having the fierce-looking Gasim in love with her and had felt unjustly deprived of an unexpected gift when her mother insisted on their leaving. She had finally deposited the children here in Djalal-Ogly with Kekele, a prosperous and pious peasant who mothered them. By now Kyra had stopped feeling aggrieved. Anyway, she was through with all her silly adventures.

A clanking of horse's hooves approached rapidly from the far end of the street. The horseman rode past without seeing her but reined in at Kekele's gate. Without dismounting, he remained still for a while, then urged his horse closer to the lighted windows. Kyra could now make out the familiar tall silhouette with the sheepskin hanging loosely about the man's shoulders. Reluctantly she slid off the statue and took a few steps forward.

"Gasim," she called faintly.

The man pulled so hard that his horse almost sat on its haunches, then whirled around and was instantly at Kyra's side.

"I did not see you in the dark." He jumped down and took Kyra's hands and stood bending down to her. "I was just about to knock at the window."

"I know, that's why I called. But don't you know they would never have let me come out to you? Why did you come, Gasim?"

"If I tell you I'll make you angry again. But I was frantic and didn't have a moment's peace for fear that your mother would suddenly take you away."

"Please whisper, Gasim, or I'll get into trouble," Kyra tugged at her hands which hurt because he was holding them so tightly.

"We won't stay here then. Come and sit with me over the ravine. You trust me, don't you? I'll lift you onto the horse."

Without waiting for an answer, he lifted her off the ground and swung her up onto the saddle. He started to walk alongside holding the bridle.

"Your poor Djigit, Gasim, he's so hot." Kyra began.

"It's twelve miles from Kara-Kala. But there's plenty of life in the animal still. I'll show you."

"Don't, don't—"

Gasim had suddenly jumped onto the horse's back, pushing Kyra forward off the saddle and holding her tightly. He whistled piercingly and the horse was off.

"Stop!" shrieked Kyra.

Crushing her closer to him, Gasim was shouting in her ear, "This is what I've always wanted to do—carry you off. It's the only way I can have you."

Bending over, Kyra bit hard into the hand that was holding her. For one brief second he let go of her, then caught at her again as she started to fall. Where the road turned and began twisting uphill, he stopped the horse abruptly.

"Badly frightened?"

"I hate you!"

"If that's true, I'll turn Djigit toward the ravine and dash us both down to death. Do you understand?"

Tightening inside, biting her lips, Kyra did not answer.

"Kyra!"

"To hell with you. Dash!"

"You hate me so much?"

"I don't hate you."

Djigit was walking slowly back toward the village, snorting and head down. Gasim slid off the saddle and threw his sheepskin about Kyra's shoulders. It smelled of him and leather and horse sweat, and the rough wool tickled Kyra's bare neck and arms.

"Forgive me, I'm a beast, forgive me. My little beauty, my treasure, don't be furious."

"I'm not anymore. Oh, Gasim, before you came I was thinking of such entirely different things. I can't explain—you wouldn't understand. Why did you come here tonight?"

"I had to talk to you again, find out if your mother was taking you away to Alexandropol."

"She's already left for Alexandropol because, you see, it could not be postponed any longer. She wanted very much to take us along, but there isn't any room for us at the American House there and besides, she'd been told that it's so terribly hot down in the plains. Gasim, you know, it's awfully funny but Mother's scared of you. You're sort of a brigand to her. Yesterday afternoon Olga Ivanovna came to stay with us for the time being. She's the woman who shared our apartment in Tiflis. I don't like her at all. But Mother asked her to come on account of you. She suspected you might come down to Djalal-Ogly."

"I blame myself day and night. Just to think if I'd been sensible those few days that you were in Kara-Kala with your mother, she might then have left you there all summer instead of in Djalal-Ogly. I was such a fool! But Kyra, if you only knew—that first night when you arrived in the rickety cart and stood under the lantern, all tired out and pale and small, right then I wanted to snatch you up in my arms. And the hailstorm in the hills—do you remember?"

"I remember you held me so tightly, you bruised me more than the hail did." Kyra was now able to laugh.

"My little bird, will you promise me just one thing? Let me know if your mother sends for you. I can't let you go like this. I know you're not for me. An uncouth, crude animal like me, I'm not fit to kiss your little feet. But you've made your way into my very soul. How can I let you go?"

The cornfields rustled on either side of the road, and a white half-moon was now hanging over them, causing them to look aloof and mysterious and not at all like the dusty cornfields of hot afternoons. The road too had become lighter. Sideways, Kyra stared at Gasim, but his head was turned toward the hills, and she could only see his shaggy astrakhan hat thrust deep down over his fierce shaggy eyebrows. Noiselessly he stepped in his heelless, soft boots, one hand on the horse's neck, the other resting on the hilt of his dagger. A dog barked somewhere. They were reentering the village.

"Don't come any farther, Gasim, the moon makes it light."

Lifting her down from the saddle, he held her so that the moon shone bright in her face.

"God knows I would not harm you, I would not touch you against your will. I'd rather chop my hands off. Your little face is so white and you have such little hands. I'd lay my soul down for you."

When he had ridden off and she could hear Djigit's hooves no longer, Kyra turned and ran down the village street. At Kekele's gate she paused to get her breath and smooth her hair, then humming, she began feeling her way through the dark entrance hall.

"Is that you, Kyra, at last?" came Olga Ivanovna's exasperated voice.

Kyra pulled open the door of their room, Kekele's parlor, and faced Olga Ivanovna innocently.

"Why, did you want anything? Would you like me to bring some water from the well?"

"What I want to know is where you have been. I went to the gate three times looking for you."

"Oh, I just took a walk. It's such a beautiful night."

"Beautiful night, indeed! You've been told time and time again that it's not safe to wander about alone. After I promised your mother not to take my eyes off you. Maybe you're lying to me, anyway?"

The devil take you, Kyra thought fiercely. If you don't shut up I'll elope with Gasim the next time he comes down. There, you old witch! He'll carry me off into the mountains and you'll never set eyes on me again.

Still grumbling, Olga Ivanovna went back to examining her mattress for bedbugs, and Kyra strolled over to her sisters who were lying on their stomachs on another bed, playing cards. Before undressing, they went into the yard and made their way between the chewing and heavily sighing cows and the pigs who grunted sleepily, toward the far downhill end where the outhouse stood.

"Be careful of the cows, and come back quickly," Olga Ivanovna shouted after them.

The heat that day had been heavy, and a breeze arose only after sunset. Nevertheless, Olga Ivanovna, who had been sitting on the bench in front of the house, went indoors early, half whispering to Sonia, "I want you to get a good rest, Sonia, and besides, there are certain things I expect you to do before going to bed."

"What does she want of you?" growled Kyra.

"I'll tell you," Sonia whispered excitedly, "but we better walk a little down the street because if she catches me telling you—"

"For goodness sake, what is it? Can Tassia hear it too?"

"All right, she can hear it too. But it's something awfully important. What will you give me if I tell you?"

Sonia was plainly making the most of her important news.

"All right, what do you want?" Kyra unwillingly surrendered.

"Promise never again to call me monkey-ish brat as long as you live," Sonia answered solemnly.

"Oh Sonia, but you do ape so. You don't know white from black. You swallow all the propaganda at school. Mother has said it's because you're so much younger and that life will be easier for you. All right, I give you my word of honor, and should I forget, Sonia," Kyra admitted honestly, "you'll know it was a mistake and I'll take it back."

"And you, Tassia, too?"

"Word of honor."

Stopping in the middle of the street, Sonia faced her sisters. "Olga Ivanovna wants me to help her pack because we are leaving Djalal-Ogly tomorrow morning."

"What!" Kyra shouted incredulously.

"Don't shout so, Kyra." There was a ring of condescension in Sonia's voice. "We're leaving for Alexandropol first thing tomorrow morning. The horses are ordered and everything is arranged."

"Why did she say nothing to us?" Tassia interrupted.

"Why, if she had told you, Tassia, she knew you would repeat it to Kyra. And of course she does not want Kyra to know because of that Gasim. You know what I overheard her say to Kekele? Gasim is a wild mountaineer, and she won't be held responsible. If he finds out that the girl—that's you, Kyra—is being taken away, he is capable of abducting her. Kyra, tell me, will he abduct you?"

"He might, and it would serve her right, the low, ignoble double-crosser." Kyra uttered dramatically, "I wish I could do something beastly to her. Besides, I promised Gasim that I would let him know if I'm taken away. He told me to send Kekele's nephew, Varoum, to Kara-Kala with a message, but what am I to do now that it is so late? Varoum goes to bed as soon as he's through with the cows, and there's no way to get to him." Kyra was concentrating on the immediate situation, on the problem that posed itself.

"Then you want to be abducted?" Sonia was plainly thrilled.

"I'm going to get up at sunrise tomorrow and send Varoum to Kara-Kala," Kyra continued, not liking to admit to her sisters or even to herself the childishness of her defiance. "As to abduction—let fate intervene."

20. A Reckless Adventure

The light phaeton which was to carry Olga Ivanovna and Sonia had been waiting for some time at Kekele's gate, but the cart was late. At last, wheels screeching, the cart drove up too, its driver Papoush climbing down in a leisurely manner. Before starting out for Kara-Kala that morning, Varoum had promised Kyra to let Papoush know that he was to take his time. Grumbling impatiently, Olga Ivanovna began supervising the loading of the luggage into the cart so as to leave enough room for Kyra's and Tassia's legs. Kekele and the neighbor women seemed saddened by the departure. Pretending she had to fix her sandal, Kyra ran up to the stone sphynx and leaned against it for the last time, her fingers caressing the curlicues on the strange beast's forehead.

"May God grant you a safe journey." Kekele bowed to Olga Ivanovna, her head in its black kerchief bent resignedly to one side.

"Thank you for your good wish. Well, with God's help, we're ready to start at last. Kyra, why are you dawdling? Climb into the cart." And Olga Ivanovna settled herself heavily into the phaeton.

Bare-legged children and barking dogs ran after them to the end of the dusty village street. Beyond the village the deep bumpy ruts in the road, reminders of the impassable quagmire caused yearly by rains, smoothed out gradually and the horses broke out into a trot.

"Don't worry, little lady," Papoush turned around, his toothless mouth in a grin, "long ago Varoum has reached Kara-Kala. He's a good horseman, Varoum. By now they must be on their way after us."

Kyra nodded to Papoush to convey the gratitude she felt she owed him, and for a few minutes continued to stare at Papoush's back in a grimy homespun cherkesska and the long-furred papaha shapeless on his head. Drowsy from the heat and too few hours of sleep, she felt dispirited. The jolting and screeching of the cart made it difficult for her to think, or to sleep, and finally she gave up. "Let it happen, whatever happens," she said to her sisters.

Midmorning, Papoush pulled up behind the phaeton by a brook dribbling over rocks and between boulders. The horses, unharnessed were led to a small clear pool cupped in a rock below the road, while the girls, cramped and stiff, splashed their hot faces a few steps above. Olga Ivanovna drank gingerly from an enamel cup she had brought along and then, opening a basket, handed corn bread and hardboiled eggs around. There was no shade anywhere. To the right of the road a rocky low hill rose in terraces, while to the left the slope widened and leveled itself out into a glowing monochrome valley.

No sooner had they started off again than a thud of horse's hooves sounded behind and a rider appeared round the bend of the road.

"Gasim," Kyra shrieked, then muttered stammeringly to Tassia, "what am I to do now?"

"Well, you sent for him, didn't you?" Tassia sounded grumpy.

In her apprehension, Kyra sat bolt upright and stared at Gasim unblinkingly, like a hypnotized bird. He had his papaha off and was waving it, then suddenly he thrust it back on his head and dashed at the cart at breakneck speed. Their hands to their faces, Kyra and Tassia screamed. In a moment his horse was panting alongside of them and Gasim had leaped from the saddle down into the cart. He attached Djigit's bridle before sitting down.

"You brigand, you thief, how dare you!" Olga Ivanovna shouted from the phaeton. Hands waving and grabbing at the hood, she was trying to get out, her anger making her even clumsier than usual. Gasim called out something in Armenian to the coachman. Immediately the phaeton started off again, Olga Ivanovna falling back and disappearing from view.

"The old lady has a nasty temper," Gasim sat down in the cart, crossing his legs under him. "The driver will tell her that this is not the place to stop and argue. He will tell her landslides happen here."

"How are you, Gasim? I'm sorry this cart is so uncomfortable," Kyra said timidly, not knowing how to act toward a possible abductor.

"It's a fine cart, it does not go fast," grinned Gasim, "but it won't be so fine later on. A storm will come up before sunset. Look how the air trembles over the valley. Forgive me that I always bring storms to you."

"Well, I'd sooner get drenched than baked by this dreadful sun."

It seemed to Kyra that Gasim's coal black eyes never wavered from her face, and that there was a tense, greedy look in them which did not square with his joking words. She would have liked to ask him what he was planning to do with her now that he had caught up. Surely he had not galloped all the way from Kara-Kala just to sit in the cart, staring.

When they had to pull up to give the horses a rest, Olga Ivanovna climbed out of the phaeton and hurried toward the cart. Gasim stood up in the cart, his arms folded. They watched her approaching, red-faced from fury and heat, head high.

"You savage, you brigand, what do you come bothering good people for? Go away immediately or I'll— Get on that horse and be gone with you!"

"I'm sorry to contradict a venerable lady, but it is not my intention to leave."

"Get out of that cart. I forbid you to stay in it."

"The young ladies have permitted me to stay."

"Kyra, come with me immediately. You come with me in the phaeton." Olga Ivanovna made a step forward, tried to grab Kyra's arm.

"Leave the girl alone. She is staying where she is. It will be better to leave her alone." Gasim hadn't moved, only his voice had changed.

"Do you hear, Kyra? Follow me back to the phaeton." Olga Ivanovna had succeeded in catching hold of Kyra's wrist.

"If you try to drag her by force it will go badly for you. I warn you, you'll regret it very much indeed. I don't make threats idly, I assure you, lady."

Dropping Kyra's hand, Olga Ivanovna made a step back.

"Now, Kyra, be a good girl. Come of your own free will. Tell that—"

Kyra shook her head.

"Go in peace, lady. Return to your carriage. The horses are rested and you should get started. A storm is coming up." Gasim sat down.

Olga Ivanovna turned and, fuming, retreated.

Keeping in rhythm with the horses' steps, Papoush began to sing. It was a wordless, dragging tune, without beginning or end, repeating itself again and again monotonously and sadly. It reminded Kyra of the hills, always more of them, one back of the other, indefinitely, all alike, all swinging up and then down, yet never quite identically.

In the afternoon clouds began piling up over the hilltops, then pushed down rapidly over the slopes, spreading in a thick screen over the sky. The phaeton, its hood pulled all the way up, rolled faster, and Papoush too whipped his horses, the cart shaking and groaning in all its joints. There was a village some distance away where they could find shelter. Gasim reached for his burkah * folded under the saddle and made sure that Djigit's bridle held him fast to the cart.

"Thunder frightens the horse," he explained, then sat back again, holding the burkah, waiting for the first drops of rain to fall.

He wants it to rain, thought Kyra, he's waiting for it to begin so he can throw the burkah over us and then hold me

---

* Burkah: a cloak made of goat's or sheep's wool, felted to be smooth inside but rough outside, usually black and semicircular in shape.

in his arms. But I won't let him, I won't let him. I'll hit him if he touches me.

"I don't want anything on me. I want to get wet," Kyra exclaimed challengingly, kneeling in the far corner of the cart, head thrown back against the wind.

Gasim covered Tassia with the burkah, and without looking in Kyra's direction, swung over to Papoush's side in front. Thunder rumbled heavily. Large cold raindrops fell on Kyra's neck and arms, and she started to shiver uncontrollably.

"Stop showing off," Tassia shouted indignantly.

"I'm not," but at that moment there was a terrific glare of lightning and with a cry Kyra hurled herself down and began crawling under the burkah as fast as she could. Mortified, her wet dress clinging stickily, she buried herself in the hay.

The sky had taken on a malignant purple-black tint, lightning zigzagging and darting fiercely against it. Hoarsely and croakingly, the mountains echoed the rolling and roaring of thunder. It seemed as if the whole world were being rent asunder. Rain pelted the burkah with a soft persistent plopping sound and the cart swung wildly from side to side as the horses galloped downhill.

"Tassia, I'm so afraid," moaned Kyra, wriggling closer to her sister.

"So am I. But get away from me, you're wet."

Forgetting all her resolutions, Kyra stuck her head out from under the burkah and screamed Gasim's name. The roar of the storm smothered her voice, and he did not even turn around. Kyra saw his tall body leaning forward, intent on the road, and it was he, not Papoush, who was holding the reins. Resignedly Kyra pulled the burkah over her head again.

Suddenly the cart swerved, bounced crazily over stones and stood still. Some suitcases had rolled down and lay heavily across Kyra's legs, and her head had hit against the cart's side. Loudly and angrily Gasim was shouting at someone and from ahead came a muffled voice in answer. The rain was now coming down in such a blinding whirling torrent that

Kyra and Tassia could not distinguish anything of what was happening ahead of them. Tilted crookedly, the cart stood at a strange angle to the road, and immediately to the right a gray indistinct mass of a hill towered over them, while to the left there was a void of nothingness. Struggle as she might, Kyra could not pull her legs out from under the pile of luggage, and to make it worse, no one seemed to care about her and Tassia's plight. Gasim's and the driver's voices and an occasional flash of their lantern came from somewhere down the road. After what seemed ages, Gasim uplifted the burkah and his dripping face bent over them.

"There's a roadhouse in the valley about a mile away. You'll have to walk there. The road has been washed away."

"But we can't get out from here. What happened when we stopped like that?" Kyra said plaintively.

"I almost crashed into the phaeton. We'd all be lying down there if I had." Gasim pointed grimly to the void on the left. "The phaeton had to pull up without time for warning when the driver saw there was no more road ahead."

With her first steps away from the cart, Kyra sank shin deep into the sticky, semiliquid mud and almost fell face forward.

"Keep away from the precipice side," Gasim roared.

The horses stood unharnessed and the luggage was being roped across their backs in the manner of saddlebags, a basket or a suitcase dangling against each flank. Sitting all by herself in a helpless small heap right in the middle of the road, Sonia was crying wretchedly.

"I'm stuck, I'm stuck for good."

Struggling against the driving rain and weighed down by the burkah, Kyra somehow managed to stagger to her side.

"Please, please try to get up, Sonia. You're in it up to your middle." Kyra herself was on the verge of despair as she tugged at her sister and slipped about, unable to find any foothold. Presently Gasim picked up Sonia and lifted her onto Djigit's back.

"Hold on to the saddle, Sonia, but don't touch the bridle."

The pack horses were led ahead, Papoush and the other driver nudging them and swearing encouragingly. Her skirts tucked up, a parasol against her shoulder, Olga Ivanovna marched in grim and outraged silence. She gave Kyra one wrathful look and then turned her face away in powerless scorn.

"See that look," Kyra screamed gleefully to Tassia. "The old witch knows she's now completely dependent on Gasim and she can't swallow that."

Gasim was leading Djigit, with his free arm guiding and supporting Kyra and Tassia by turn as they slid about in the mire. Where the road had been washed away, there was but a narrow crumbling ledge littered with boulders and rocks. One by one Gasim led the children over the debris, keeping them close against the hillside and shielding them with his body against the tearing force of the storm.

It was a difficult descent. Kyra had no choice but to hold on to Gasim who neither glanced nor spoke to her otherwise than to shout directions to both her and Tassia. It was humiliating to depend on one so scornful and angry. Damn this storm, damn her for refusing his burkah! She knew he had sensed immediately why she had refused it and that he took it as an insult, a blow to his self-esteem. Had he not given his word that he would not touch her against her will? How could she explain, much less justify that in her unwillingness to accept Olga Ivanovna's dictates she had disregarded what her sending for him might have meant to him? Then confronted, as she was, with the consequences of her own reckless action, fear had made her childishly defiant. Fool, fool, fool, Kyra blamed herself, how could she have been so thoughtless! Now that she needed him, it was as if she had stopped being Kyra. To Tassia, and particularly Sonia, he was paying more heed. Even to Olga Ivanovna he called out encouragingly. Olga Ivanovna had lost all her arrogance together with her parasol, which the wind had immediately whirled out of her hands and sent careening down the precipice.

At the foot of the hill raged a stream, and where the road had led down to a bridge there was nothing but scattered planks and black whirling water. From a bluff on the opposite shore a reddish light flickered. It was the roadhouse. In answer to shouts, dark figures with lanterns hurried from the house to the water's edge, pointing out a place where the stream could best be forded. The pack horses were driven across first and were unloaded. The sky had become entirely black but there was not much rain any longer. The children stood huddled together, not speaking, each feeling the terror of the others, intensified by Olga Ivanovna's groaning somewhere back of them. Then Gasim approached, holding two horses by their bridles.

"Now we are ready for you. Who is coming first?"

Kyra stumbled forward and Gasim lifted her onto the saddle. "Gasim," Kyra whispered despairingly.

He paused for a moment. "Don't be afraid, it's shallow here," was all he said. He rode into the stream by her side.

Inside the roadhouse it was smoky and hot. Swarthy men wrapped in sheepskins and burkahs sprawled on the floor around a brazier. Gloomily they looked at the newly arrived, and a few moved over to make room. The proprietor brought a bench for Olga Ivanovna, and the girls knelt by her side as near to the fire as they could get. Papoush and the other driver sat among the shepherds and they talked to one another in Armenian, slowly and solemnly and without gestures. Gasim squatted silently a little way apart, his cherkesska off, his tight-fitting long black beshmet * making him look like a crouching panther. After a while Olga Ivanovna hung a blanket across a corner of the room and made the children go behind it and strip and change into dry clothes she had pulled from the suitcases.

The wiry little innkeeper was bustling around preparing

---

* Beshmet: a high-collared shirt worn under the cherkesska.

their supper. There was the flat chouvash bread, goat cheese, wine in earthen jars, and pieces of lamb roasted over charcoal. Greedily the children snatched at the food, wrapping the dripping hunks of lamb in the bread, as Gasim and Papoush were doing. Olga Ivanovna had regained her composure and was complaining of the smoke and the smell and that there was not a fork and knife to be had. Grinning and scratching his head, the innkeeper listened to Olga Ivanovna whose laments he was unable to understand, but he chose the tenderest, juiciest pieces of lamb and handed them to her with a low bow of hospitality. "Eat. Good lamb. Eat, venerable lady."

The smoky heat and the wine were numbing Kyra. She was half-dozing, one hand over her eyes, when a draft of cold air and a slamming door made her look up. Gasim was no longer in the room. Immediately she was seized by the urgent need to explain or somehow make him understand that she never doubted him, that she had wantonly and unworthily hurt his feelings. He had in all probability saved her and her sisters' lives, but that was not the immediate point, for honor in the mountains meant more than did life itself. It was a terrifying thing to do to slip out like this at night. Still, she would do it. She waited, glancing cautiously around, listening to the breathing and snoring, to Olga Ivanovna asthmatically whistling through a handkerchief over her face. She tiptoed to the door and quickly crossing herself, pulled it open.

It had stopped raining. The sky was crowded with fat, rolling whipped-up clouds, lavender-gray when they swam past the moon. Somewhere a sheep bleated, nearer she could hear horses snorting and stamping from foot to foot. Splashing into puddles, Kyra made her way to the middle of the yard and stopped. A dog began barking fiercely.

"Who's that?" came Gasim's voice in Armenian.

Now she could see him leaning over the side of a wagon. She walked slowly in his direction. When he recognized her, he made a sharp gesture, obviously taken aback by surprise.

"What happened?" His voice was hoarse.

"It's stuffy in there and I wanted to—" Kyra began slowly, not looking at him.

"You shouldn't be here." Gasim interrupted even more gruffly. She had now approached the wagon and tried again, "I had to tell you—" Gasim was not listening. He grabbed her shoulder and pulled her up against the wagon. Then without a word, he rose to his feet and dragged her up by her arms. Kyra tried to speak but he crushed her against himself, and all she could do was whimper from pain. She tried to wriggle out of his embrace, weakly at first, then as his grasp tightened, pushing against his chest with both hands. Not seeming to feel her pounding fists, Gasim jerked her forward and then down. As she fell, he threw himself at her, his mouth brutally on hers, kissing and biting. For a few seconds Kyra lay terror-stricken and dazed. A sentence from somewhere swam into her mind: she had forfeited her immunity. Then every inch of her began squirming and struggling to free itself from under the relentless weight pinning her down. As he let her head slide back to grip her body in both hands, she managed to cry out, "Gasim, in honor I came to you—"

The words seemed to reach him for his hold slackened and then he was crouching at her feet.

"Why did you come?"

"To ask forgiveness."

It was a while before Gasim spoke. "There you were, all of a sudden, and I lost all sense of what I was doing. You came of your own accord. I had made up my mind to carry you off at dawn, whether by force or not, I did not care. I had to wait till dawn—the horses are all done in. You came in trust and I, a savage, almost committed a crime. I will not take you forcibly. It must not happen this way. You must come back to me of your own free will at sunrise before they start tending to the horses. Go now, unhurt, unsullied. Alone in the mountains, knowing that you are mine, entirely mine forever, I swear I will be gentle and I will make love day and night and I will fulfill your every wish. Bless you, my golden one."

He lifted her to her feet and set her on the ground. As she stumbled toward the inn's door, her mind was made up and at peace now that she had made honorable amends.

Exhausted, her sisters and Kyra slept on until the sun was high in the sky, and it was Olga Ivanovna's proddings that got them up when the horses were harnessed and ready to start.

Gasim and Djigit were gone.

By noon they had laboriously ascended to the pass over the mountain range. The plateau was bald and windswept and one had a feeling of being very near the hot sky. To the south the descending hillsides were matted with dark uneven woods, the road continuing to wind in narrow parallel loops until it hit the stark plains. It was not pleasant to stare down the precipitous slopes, so Kyra and Tassia had moved closer to Papoush. Pointing with his whip in the direction of the plains, Papoush began telling them of the Turkish invasion when, after the collapse of the southern front following the Russian Revolution, the garrison troops had deserted their posts and left the frontier open but for a contingent of Armenian volunteers led by a handful of former Russian officers. The massacre did not take long.

"Like fierce beasts the Turks swept over the plains, killing, burning. Our villages became slaughter grounds with bodies piled in heaps. There's a valley some ten miles from Alexandropol where more than three thousand were put to death in one day. Just corpses on top of corpses till the air stank for miles around. Later the Americans tried to burn and bury them. The merciful God himself must have brought those foreigners here. They took care of people who had fed on grass like cattle, living corpses as they were spoken of, children with arms and legs thinner than my finger. I've seen them. And then the plague came, cholera and typhus and whatever else—I'm not a learned man, I don't know the diseases—but thousands more died. And there were those who went mad—"

"And now, Papoush?"

"You'll see for yourselves, little ladies, you'll see the orphans in the barracks rebuilt by the Americans for their shelter and protected by good strong barbed wire from marauding bands that still roam the countryside. What is there more to tell? By now the Turks have gone from around here—I have no knowledge as to who made them leave—but they kept all the fertile land south of Alexandropol and their new border is just a few miles off, along the river—the filthy dogs! They have always hated us Armenians, because we are Christians. The Americans are Christians too, although not in our way. May God reward them!"

"In Tiflis, too, the Americans have soup kitchens and distribute old clothes," Tassia said pensively, "but the clothes end up somehow in the black market, and the soup is not very good, but that's because there are so many hungry people and they have to keep adding water to the soup. We went there when there wasn't any food at home."

After they had made the last hairpin turn, the road suddenly swung out from among the trees, circled a narrow ravine, then flattened and straightened and, pale with dust, continued through treeless plains of a harsh dirty yellow.

Kyra whispered unhappily, "And it's all because of me that we ended up here."

The high regard in which their mother was held enabled her to place the children in the American personnel compound, an enclosure on the dust-swept plain with sentries at its one gate, but some miles away from the nearest refugee post. Olga Ivanovna, pointedly relieved and self-righteous, was sent off to Tiflis in a half-truck on its weekly run to the city-based headquarters. Sonia shared her mother's bed. Kyra was lodged most uncomfortably, for by day her folding cot and she herself had to make room for a washing tub and the laundresses. When she took to spending long hours at the stables where the grooms were elderly local horsemen, no one missed her or minded, for she seemed to have found a harmless and useful occupation in trotting the horses for exercise within the limits of the compound.

Tassia was the lucky one. She was taken in by Mr. and Mrs. Woodcock, a missionary Quaker couple who had a cottage of their own on the grounds and who had taken a great fancy to her because they thought she resembled a daughter of their own back in Ohio. Mrs. Gladys Woodcock was wont to repeat that she would gladly adopt this beguiling and sensible child, and that one way or another she would certainly see to it that the girl got a proper education. She had sent to the United States for proper clothes for Tassia who, although skinnier, must be roughly the size of her daughter. To Kyra's bewilderment, Tassia was changing rapidly from her forlorn self as the ex-president of her class in the Labor School into a well-fed, rosy adolescent, content and brightly facing the future. How unpredictable is life! Her involvement with Gasim which she recognized as senselessly and provocatively reckless, had unexpectedly brought about this good thing for her sister. But what if Gasim had made true his threat, had abducted her and made her his bride?

21. Nothing But Extra Mouths

The children had returned to Tiflis unscathed, but their mother had not been as fortunate.

Kyra sat crouched on a small stool, her head pressed against the door of her mother's sick room. From within came the same dreadful sounds, strangled breathing and coughing interrupted by short low moans. A tear fell hot upon her hand. She felt others sliding down her cheeks, yet she wasn't crying: she hadn't the strength to cry any more. Catching her unawares, the conversation she had overheard forced itself back into her mind.

"There isn't much chance of her pulling through, poor thing," Olga Ivanovna had repeated several times, "she's so weak now."

"She came back from Armenia all done in, and anyway she's been overworking for years with those children to support. Such an infectious illness, too—diphtheria," Russudanna Georgievna had added.

The two women had stood talking in the front hall, but the door was ajar.

"The doctor said he was unable to get whatever medicine she should have, so unless—poor woman, poor woman!"

"What on earth will happen to the children?" Russudanna asked shrilly. "Theirs was a large clan but, as far as I know all perished, at least those who did not manage to escape abroad. Why, they'll starve within a week. Nowadays who can afford to feed extra mouths?"

"It would be better if God took them all."

Fists at her ears so as not to hear anything further, Kyra had cried herself into utter exhaustion, then remained slumped against the door, unthinking, emptied.

Now she would get up. It was madness to pay attention to those two women's words. It was in their mean natures to believe the worst. She should have realized that. She would bathe her face in cold water, she would hold herself tightly in hand. Where were her sisters? When had they eaten last? Had either Tassia or Sonia gone to fetch bread after school? With nyanya never leaving their mother's side, it was up to her, as eldest, to see that there was bread and cheese or sour milk in the house. Rapidly, thrice, Kyra made the sign of the cross against the door of her mother's room and forced herself to stand up.

She went into the children's room. It, too, was in darkness except for the pink glow from the stove. Recently coal had become available—perhaps because of the Americans? Curled up on the floor in front of the stove, Sonia lay hugging Vasska, a huge gray alley cat whom she had befriended and painstakingly taught to jump in through the window. Kyra was on the verge of saying as usual, "That filthy beast again. Wait till you catch some horrible disease pressing your face to him," but somehow the words did not come after all and instead she just stared at Sonia's face, pink from the pink glow of the stove, small, round, and childish. Surprised at the lack of comment, Sonia glanced up apologetically. "You know, Vasska is keeping himself much cleaner nowadays. See his paws? And the white on his breast is really white. Vasska, my darling beautiful Vasska!"

The animal purred loudly. Sonia, happy, clasped him to her.

Kyra moved nearer the stove, stood irresolutely. Stretching out a hand, she was about to stroke Vasska's head, but he glared at her, hissed, and tearing himself from Sonia's arms, bolted onto the windowsill.

"I was only going to stroke him," Kyra said humbly.

"How was he supposed to guess that? He knows everyone here hates him except me."

Sonia got up to open the window and let Vasska out, then came back sucking her scratched hand.

"He only scratched me because you scared him."

Kyra slid to the floor at Sonia's side. "Where is Tassia?"

"How do I know? You both went away and I've been here all alone; then I called Vasska."

"I was only in the dining room. You know Olga Ivanovna has moved out until Mother— She's going to stay upstairs with Russudanna Georgievna."

After a silence, Kyra added desperately, "Look, aren't you hungry?"

"Not especially. I had some soup. Nika's mother gave me two whole plates, and she also gave me some herring to take away for you and Tassia. I've eaten some of it, but there's more there on the table, and I also went to get the bread."

"I wonder if Tassia has had anything to eat."

"How do I know?"

"She'll probably be hungry when she gets home."

"Well, there's the herring for her."

"Maybe I better get more coal for the stove."

"There's more in the pail here. Look Kyra, please let's talk. Will you talk to me?"

"But I am. I just said that I was wondering if—"

"I don't mean that way. Oh Kyra, you know, the kind of thing you always tell about—supermen and yogi and will power, you know, like closing your eyes at the movies when the most exciting part is about to begin. Remember, you told me last time how to concentrate? You were reading some very fat books then, Ramacharaki or something like that."

"Well, I've told you all that."

"Then something like sex and character, remember? A man isn't a man, and a woman isn't a woman—oh, you know —and about geniuses."

"Sonia, you do get things mixed up. A man isn't a man— that does not mean anything. What I told you was that there is no such thing as absolute man and absolute woman, but just approximation. A certain percentage of both in each person, and the degree of the percentage determines your sex, and in the middle you have hermaphrodites—that was Otto Weininger—and that genius is a male characteristic, and talent is quite another thing. Also I told you about Nietzsche's superman, but don't get that mixed up with yogi—that's plain nonsensical."

"But of course I'm not getting them mixed up. Tell me some more, please."

"I don't want to tonight, Sonia."

"Don't be mean, Kyra, you're sitting there doing nothing, so why can't you talk? You chased Vasska away too, why don't you want to talk to me?"

"I just can't tonight."

"Kyrochka, remember when you told me about reincarnation and also black magic? That was awfully nice." Sonia's voice was so wistful that Kyra gave in.

"I'll tell you about the Absolute, if you want to. Only I'm not going to talk very much. I'll tell you about it, and that's that, and don't ask for more."

"All right." Sonia rolled over so as to better face Kyra. Then suddenly she snatched Kyra's hand and kissed it.

"You'll never know how much I love you!"

"Oh, Sonia!" Dear God, don't let her start in crying again. If she started crying, she would tell Sonia what she had overheard. Sitting rigidly upright, Kyra began to talk very rapidly.

"Look, Sonia, I'm going to talk fast so just stop me when you can't understand something. You see, all matter is one; there is only this one matter and everything, everything is a form of it. Take a chair or a table, or this stove, that's the crudest lowest form of it—all material things, our bodies included, is its lowest form. To simplify, I'm only going to mention three of the most obvious gradations, though actually it's a continuous infinite gradation. Well, the second, the higher manifestation of this same matter is thought. Also emotion, you know, like loving, hating, being afraid. You see, it's all really the same thing as thought. They are both attributes of us as conscious beings. Look, I'll explain it this way: every thought anyone ever thinks does not just disappear. It goes on existing outside, apart. If you could but see, you'd see thoughts all floating around you. Some are pure colorless ones like concentrating on astronomy or solving some mathematical problem, just pure thought, and some would be brightly colored, for example, if you thought about someone you loved passionately the thought might be purple, or maybe black if you hated, or just kind of little gray ones if it's a petty little thought as: it's time to go to bed, or what dress shall I wear? They're all kind of swimming and jostling each other all around us. And of course we are influenced by the ones which are the nearest us, at least, they can influence our aura, our astral body which is also one of the intermediate manifestations of matter. Now, in the highest, the purest form, this matter is Absolute, or what we call God. Our souls are particles of the Absolute, and after our death join the Absolute. Now I imagine sometime eventually all the cruder manifestations of matter will somehow move up higher and higher and nearer and nearer to the Absolute, and then all matter becomes Absolute. Why, that's the aim, the end, the completion. Do you understand?"

"Will that be the end of the world then? Oh Kyra, can you see thoughts? Can anyone see them or is it impossible? I'd so love to see them, but anyway I'm glad they're there, and not everything just empty. Kyra, does everybody know about them?"

"Well, no. You see, one can't really be quite sure about things like this; one can only have theories. That's my theory. And of course some people can see astral bodies, so why shouldn't they see thoughts?"

"Kyra, then is there a sure way of telling when the end of the world is near? Nyanya says it's near now, but we still have chairs and tables."

"What do you mean?"

"Well, you said chairs were the lowest, and when everything begins moving up, wouldn't they be the first to disappear? I mean when they become something better they'd stop being chairs."

"It's not as simple as that. It may happen another way. Gradually our bodies, our senses like touch, smell, sight, and so on will become surpassed and a new set of senses will be acquired. As for example, seeing thoughts and astral bodies, we will begin living on that plane, a higher plane. It's only our limited unrealized consciousness which makes us see a table as a table. After all, actually it's all this one matter. Do you understand? It's not the question of the table disappearing, but us living on another plane with our senses, then we would no longer know matter in the crude shape of a table. Maybe it's too difficult for you to understand. Anyway, I myself have not thought of the Absolute for a long time. Perhaps a few things need to be changed in my theory. That was before I'd read any psychology. You know what psychology is? That's what I'll tell you about next time—remind me."

"Kyra, I wish you would teach me something every day,

oh, how I wish you would! And honestly, I don't get things
mixed up. It's only that I can't remember the words, and it
sounds all wrong when I say something, but I remember things
you've told me ages ago when I was very small—all about the
Greek gods and women gods and simply women and how
they fought all the time among themselves and were beastly
jealous. And about entirely different gods, the Persian ones.
I even remember their names because I liked them so, and
Kyra, you won't laugh at me? Well, when I'm alone with
Vasska, I don't call him Vasska, I call him Ormuzd, and
Ahriman is Olga Ivanovna. You know, it's really very funny,
I've called her that to her face and of course she does not
know what it means. Once she asked me. Of course I couldn't
tell her it was an evil god. All I said was someone she re-
minded me of. It was funny!"

There were quick steps along the porch, then the door
flew open and Tassia ran in, panting, laughing, shaking off
her coat.

"It's actually snowing! Look, look, it's on my coat and
my face is all wet. I love snow! It's marvelous! How I wish
it would really snow hard, a real snowstorm."

Still chattering breathlessly, she pulled off her coat and
tossed her beret on the table.

"Galia, Nina, and I went down to the Koura. We stood
on the bridge and the wind was blowing, it was blowing like
anything, and all the people who passed were walking bent
and all huddled up in scarves and things. They must have
thought us crazy. You see, we stood there and sang. We had
our hats off and we were singing into the wind. Then Galia
and Nina had to go home because it's so late and they'd get
scolded, but I stayed on all by myself, and it was wonderful."

"And now you'll catch cold." Sonia imitated nyanya's
tone of voice.

"No, I won't. I'm hot, I ran home. Why are you sitting
in the dark? Is Mother asleep? Can I talk to her through the
door?"

Kyra shook her head, then lest Tassia ask any more

questions in that brisk easy way, she murmured, "Asleep."

"Let me get in front of the stove too. Move your legs, Sonia. No, Kyra, don't you move, I did not mean you, there's lots of room if Sonia stretches her legs the other way." Tassia held her reddened hands to the flame, then pulled them away with a little cry, "Oh, my chilblains! When your hands are cold they hurt; when you try to warm your hands they itch and burn like a thousand devils. Lord Almighty, what are chilblains for?"

"You know it's because we don't get enough fats," Sonia answered reasonably.

Tassia began pulling off her shoes and stockings which were wet and covered with mud. One of her damp pigtails brushed against Kyra's hand. Sonia was squirming, trying to worm as much of her body as possible into a position directly in front of the fire. There was a long silence, and presently Kyra spoke in spite of herself, a new wave of despair wrenching it out of her.

"Mother is going to—" then her voice was cut off by the strangling swell in her throat.

"What, Kyra?" Busy with rubbing her toes, Tassia hadn't looked up. Sonia too had remained with her back toward Kyra.

Kyra began to cough chokingly, her tear-drenched face turned aside, hidden in her hands, her fingers spread so as to cover even her puckered temples.

"What's the matter, Kyra?" Tassia's whisper was quick and frightened.

"Choke," Kyra managed to enunciate. When Tassia leaned toward her, she sprang up and ran across the dark room to the window. She kept up her coughing as she pulled the window open and lay across the sill.

"Shall I hit your back or do you want water?"

"Water." She lay there grasping the window ledge, trembling uncontrollably, the cold air stinging and drying her face.

"Kyra, what did you begin to say about Mother? What

is she going to do? Did you speak to her? Is she worse?" Tassia
was gripping her shoulder.

"Tell us, Kyra." Sonia's voice too sounded frightened.

"No, it's nothing—I did not mean to—it's nothing."

After a minute she pulled the window to, and followed
Tassia back to the stove, obediently dropping to the floor
and only trying to lean far enough back to keep her face from
the glow of the embers. The image of Tassia on the bridge in
the dark and the wind came back to her. Below the bridge
the Koura rushed dizzily. If her mother were going to die, she
would also, and so would Tassia and Sonia. They would go
down to the bridge over the Koura, wait till it was deserted,
and climb over the railings. That way God would take them
all—the solution Olga Ivanovna had seen as best for them.
Russudanna Georgievna obviously had no solution to offer
with her "No one today can afford to feed extra mouths."
Mouths, they were nothing but mouths; she, Tassia, and Sonia
were nothing but mouths, it seemed.

Tassia touched her arm. "What a strange expression
you have on your face. I've never seen you like that. What
are you thinking about? Listen, are you sure Mother isn't
worse?"

Kyra shook her head.

"It must be way after twelve. Look, Sonia's asleep. Sonia,
wake up and undress. We better have some light."

"No, don't, Tassia. It's nice with just the stove. I'll close
the stove only after you're in bed."

Making a pretense of undressing, she waited until her
sisters had got into bed and were still in the darkness. She
closed the stove. Stealthily she crept from the room and back
to the stool at her mother's door. It was quiet behind the
door. With her ear against the keyhole, Kyra waited.

"Nyanya," she whispered presently.

She heard nyanya moving, shuffling in soft slippers across
the floor.

"It's me, Kyra."

"Shsh—she's asleep. Better pray to the Lord," nyanya whispered back through the keyhole.

Kyra slid off the bench to her knees.

22. The Wall

Slowly Kyra began to descend the broad marble staircase of the former Nobles Assembly, now the local headquarters of the Workers Union. She had waited three hours to see Comrade Ivanchuk, a petty official, and as usual, was leaving without having been called in. "You can wait," she had been told, and day after day she waited. She watched other people entering his office, some knocking, others just sauntering in. Those were mostly young men in leather jackets exuding self-assurance, and earnest crop-haired young women with papers under their arms. Kyra stationed herself immediately in front of the door to remind those inside of her presence, of the answer she was awaiting to her application. In her weariness and exasperation she would sometimes be on the verge of walking in without being summoned, but no sooner did her fingers touch the doorknob than she backed away, defeated.

It had been that way ever since her mother had started to recover and Kyra had gone looking for work. It had been that way earlier, when in the fall she had tried to enter the university. "Your social origin? Your father's occupation previous to 1917?" The inevitable stare and shrug of the shoulders as she braced herself and answered—the careless dismissal.

Kyra tried to leave some of the bitterness behind her before facing the sunny street. Her mother was almost well at last. She tried to cheer Kyra up by assuring her that she really preferred her not working yet—she was barely seventeen; that there was plenty of time for work in the years to come, and that the bad times would inevitably come to an end. Russia had to reconstruct herself. There was bound to be work for everybody. If the N E P * continued there would be large private enterprises which would need lots of people. N E P had been started by Lenin. His successors would surely continue the newly relaxed program. But rumors had it both ways. At Lenin's death, some people said that things would become more normal and easygoing; others thought that, after a respite, it would get much worse.

Kyra stopped at the curb. There, across the street from her, stood a recently opened private store, its windows full of wonderful things. Kyra knew every item by heart—a mound of butter, the loaves of white bread, a side of pink ham, two graceful strings of sausages, blue tins of caviar, a huge white fish with a green twig in its mouth. Would a day really come when she could enter and give her order with confidence? I'll have half a dozen sausages, please, and a loaf of white bread, and add a quarter of pound of butter to that. At present only the wives of commissars and speculators could afford to shop in private stores. Once she had been inside. Eva's brother had taken her in and bought her three doughnuts with the jelly oozing out as she bit into them.

Eva was expected to go to Moscow very shortly. The whole family would join her father, who had gone to Moscow and was now evidently beginning to do very well trading in something.

On the day set for the state funeral for Lenin, processions marched along Golovinsky slowly and endlessly. There was so much tension that it seemed the houses themselves would burst open. Kyra had marched for hours and hours in cold drizzling rain which at times became snow, then turned into rain once again. Her feet were wet and numb and her chilblains ached, and whenever the procession halted she was afraid that she'd be unable to resume walking. Funeral marches

* N E P: New Economic Policy.

never stopped playing. Carried back and tossed by the wind, the sound seemed part of the cold, cruel day, relentless, inevitable. Kyra wept from pain and tension.

She marched between two girls about her own age, one sullen and blue-nosed with the cold, her little dark eyes stubbornly glued to the ground, her shoulders hunched; the other, clumsy in a man's heavy overcoat, whispered questions to Kyra under her breath about whether it was true that Lenin had died a long time ago but that it had been kept a secret from the people, and whether it was true that they would be given hot tea and rolls after the speeches on the square. Kyra tried not to listen to her. Gradually there grew inside of her a strange immense emotion, a new emotion born of the unceasing music and crowds silently moving, crowds wondering as they moved where they were being led to on this solemn day, where they would be led on solemn days to come. What forces beyond their control were to govern them? It was a fateful day for every Russian. All over Russia people were marching today. She was marching with all Russians from the past, through this day and toward a future. This was a day which would never be forgotten.

When she had come home, before even throwing off her wet clothes, she pulled out her diary. Leaning on the windowsill, looking at the now empty and quiet Golovinsky, she tried to think of words which would express this great thing taking place—words which would go beyond her, beyond her emotion, which would hold the consciousness of everyone of this day. She wrote, "We are Russians—" then she gave up. Nyanya was calling to her crossly to take off her dripping coat and have some hot tea. She and Tassia and Sonia drank many cups while nyanya rubbed their feet with a rough towel. Russudanna Georgievna had come down. She said, "Well, that's one less of them. Hope the others follow suit. The murderers!"

"Vampires, bloodsuckers, dragging little children around for hours in weather like this," nyanya muttered.

"I always hated him so, but I did not today," Tassia said quietly.

"I walked next to a girl who cried about him, but she looked like a crybaby anyway, and besides she did not have any gloves and her hands were blue like a dead man's. I liked the funeral marches though—they're like a lullaby, only more so." Sonia looked quite satisfied with her day.

Kyra had not found anything at all to say.

Lost in thought, Kyra had not heard Eva calling until her friend grabbed her arm and laughingly shook her. Then, without waiting for a rejoinder, Eva continued excitedly, "I have great news. I'm leaving for Moscow at the end of next month. We just got a letter from Father. He's finally been able to get an apartment. I'm to have a room all to myself. Just imagine it! Oh Kyra, I'm so happy. And yet, in some ways, I'm not. I'll miss Lilly and you so terribly. I'll never have such friends again. You know how much I love you both, don't you? Sometimes you've both accused me of being cold, but that's only my way. I can't act as demonstratively as Lilly. I can't show my affection by just looking at people, the way you do. But I'll be horribly lonely without you."

"Eva, Eva, I so wish you weren't going."

"Look, we can't just stand here. Walk with me. It's such a beautiful day. I've just left Souren. I've spent the whole morning with him. Oh God, I'm so sad really. Come and walk with me. Where were you going?"

"I was about to go home but I won't now. I was at the Union, but all in vain again. I don't want to go on being depressed, though, so let's not talk about it; let's talk of other things, please, Eva."

"You know, it's days like this that I'll miss most in Moscow. Just strolling in the sunshine with no place to go, meeting people, talking to them, and strolling on again. Meeting Souren. Kyra, do you think I should marry Souren? He wants us to elope. His family feel just as bitter as mine about us becoming engaged. When he's kissing me, it seems to me that nothing else matters in the world, and that I should go off with him, and the hell with everything, but then— Oh, why did he have to be an Armenian and me a Georgian! It's fantastic, even barbaric, that it should make any difference, but it does, even to me. How deep-seated those things are— no reasoning changes them. I shall go to Moscow. I shall meet new people. I'll be able to tell better how much he means to me."

"You'll never marry him, Eva, if you go to Moscow. Remember what nyanya said when she told your fortune. 'You are to marry an important man.' "

"Yes, that was strange, wasn't it? 'You will go away to a very big town and you will live well. You will live better and better, but there is danger around you. Great danger. You will marry a man, an important older man, and you will live better than ever for a while.' Then, remember, she suddenly mixed up the cards and would not say any more. She scared me, you know. That was before I even knew about Moscow. It makes me feel very strange, almost as if I were moving to a predestined end. What else could she have seen in the cards? What dangers? I suppose it's silly to believe in fortune-telling."

Kyra did believe in nyanya's fortune-telling, and now she suddenly remembered what nyanya had told her after Eva left. "She won't keep her pretty head on her shoulders if she marries that man in the cards. It's a bad end she'll have, Kyrochka. High she will fly, mark my words, but not for long."

Kyra felt horror stricken. "Oh Eva, don't go to Moscow. I don't want you to, please don't. Darling, darling Eva, don't go."

"But Kyra, only think! I'll have a room of my own, and I'll go to the opera and to the theater, and I'll meet clever people through my aunt. She knows everyone in Moscow because she's married to a famous professor. I'll go to exhibitions and museums, and also to the races and the cabarets and—I'll see so much, and I so want to see a lot. You know, we've seen nothing, nothing at all. It will be marvelous, Kyra."

"Oh, Eva!"

"Look, Kyra, maybe I'll go to Paris some day. It isn't really impossible. I'll sit in a café on the boulevard and I'll sip a cognac, and I'll wear a veil, and there will be music played by negroes in purple jackets, and a long row of black shiny cars. And at night I shall dance in some immense hall and there will be rare flowers and champagne and oysters."

They walked silently for a while. A squadron of soldiers, boots clanging on the cobblestones, marched by singing the Internationale. A heavily laden arba drawn by water buffaloes turned in from a side street, and they had to pause to let it go by. Somewhere a boy's guttural voice was shouting monotonously, "Charcoal, charcoal." Groups of men stood idly here and there by the trees edging the sidewalk and many raised their hands in salute as Eva passed, and stared after her. The street became more and more crowded with sauntering people and the small balconies overhanging the street were crowded too. Passing Lilly's house, they met her cousin Gleb.

"Lilly's secreted in my room, scribbling as usual," he told them; "She cut her lecture again, silly girl!"

A party member of long standing and with excellent connections had promised Lilly he would back her for a position in the foreign section of the library attached to a trade mission. Although impressed by Lilly's ready intelligence and ingenuity, the man had made it a condition that she acquire the rudiments of the needed skills before pushing the matter further. As sensible as the request had seemed, and as readily as Lilly had jumped at the opportunity to obtain work so painlessly, they had not reckoned with Lilly's inability to stem her flow of poetic self-expression, so utterly inappropriate to the demands of the day.

Eva took Kyra by the elbow. "I know you're really still thinking of that beast, Comrade Ivanchuk. Let's stop at Gleb's for a minute, Lilly always knows how to cheer you up." To avoid Princess Argadze, they went through the yard and up the back stairs. But it was with deep sighs of self-recrimination rather than her usual little shrieks of pleasure that Lilly met them. "Slap me, pinch me, punish me somehow," she cried out. "Here I sit writing like a fool, and I've missed the library lecture again. I must have been born with the slogan, *Le plus lourd fardeau c'est d'exister sans vivre*. As long as life is alive, even if it's alive with suffering, that's better than a slow, gray, unfeeling and unthinking existence, and for me writing doubles, triples the feeling of being alive. Kyra, my nice, my intelligent one, do something, say something to help me."

To her own surprise Kyra started laughing. It was loud, rude laughter and it puffed out of her so violently that she had to lean against the wall. The next moment she snatched Lilly's hand and kissed it. Lilly's arms went around her. "You've been to see Comrade Ivanchuk again this morning, haven't you?"

"Yes." After a silence, Kyra said slowly, "I have also thought a lot about life. Listen. I've read it somewhere, or maybe I've only dreamt it but life is like an endless field, barren and muddy looking, and there is an immense wall, a wall of heavy unclear glass, which is moving relentlessly and slowly across that field. Men are on the field, doing all kinds of things. As the wall moves up to them they run and struggle and try to escape that horrible wall. They cannot, and the wall mows them down, levels them with the muddy earth and passes over them. It reaches other groups and those in turn claw at it and kick at it, but it mows them down, too. Always the ones at the farthest end of the field see the wall approaching and through its unclean glass they see their former companions leveled out with the earth. They can do nothing about it. They prefer not to look, and just keep on doing things hastily, senselessly—"

"How ghastly, Kyra. I suppose the wall is death."

"I suppose so. But something different occurred to me as well. That wall is not death but life itself. I don't know if I can explain. It's the forces of life beyond one's control that mow people down. People go under during life. I've seen people over whom the wall has rolled, haven't you? Older people who have lost everyone and everything dear to them because of the Revolution, for example. Not my mother, nor yours, Lilly; and we three, we're skipping ever so hard to keep away from that wall."

Eva took Kyra's face between her hands. "My poor darling, we cannot afford to philosophize, we who may be 'liquidated' before we've had time to live. So let's concentrate on the skipping."

"Anyway, I don't really believe what I've just told you, at least not very often."

"How is that?"

"You see, it leaves no place for God, for a Purpose, for Truth. Eva, Lilly, have you read *The Brothers Karamazov?* Yes? Isn't it the most extraordinary book you've ever read? Do you remember, near the beginning, Ivan Karamazov's conversation with Alyosha in the tavern? Do you remember what he says about God? Let's see if I can get it straight for he takes pages and pages to explain it—that he believes in God but he cannot approve of God's scheme. That God should not build His scheme on so much human suffering. However high and glorious the scheme, it cannot be accepted at such a price. When I go past the Cheka or hear about the senseless killings and torturing, I think that maybe God is not all kind and merciful and good—all those one-sided things. Maybe He is unfeeling as far as men are concerned. Or maybe He is neither kind or cruel, nor good or bad, but is beyond any attribute or any set of attributes. He is everything. He is everything. He is so much everything that maybe evil is included in Him. That's the only way I can understand it."

"Kyra, Kyra, don't get yourself in such a state. I'd dearly love to wring that Ivanchuk's neck, the puffed-up turkey cock, the vile bureaucrat!" Lilly cried out savagely, while Eva, silently, embraced Kyra again.

PART VII

23. Mother and Daughter

The light breeze from the window which Kyra had left ajar kept the candle flickering uneasily, the small circle of light on the table ever moving, distending, then shrinking, gliding haphazardly about. Elbow resting on her open diary, Kyra began molding the soft wax back into shape as it dripped. She scorched her nail and gave up, sliding lower into her red armchair, finding the familiar comfortable support of its triangular back. Tassia was muttering and twisting in her sleep, and after a moment Kyra sat up again to stack more books around the candle and diminish the light in the room. Her eyes fell on the half-written page of her diary.

There really wasn't anything more to add. Day after day it was all the same and equally futile. God, would it always be this way? If she could only get a job—but not through Volodia. There were bruises on her arms where his fingers had clutched her. Her lips also felt bruised. Damn him. Still, if he was really willing to get her a job— Undoubtedly he had pull. With an official car in his hands it was easy to do favors, and favors naturally had to be repaid. No, she would go on trying alone. Levan had found work. Of course, he had had a couple of years at the Engineering School, and now worked as a minor draftsman on a hydroelectric construction site on the

Koura in Mtskhet, some two hours from Tiflis. Darling Levan. She was so fond of him, and she missed him frightfully. With Eva in Moscow and Levan away most of the time, she felt deserted. There was still Lilly who was amusing and clever and whom she loved, but Lilly was not of much help. And recently something odd was happening to Lilly. She seemed distressed and nervous and as depressed as it was possible for her gay, easygoing self to be.

Pushing her armchair back a little, Kyra turned toward the window and pulled the shutters wider apart. It was such a peaceful gentle night with the small warm breeze and a sturdy lopsided moon and plenty of stars. One could almost make out the line of hills beyond Tiflis, and the town with its rare lights seemed to be lying asleep so defenselessly, so patiently, so strangely confidently. There, on the opposite side of Golovinsky were shuttered, balconied houses with the familiar tall cypress bending slightly over one of the roofs, and the row of dim blinking street lanterns. One could make out where the Koura was by the lights along the bridge, and somewhere in the distance beyond the Koura where the town climbed upward again there was a late trolley car slowly, steadily advancing its one yellow eye. All was as it should be, or at least it seemed that way. But, oh God, everything was sad. "Your social origin, YOUR SOCIAL ORIGIN. Liquidate the hated class enemies of the victorious proletariat, tread them underfoot, starve them out." So what was she expecting? She was being highly unreasonable. Things could so easily be much worse. She really was quite lucky. Her mother was working again and she was left free to enjoy herself. She murmured a line from a poem of Lilly's, "For one should take from life as much as one is able—" She damn well would. She'd rather die and be done with it than just sit back moaning and sniveling like Olga Ivanovna and Russudanna Georgievna. Of course they were old and she was young, but she would kill herself before growing old that way. She must get something from life, something, anything, whatever she could. Come on, friends, bring vodka and wine. Let's drink to liquidation. Not noisily but, oh, very quietly, so no one would know. Quiet, quiet. Mustn't wake Tassia and Sonia. Now keep still. Damnation, what was happening to her?

Kyra sank her teeth into her forearm, pressing in fiercely till the pain quietened the tumult in her chest. Slowly she let go, then sat staring at the hideous red circle with its beads of blood. Serve her right! Now she would find something easy and pleasant to think about before going to bed. Otherwise she might see the nightmare again—those horrible, horrible screams, a man running and stumbling and falling and running; the street never ending and narrow between tall dark walls; then the distant rumble of huge motor lorries; then clanging and thundering, ever approaching, approaching. Now really she must think of something pleasant.

She began to remember Rezo Garidzé's party where she had met that strange person, Jan. The night had begun so wonderfully. It had been very late when she had sneaked out of the house. As soon as in the dark she had caught sight of Levan who was waiting for her outside the gate, she started in explaining that they had stayed in church long after midnight because Olga Ivanovna had had to kiss half the congregation and wish them "Jesus has risen," and that afterward they had eaten and chanted, and her mother had not gone to bed till just now. Only then did she see that there was someone with Levan, and when that someone approached, Kyra, thrilled into silence, recognized Jan Karitsky. Jan Karitsky, the dancer, Jan Karitsky whom every schoolgirl in Tiflis worshiped, Jan Karitsky who sauntered along Golovinsky, shoulders hunched high and forward, hands deep in pockets, seeing no one, keeping his gray arrogant eyes fixed immovably at an angle which skirted the faces of other strollers. As he kissed her hand, he had said, "So you've had to escape through the window? Our host will be honored to learn it. I sincerely hope your mother sleeps soundly and wakes late to find you safely tucked into bed. Well, Jesus has risen!" Once again his lips touched her hand. "Indeed He has risen!" Kyra answered automatically, suddenly feeling horridly ashamed of herself—Easter night, sacred night, the purest of all nights, and here she was sneaking out in the dark, betraying—a Judas. Forego party? At least 'she must get home before daybreak. And if Jesus, who had just risen, wanted to be kind to her mother, He would arrange it so that she would slip back unnoticed, and thus spare her mother an unhappiness.

In the izvozchik on the way to Rezo Garidzé's, Kyra had worried about her dress. It had just been made over for her from an American petticoat, and though the material felt almost like silk, it was pink—light pink—true—but pink. If only the petticoat had been a shiny black. Still, she remembered Levan saying to her earlier, before church, "You look like a cool, soft little mermaid." Of course mermaids never wore pink. Unthinkingly, in the izvozchik she had asked, "What color are mermaids, I mean the usual kind?" and Jan had answered, "Oh, just the very usual variety? Silvery in moonlight, dead white under water. Now, their hair varies. Golden tresses for the German ones. As I remember, our Polish ones had raven black straight hair with seaweed or something entwined in it. At least, that's what my nurse said."

After they had arrived at the party Jan obviously forgot her existence. She had watched him and the dancer Alek Ratoff from across the room. How beautiful they looked dancing the tango. Jan obviously preferred men to women. There was something in Jan which aroused tenderness, almost pity, something lost and desperate. Probably every bit was true of what people said about him, even that he'd been in jail for thieving. But then all bezprizorni * were thieves—how else could they live? How old could he have been when the revolution came? Thirteen or so, all by himself in frozen, hungry Petrograd, his family far away in Poland, his school closed down, left alone, all alone. For years he must have just roved about from town to town, maybe joining up with some gang at times, running away from where there was fighting, looking for places where there was more food to be begged

* Bezprizorni: homeless children.

or stolen, sleeping in doorways like the bezprizorni in Tiflis, all in rags and sores and lice. Poor Jan!

But when, some two years ago, he had appeared in Tiflis, already well dressed and with his arrogant air, there was the rumor that some wealthy foreigner had befriended him. From her reading of French novels, and her observation of oriental practices, Kyra knew about pederasty. Young boys had recourse to it whether they liked it or not for it was a means of survival. It was better than starving to death.

Kyra swung around, listening. It sounded like steps in the next room. Now the handle of the door was being pressed. Softly the door opened. Her mother stood on the threshold. Instinctively Kyra reached back to close her diary, then waited perched on the edge of her chair, uneasy and avoiding her mother's eyes.

"Why are you up so late, Kyra? You're not even undressed. Aren't you feeling well? I saw light under the door and was worried. It must be after three."

Her mother spoke in a whisper, but even so Kyra thought she distinguished reproach in her tone.

"If you think I just came home, it isn't so. I'm just not sleepy, that's all, and I wanted to write a letter." Kyra knew she was answering rudely and felt sorry even as she spoke, but somehow couldn't help it.

"Well, as a matter of fact, I, too, have been awake." Her mother had waited a few seconds before speaking. "If you're not sleepy I'd like to talk to you. Maybe this isn't the perfect time, but I seem to see you so seldom what with my being away all day, and you out in the evening, and besides there are always people around. Come with me to my room—I don't want to wake the children."

Reluctantly Kyra rose. Her mother's tone had been firm.

"I'll come in just a second, Mother, all right? I just want to put it away—"

Her mother nodded and left the room, closing the door. Frowning and biting her lips, Kyra remained still for a moment. Then she thrust her diary under the mattress of her bed, felt with her hand a little farther along, pulled forth an envelope of tea leaves. She took a pinch of the tea, put it on her tongue and chewed vigorously, her face all screwed up from the bitterness. Still, it was better than having her mother smell wine on her breath, especially when she had evidently been brooding as it was. She spat the tea out onto a piece of paper, rolled the paper into a ball, stuck both it and the envelope back under the mattress, took a few deep breaths with mouth wide open, and tiptoed to the door. In the dining room behind a screen Olga Ivanovna was snoring. She tiptoed past her but not as noiselessly as she had past her sisters.

Her mother was sitting in the center of the small room on the hard chair by the desk. Her clasped hands were stretched in front of her across the desk and her eyes were lowered as if carefully studying those hands. When she heard Kyra entering, the clasp loosened, fell apart, and she looked up without smiling or speaking. Kyra went to sit on the end of the bed, also silent, still frowning. For a moment they just looked at one another. Kyra noticed that her mother's braids had become undone and tousled as when one's head has twisted and tossed on the pillow. Over her nightgown she wore the now tattered raincoat which had once been their father's, and which her mother used in place of a dressing gown. As Kyra gazed on, she was suddenly shocked by the realization that her mother looked old—not just weary or unwell, which the children had become accustomed to—but no longer young. Long slanting furrows lay on either side of her mouth, lines were deeply cut into her forehead, the once-smooth delicate skin stretched tightly over the high cheekbones now looked loosened and dull. It can't be, it can't be, Kyra repeated to herself. Thirty-nine, her mother was thirty-nine. In a way that was old, but it was unthinkable that her mother would just get to look old like anyone else. It was absolutely neces- sary that her mother stay beautiful. Tired yes, and worried sometimes, but always beautiful and ready to smile. It shouldn't be otherwise. Half squinting, Kyra tried looking from another angle, then stared straight into her mother's eyes. Oh, that was better. Her mother's gaze was clear and strong and right.

"Why don't you answer me, Kyra? Why do you stare like that?"

"Oh, Mother, Mother—" Kyra threw herself off the bed and down on her knees at her mother's side, arms tight around her mother's waist, face buried.

"Kyra, Kyrochka mine, don't get upset. Stay quiet a minute, calm yourself. Oh, my little girl, I know you're really good and sensitive and kind, and it's so hard for me to bear the things you're doing to yourself. You're so highly strung, so impulsive, so heedless. I'm afraid for you. I'm afraid you may hurt yourself terribly one day. It's difficult for me with you—you know you are very difficult, I don't mean it as a reproach—you are unusually intelligent and yet childishly, recklessly foolish when it comes to your conduct. Now go and sit down and let's talk, and believe me, my little girl, that I'm not blaming you blindly, I would only like to help."

Slowly Kyra rose and went back to sit on the bed.

"You see, Mother, it's not that I'm childishly foolish, or maybe I am, but not in the way you think. I think I know what I'm doing. I do it because I mean to do it."

"But you can't set out meaning to do yourself harm. And you're harming yourself as a person, you're tearing yourself down physically, emotionally, spiritually. It's easy to lose one's integrity bit by bit, almost unnoticeably at first, then faster because caring less, till nothing remains but weakness, self-indulgence, and unhappiness and disgust with yourself. You can't mean you want that, Kyra."

"Of course not, Mother, but, Mother, I probably want the same things you wanted when you were young, you know, what everyone wants—oh, to just have something pleasant and gay, and also deep and important, all kinds of things that are in life. I mean, you went to balls and the opera and places like that, and you met polite, well-educated people, men like Father, and you also went sleigh riding and hunting and on picnics, and everything was all prepared for you and easy to do. But now it's so different."

"My darling, I know. There's nothing in the world I would not give to make it possible for you to have a normal happy youth. It's not in my power. I can only feel pity for your whole unfortunate generation. But, my darling, be proud, don't accept dregs instead of wine. You can't be happy with dregs, you're not made for it, you're not happy even now, not even when you've forced yourself to be gay. Something good will come in your life, wait for it, keep yourself for it."

"But what good can come? Will anything come? No one will give me anything. No one wants me to have anything. I might as well get what I can get, and there isn't much to choose from. If I can get the least little things, even dregs, why shouldn't I?"

"Kyra, I'm talking to you as to a grown-up. Don't you think that we too, that I too, have had desires, desires I wanted to give in to, but that I did not give in to? Don't go imagining that self-indulgence is something new and peculiar to your time, it's as old as the world. There always were that kind of people, and it's not an attractive kind. You're rationalizing your bad conduct so that you may continue with it."

Hand clasping her throat, Kyra fidgeted on the bed, confused and unhappy. Maybe her mother was right. Maybe she was rationalizing, deceiving herself. She drank too much. And there was the time she had danced naked in front of Gleb. True, Lilly had challenged her, and what was the harm, still —If technically she remained a virgin, it was certainly not out of virtue, but solely out of fear of pregnancy, fear of the fate of Nina Tamidze who threw herself to her death in the churning waters of the Koura. Well, instead of facing, admitting her weakness, she realized she deceived herself into thinking of it as a positive thing. But there was something else, something else. It wasn't weakness the way her mother meant it. Weakness to give in to something one shouldn't give in to. For she had never even tried not giving in. There did not seem to be any reason for not giving in. What difference did it make?

"Mother, I'm all mixed up. Listen, Mother, listen. What was it, what made you not give in to some desires? I don't mean anything like blowing up houses or starting fires or shooting your enemies, but just little things. Didn't you ever say to yourself, oh, who cares, what difference does it make? And then how could you still refuse yourself it?"

"But everything makes a difference, Kyra, to your own self-respect, self-regard."

"But I don't know what my self-regard is, I mean when I'm at the Labor Union, or before that in school. Oh, Mother, I think something is missing in me."

"Also, don't you want other people to regard you with respect and to know you're worthy of that respect, of their high opinion? How would you like it if I, your mother, was thought badly of? Why, then, don't you want respect for yourself?"

Kyra squirmed and frowned and scratched herself. Of course her mother was right, but there still was something else.

"Look, Mother, when you were good, when you made yourself be good, it was because there was some point in being good. In one way or another you got reward for it, just what you've been saying—respect, self-respect, it's like nyanya will be rewarded by going to heaven. Do you see what I mean? But who's going to reward me for anything? If I turned into a saint and *une petite fille modèle,* all rolled into one, would anyone care? Would they give me a job? Would they accept me at the University? There just does not seem to be any point. Oh, I don't mean to sound horrid; maybe you didn't think of reward, but that was how Grandmother acted, and Great-grandmother, and they all expected you to— It was all kind of set out and arranged, and somehow you were part of something and you couldn't let it down and you lived up to something. You know, like the people in *War and Peace* and Tatiana in *Evgenii Onegin.* Don't think I don't understand that it was important to them, and that really it was important altogether. Oh, I'd so like to feel that way and live and die for something important and be part of something important.

You know, Mother, I could, I could have, I really could have."

"My little girl—" Her mother's voice was so full of pain that Kyra jerked her head away and started tracing with her finger the design on the blanket. Several minutes went by, then her mother moved something on the desk, changed her position in her chair, and when she spoke her tone was once more calm and firm.

"What is gone is gone and there is no use romanticizing the past which had its wrongs too. Many wrongs and evils. Let's go back to your problem in a more realistic way for a minute. Look, it will begin to get light in a short while and we have had no sleep. But now so much has been said. Kyra, I realize the fault is not yours entirely but that doesn't help either you or me. The problem can't be solved in a moment of emotion—in the long run it's a matter of belief and choice. What you said earlier—that it didn't make any difference, really—that frightens me more than ever, Kyra. I can't accept it. You must understand that."

"Mother, I do understand and I don't blame you at all for feeling that way. And I wish I was different and the way you'd like me to be."

Kyra was sitting up straight now, feeling strangely calm and reasonable.

"Do you understand that I feel it's my duty, my responsibility to look after you and take care of you even against your will. Someday maybe you'll be thankful, but anyway I can't, I just can't sit back and watch you doing what you do to yourself."

"No, I suppose you can't," Kyra admitted seriously, impartially.

"Perhaps I'm exaggerating, perhaps I'm lending too much importance to what may be just childish imprudence and love of fun. It's so long since you've told me anything about yourself, Kyra. Perhaps I am misjudging you in my anxiety. But this staying out late every night, whom are you with, what kind of people, doing what? Wine on your breath so often.

You avoid kissing me sometimes. Don't you think I know the reason why? Maybe your theories are just theories, the way it is so often in one's youth, but it's such a dangerous way to think and see things. It excludes any need for restraining oneself. And with your emotional nature—then also this sense of futility. How can I best help you?"

"I don't know." It really wasn't in her mother's power to help her. Should she promise her mother something—but what? To give up everything she was doing now and instead— but what instead? What? She couldn't just sit and think all the time. There wasn't anything worse than letting oneself think for a long time—then she'd really do something foolish. Oh, if she'd only been able to enter the University. Literature and psychology and philosophy—that would have been her choice. Could she promise her mother anything? If only she could. It was beastly of her not to promise, it was cruel. But what?

"Don't promise anything just to please me." Her mother seemed to have read her thought. "More than that is needed. A change of attitude. Will you think over the things I've said? You know it is very serious. It's a question of shaping your life. In the meantime I'm sorry I can't let you go to Mtskhet, but especially after Easter night I don't see how I can. I hope you don't think me unreasonable. Oh Kyra, I wish I could trust you."

"I don't think you're unreasonable, but I wish you'd let me go to Mtskhet. As I said, I will be with Lilly and Levan, my closest friends, and surely they would see that no harm comes to me."

"I have always discounted Lilly as a good influence, anything but that. Besides she is impulsive and self-engrossed, and would pay no attention to you. Perhaps if Eva had been here and going along, I might have hesitated, for I recognize that she has common sense and is in full control of any situation. As for Levan, I know his deep affection for you, but shell-shocked as he was, true, some years ago, his stability must remain questionable."

234

Her mother knew nothing about Jan. Further persuasion became useless when her mother added, "Until I am convinced that I can trust your judgment, you will just have to accept mine, if only for your own sake, to keep you from blundering into wrecking your life. In the meantime, I demand obedience. I don't like talking to you this way but you leave me no choice, no choice whatsoever, Kyra."

Her mother's face looked very pale and weary, the mouth drawn into a straight bitter line that Kyra didn't remember having seen before, the eyes heavy with sadness.

"Now you must go to bed, Kyra. Good night, my poor little girl."

"Good night, Mother." She caught her mother's hand and kissed it.

She crept past Olga Ivanovna into the children's room and relit the candle. For a moment she stood staring into its flame, then quickly began undressing as if her resolute movements took the place of any mental resolve. She got into bed still unthinking, preoccupied only with rearranging the lumpy pillow and the worn sheet split in the middle.

24. Mtskhet

Kyra crept out of the house before dawn and sat in the old Georgian cemetery until it was time to meet at the station for the trip to Mtskhet. She had forsworn going, but when she learned from Levan just the evening before that Jan had in the last moment promised to join them, however reluctantly, she felt unable to abide by her resolution. It was, after all, her pleading with Levan that had made him persuade Jan to go, since this was against Levan's own inclination. She knew that Jan's admiration for Levan, which Levan did not reciprocate, had made Jan change his mind. Jan, the "exquisite" Jan, was not one to take to the discomforts of an overnight countryside outing.

Someone threw more wood on the embers and in a minute flames were darting and leaping against the black of the night, illuminating the circle of faces, the soiled tablecloth, the empty overturned bottles, the remains of the food. Kyra started, and tried to emerge from the trance in which she had been staring at the embers with the thin blue tongues gliding over them so smoothly, disappearing, reappearing, swift and delicate. Now that she too was visible, she had to pull herself together. The singing which had faltered with the sudden light, continued plaintive, monotonous. Everyone was singing except Kyra and Jan, and even Jan joined in at intervals, humming. The three peasants squatted together a little distance away from the tablecloth, the older of the three with the clipped graying beard, leaning over toward Levan, his big fist posed on Levan's boot. Levan lay stretched out across a burkah, one hand under his head, the other around Keto Lagvini's waist. Lilly and Vahtang and the engineer from the Construction were huddled together at Kyra's side. The engineer had made several attempts to pull Kyra toward him, but she had resisted, and by now he had forgotten her. With every nerve of her body Kyra was conscious of Jan sitting, arms hugging his knees, to the left of her. She never turned to look at him, but she felt his slightest movement, every deep breath he took. Around them the trees of the orchard stood in a black heavy circle, and in comparison the clouded sky seemed light and terribly far. The smell of scorched meat still rose from the fire, though they had finished the shashlik some time ago.

Vahtang swung forward, reaching out for a bottle. When he found one that was full, he handed it to Kyra with a bow. Head thrown back, she gulped quickly and greedily, knowing that Jan was watching her, wanting to release herself in drunkenness from this enervating awareness of him. Reluctantly at last she returned the bottle and hid her hot face in her hands. The unceasing song was floating past her, it ebbed and eddied and whirled, threatening somehow to engulf and drown her.

"Let's go." Jan had spoken very quietly, without using her name, without a gesture toward her, and only when she had half risen did he touch her arm. They went so swiftly and suddenly that Kyra found it hard to believe that she had moved from her place in front of the fire. Either she was imagining this, or she'd always been walking toward the dark trees, her arm held by Jan. They were among the trees now, in the secret padded inner darkness of the orchard. Jan stopped her and kissed her, then they walked on, arms outstretched, careful. The sense of reality returned to Kyra, and added to it was joy. It was an apprehensive joy, unsure of its right to exist, ready to flee at the first wrong word. It just can't be, it just can't be, Kyra kept remonstrating to herself. This is what I wanted, what I bullied Levan into arranging, what I ran away from home for, so it just can't be true. Jan feels nothing for me, I know it without any doubt, otherwise he could have seen me anytime so easily and not waited for me to do all this. He could have talked longer the times we met on Golovinsky, and not the few aloof words. I must realize he is not too much in love with me at all. I'm nothing to him one way or another.

The silent moving through the darkness with him was joy in itself, the pressure of his arm against her side—it was such joy that it made her body hurt. His not speaking, only holding her tighter when she stumbled meant that he too was feeling something.

"You have not asked me where I'm leading you," Jan's voice sounded odd, as if he had had to make an effort to break the silence.

"Where?" her own voice turned out to be a whisper.

"Are you afraid?"

"No," but it was true no longer.

Suddenly they were out of the orchard and at the foot of an open hill. "I saw this hill as we were driving up in the morning. Let's go up, there's a road."

They came upon the road almost immediately. There was a wind on the hill and it was much lighter. Kyra had drawn away from Jan and walked with head thrown back, arms swinging, feeling free and strong in the wind.

"This is marvelous, Jan, I so love wind. Look how fast the clouds are running. Do you want to run?"

"I'll only run to catch you." He seized her by the shoulders. "But you see it is not necessary, I've got you caught already."

He bent her back, mouth on her mouth, till she was off her feet and kept from falling only by straining her arms around his neck.

"Admit you're good and caught."

Kyra jerked her head and sank her teeth into Jan's shoulder directly above her. When instantly his grip loosened, she slid to the ground and was up and away before his arm shot out to grab her.

"You sadistic little beast!" but he was laughing.

"You challenged me, you know."

He ran up the road after her and when he had caught her, he kissed her more gently than he had before. They continued arm in arm, and Kyra felt she was floating to heaven rather than climbing a hill.

"Let's not go any farther. Let's rest."

Kyra could have gone on forever, but she allowed him to lead her off the road and across the stiff grass of the hillside. At last he pulled her down beside him.

"We'll sit here and rest."

They sat smoking and talking, and Kyra held on to her cigarette butt long after the tobacco was gone and there was nothing but the cardboard tip in her mouth. She had to drop it at last. Jan's arms went around her.

"Don't be afraid, don't struggle. I promise to do nothing against your will."

She wasn't struggling. She did not stop Jan when he undid her blouse, pulled it off. Naked to the waist, shivering a little, eyes closed, she sat straight and still while his mouth pressed into her flesh.

"Jan." She tried at last to lift his head.

"Yes, we better go, we better go at once." After a moment he pulled up her chemise straps and threw her blouse around her shoulders.

"We have to." But they stood long against each other, unable to let go.

They stumbled down the hill, clumsy because of their tightly strained bodies, tipsy and heavy with desire. The road was darker, more rutted and winding than they remembered, pebbles kept slipping into Kyra's sandals, and whenever she stopped to shake them out it seemed impossible that they could ever resume walking.

As they were reentering the orchard, they heard their names shouted. Kyra was about to call back when abruptly Jan's hand closed over her mouth and instantly she was falling, his free arm around her waist pulling her down. He slid to her side. Impatiently, wordlessly, his hands explored her body, then he checked himself and his caresses became long and slow and calculated. He was at her feet, he kissed her knees, her thighs. Fingers clutching knots of grass, submerged, unthinking, Kyra kept up a half-whispered frenzied refrain: "Oh God, God, Jan, Jan, Jan, oh God." Dimly his voice reached her.

"Let me, Kyra, I'll be ever so careful, I promise to be careful. I must have you. Let me—"

Animal fear seized Kyra. Striking blindly, she jerked herself free of him, jumped up, intent now only on saving herself. After a moment she became aware that Jan was making no attempt to hold her, that he had remained motionless. Only his pleading continued, "Let me, I want you."

"Don't, Jan, don't, oh don't ask me. I can't, don't beg me."

His hand reached out for her, found her, began to draw

her. Kyra moaned aloud. Desire raced through her body, she felt trapped by it as by something outside of her, something malicious, revengeful. She tried to hold back, regain strength. His pleading continued, trapping her even more securely than her own aching desire.

All of a sudden, scarcely aware that she was doing it, Kyra sprang up. She stood over Jan, repeating loudly and crazily, "No, no, no, no—" unable to stop, for fear of hearing his voice. When she did become silent, she waited trembling, miserable, but it was a long time before he spoke.

"Go away, do you hear, leave me alone, go away."

He was lying face down in an untidy heap, shoulders hunched, arms hugging his head. Kyra did not move. Then she became aware of raindrops gliding down her forehead, down the back of her neck. She felt her hair, her clothes. Her clothes were all twisted about her. Wearily she began putting herself in order, trying to find words to speak to him and afraid to speak.

"Jan, it's raining." When he did not budge she was not sure that she had actually spoken aloud.

"Jan, please get up, it's starting to rain. Please let's go back."

If she kept standing over him, she knew she would fall, her legs giving way despite herself.

"Leave me, for God's sake, can't you go—" Then moving his head a litle to speak more distinctly, more loudly, he added as cruelly as words could be made to sound, "Don't you understand—go away! If you're a virgin it would be a preposterous joke if I were the one to deflower you, a cockeyed unsavory joke." Kyra went. Between the rows of trees she stepped, carrying her humiliation as though a rock on her back. She thought the night had lasted forever, but when she emerged from the orchard the bonfire was still prancing, and to the rhythmic clapping of hands Vahtang danced the lezginka, a wine bottle balanced on his head.

Next morning Jan said, "You were quite right to hold me off last night. I apologize." But though his tone was polite,

he did not address Kyra again after those few words, joking
with Keto Lagvini and walking at her side when they went
to see the hydraulic power plant where Levan worked. It was
a rainy, windy day. The stream looked yellow and angry as
its waters whirled past them, fog hid the mountains. After
their few hours' sleep on the hard wooden cots in the barracks, everyone felt stiff, worn out and chilled. The peasants
had returned with milk and cheese and bread, and there was
more wine. They ate in a shed on the river's bank to the
pelting of rain against the eaves and the unceasing roar of
water. The peasants sat cross-legged on the threshold of the
shed, and one of them started telling a story, slow and formless and of times long past. To forget herself, Kyra at first
made an effort to follow the story, which was in Georgian,
then the voice became but a lullaby, and she was left alone
with her wretchedness.

At her side Lilly was holding hands with the engineer
and with mischievous grimaces whispering into his ear. Keto
Lagvini, in her tight black satin skirt and blouse opened too
low, leaned against Levan, eyes half-closed, a contented smile
on her plump vivid lips. There was a scowl on Levan's face,
and only when his glance met Kyra's did he take the trouble to
smile, trying to cheer her up. Earlier he had put his arm
around her, drawing her away from the others.

"Well, I told you no good would come of it, that you'd
be sorry. I'll beat him up with the greatest of pleasure if you'd
like me to, though. He is not worthy of your little toe. Now
smile, Kyrochka, come on, smile for a change."

She had shaken her head and smiled resolutely. "Dear,
dear Levan, I'm not sorry we came, and please don't beat him
up. Anyone can be in a bad mood in this weather. I'm perfectly all right otherwise, Levan."

And she'd done her best to look cheerful, to overcome
the hopeless dreariness in which she was wallowing. After all,
what had happened? Nothing. Even Jan's rude and cruel
words were understandable under the circumstances, and he

had apologized. In fact, if anyone was to blame, it was she. If only he did not ignore her so completely, if only he would speak to her. She'd lose this horrid, humiliated feeling if he'd just speak to her. He was sitting uncomfortably on a small bench almost facing her, and whenever she glanced up at Levan, Jan came into her field of vision. It amazed her to see how frail and unwell he looked in daylight—she had never been aware of it before—the grayish skin, the bruised swollen patches under the eyes, the bloodless mouth. Every moment or so his left eyelid twitched, and he held his thin hands tightly clasped as though in apprehension or impatience. He was staring in the direction of the storyteller and the open door and the river, and he never shifted his gaze.

"Kyra, you're an idiot, a complete idiot." Lilly was tugging at her sleeve and speaking in English which no one else understood, "You are completely demoralized. What's that creature done to you? With men who are *men* all around you, why pick on him? Look how you are upsetting our host. Even I can't have a good time when you act like this. Would you like my engineer instead? At least he needs no cajoling. Want him?"

"Lilly, I am an idiot, I couldn't agree with you more. It's simply that he won't even speak to me."

"Well, go and speak to him if that is all there is."

"That's easy for you, Lilly, but I can't. I thought coming out to the country would be gay and free and wonderful, but it didn't turn out that way for me, and I have only myself to blame. I think I'd better have some more wine, and as the saying goes, drown my misery in drink."

"Vahtang, pour wine in our goblets, I pray thee. Levan, Keto, Jan, I wish to make a toast. Mito, forgive me for interrupting your story, and drink to our health, we need it. Hurry, Vahtang, fill our glasses to the brim or my muse may desert me."

Sticking her tongue out at Kyra, Lilly rose, head tossed back, hands crossed on her breast.

"I drink to myself and to you
To all who ever knew
The ache of wild desire
Its raging ghastly fire
Who, for an hour of bliss
For one caress or kiss—"

Lilly kept on extemporizing till out of breath, and shriek-ing with laughter, she collapsed against Kyra.

"If that doesn't help create the right mood, I give up."
It did help. Evan Jan was clapping and laughing. Then he rose. "Now let's sing the famous old toast to women."

"To lovely women
The charming women
Who loved us, be it
For an hour—"

They continued the song in chorus and suddenly Kyra became aware of the half smile on Jan's face, and that he was looking at her. When they were through singing and as he raised his glass, he bowed slightly in her direction.

On the afternoon train back to Tiflis, Kyra could not bear it any longer. Jan was sitting, eyes closed, in the far corner of the compartment, wearily leaning back and not speaking to anyone. Kyra had prevented herself from moving nearer to him, but everyone else was sprawled comfortably, and it seemed cruel that she should be there all alone by the window pretending to watch the running hills. When she did move toward Jan, she instantly lost all control of herself and dropped against him as limply and inevitably as a rag doll. Her head slipped off his chest onto his lap, and she pressed her face against his legs and stayed without movement, hardly daring to breathe. His left arm lay under her breasts, his hip felt hard in the curve of her throat, and it was as though she had waited a hundred years and at last was at peace. Presently his free hand touched her hair, stroked it lightly, withdrew, returned once again to rest on her nape. Wordlessly, they re-mained like this till the train clangored into Tiflis.

25. Lilly and Kyra

Late one afternoon, Lilly and Kyra sat side by side on a narrow sofa in the former boudoir of Princess Argadze which served by day as a study where she gave lessons, and by night as a makeshift bedroom for her daughter.

Lilly was talking very earnestly, "As I understand it, sincere intelligent communists, like Boris, had lived with the idea, believed in its goodness, long before what is actually taking place. So in a way, it is natural enough for them to attempt to square the present with their expectations. They just don't want to, can't bear to see certain things as they are in reality, or at least they minimize them."

"I never thought about it that way," Kyra admitted. "All that stuff about building a better world—I took it for granted that it was meant for the gullible in order to seize and hold power."

"I thought so too—until I met Boris."

"It is true, we never even heard of revolution until it was upon us and people were being shot and executed and arrested right and left and there was hunger. Later, when we were given reasons for this, no good reason could balance the scale." Kyra said angrily, "So-called freedom and the Cheka!"

"Yes, I know. I suppose we were born too late to be idealistic about the revolution. But people like Boris had years in which to be idealistic about it before it took place. He is quite old, you see, he must be way over thirty. He was ready for the University when he took part in some plot and got sent to Siberia."

"Lilly, I do understand that during the old regime, it

might have been easy to dream about bettering the world, but what I still do not understand is how someone as honest and intelligent as you say Boris is can accept the evil things that have happened, that are still happening. He should deplore them. We know the past was anything but perfect. We've all read Gogol, Dostoevsky, Aksakov's *Childhood*, Kouprine, Andreev. They all had the guts to be critical of their times, saddened or outraged by injustice. At least, the best of them were. Although I was only seven or eight at the time, I will never forget a certain Madame Popov whose wish to please me or, more correctly, Mother, meant an injustice to the other children. But today those would-be idealists are glossing over the injustices instead of facing the facts."

"I know it all, Kyra, the slogan for freedom alongside the threats and demands of blind obedience to authority. Freedom! We are controlled in every little thing, and we have got to think of it as natural in a communist state. But that is not at all the way Boris sees things. Necessary sacrifices to insure the future—something like that. It's a long point of view, you see."

"That's easy for one who sprawls comfortably in his armchair and has plenty to dine on. Pretty difficult for those sitting in the Cheka and most probably being tortured, to judge by their screams. Freedom, justice, and the Cheka!"

"I think Boris is saddened sometimes. You can't expect him to admit it to me, can you? When he scolded me about not taking part in the new life, and I answered him, 'How is it to be done? Am I not always called and treated as offspring of the hated class? Am I ever given the choice of making this new life, whether good or bad, mine? Unless I repudiated my family and landed one of them in the Cheka, would I ever be accepted?' I said this and more—I'm not afraid of him—and he really did look at me sadly and did not say anything for a long time."

"Well, what did he finally say?"

"He did not answer directly." Lilly smiled ruefully. "He said people with such mental attitudes are harmful and should be liquidated for the common good. He said it quite impersonally. From his point of view, I'm undesirable, of course, the way all of us are."

"Oh, Lilly darling, poor Lilly, how awful that you should care for him." Kyra leaned over and pressed her cheek to Lilly's shoulder.

"And he cares for me too, strange as it may seem." Lilly murmured, "Wait till you have seen him with me."

They sat silently with their arms around one another in the rapidly growing dark. From somewhere came the sounds of a waltz played clumsily on the piano, voices raised in argument, and the clatter of dishes. The little room had lost its outlines. The onyx clock on the mantelpiece ticked weightily as if to reach their ears, every brittle tick had to pierce the dusk anew. They were so alone that it hurt, yet sitting together in their aloneness also held a pang of bitter comfort. Kyra was aware that in the years to come she would remember this evening, this closeness in the dark. She even tried to help the impression by stamping on her mind the dim light from a lantern somewhere farther down the street which threw an oblique glow on the rug under the window, the fragrance of Lilly's powder, the stumbling tempo of the waltz. She would remember this evening, she told herself, at the oddest moments—when she was gay and with people who were happy; when she was in horrid pain and everything seemed to be crumbling. She knew she would remember it, though she did not know yet why. Then, she had a brief sudden foresight: today, now, regardless of and despite everything, she still was inexorably hoping. A day would inevitably come when hope was no longer possible. Almost immediately the idea vanished, was lost somewhere in the dark of her mind, and afterward she could not remember what it was that had occurred to her.

"Are you thinking of Jan?" Lilly whispered. "Now it's your turn to tell me."

"There is little enough to tell you. I went to his studio last evening with Keto. Oh, I know I shouldn't have, that it was demeaning. But I had not seen him in almost a week, even on Golovinsky, and I just could not stand it any longer."

"Well, what happened?"

"That's just it—nothing. We happened to come right after they had had a dance class. The man at the piano was still there. First, Jan danced with Keto and I just sat, and finally he did ask me, but he certainly made me feel an uninvited visitor, which in fact I was. You know, it's as if he is punishing me for something, and it's not because I did not give in to him that night. Even if I had, it would have made no difference as far as he is concerned. He would, without a doubt, have thought me a bigger fool than he does now. Remember what he said? 'If you're a virgin, it would be a preposterous joke if I were the one to deflower you—a cockeyed, unsavory joke. Go away!' No, I am being punished for something else, probably having little or nothing to do with me, something bigger, more decisive, though God only knows what it is. He is purposely cruel, he means to be."

"What you are really saying—the man is a sadist. Isn't that it?" Lilly asked, concerned. "He may still stumble on a way to hurt you badly, perhaps irremediably."

"Not physically, anyway, he made no attempt to use force. But he knows how to hurt. He asked me, ever so lightly —much too lightly—if there had been trouble at home after I got back, and Lilly, you know how dreadful it had been with Mother. I did not answer him because of his tone. It was obvious he had asked it so casually on purpose. Yet, Lilly, at Keto's last party Jan spent most of the evening sitting next to me. Remember, he came late and drunk? That time, he didn't say much, but would glance at me and seemed surprised to find me at his side."

"Pervert though he is, half of the female population in Tiflis would have been glad to give their eyeteeth for just that, an hour at his side. But, Kyra, you and I are only sixteen, how can you compete?"

Lilly straightened herself in her chair. "Did it ever occur to you, Kyra, how conventional we are? We take it completely for granted, whatever else we do, that we must remain virgins or, at least, *demi-vierges*. We're plain snobbish about it, for we apply this standard only to ourselves. Let the comsomols practice free love, does it concern us? We read Victor-Marguerite, and envy the bachelor girls of Paris, but do we emulate them? We seem to have inherited this *jeune fille* notion from the world of yesterday."

"Surely that's too one-sided a view," Kyra protested hotly, "as you know from your well-traveled cousin, the philanderer Gleb. Single women abroad can get devices to protect themselves from pregnancy. Comsomols have nurseries for their offspring, free abortions, and most important, no families to plunge into despair. Lilly, when I was at the end of my power to resist, Nina Tamidze's face swam before me, the way she looked between the time she knew she was pregnant and her drowning herself in the Koura. And behind that face was her mother who, as we have been told, went near insane. She never stops shaking, and I saw her once myself. My Lilly, I know your nature too well to believe you capable of denying yourself because of an inherited notion. It's sheer animal fear of the consequences, and your mother, and my mother."

"Thank you, thank you, you've strengthened my resolve. I now see I was chipping away at it. How wonderful of you to have guessed it. You are so intelligent!"

"With Jan, my fate might have been the Koura. But cheer up, Lilly, people still do get married. Levan very badly wants to marry his girl. But, like Levan, how many young men are in a position to afford to get married and be fathers?"

"Listen! Someone is tapping on the window."

"Oh, I forget to tell you, it's Keto. I asked her to pick me up here," Kyra whispered shamefacedly.

"But I thought you were coming with me to Gleb's." Lilly did not move toward the window.

"I would have if Keto hadn't come. She wasn't sure, but—I so want to be on Golovinsky and Keto is willing to stroll all night long. Don't be angry, Lilly, as you see I'm not intelligent at all when it comes to myself." Kyra jumped up and hurried across the room.

26. First Step

Kyra walked, remembering the hot stark shock when, the previous evening on the dark sofa, Jan's hand had brushed against her cheek. With her whole body she kept remembering it, multiplying it till she swam in a vacuum of longing. As from across a distant border Keto's chatter reached her, not the sense of her words but just inflected sound, and when the inflection seemed to call for some sort of answer, Kyra giggled or said, "Oh, Keto."

It was almost midnight when, in an unlighted side street on their way home at last, they walked straight into Jan and Ratoff. Kyra would have gone past with an incredulous tardy hello, but Keto stopped firmly, her little cries of surprise putting the encounter on a less incredible plane. She started in talking of an imaginary party that they had been to and that they had just quarreled with the boys who were seeing them home, that they were disgusted, and that this was indeed a pleasant surprise for now they wouldn't have to walk home alone after all. Sensing Jan's hesitation, Kyra in vain tugged at Keto's sleeve, for Keto was self-righteously determined to do Kyra a good turn. Jan was laughing a little, a hand on Keto's arm as if giving himself time to reach some decision. Ratoff, impatient, stood a step apart.

"Well, Alek, what do you say?" Jan's voice was amused. "Why don't we take them along?"

"You're insane," Ratoff replied sharply.

"Oh, where are you going?" Keto pinched Kyra's hand to stop her tugging.

"Jan, for God's sake, shut up." But Ratoff's apprehension seemed perversely to decide Jan.

"Wait here and don't eavesdrop. I want a word with Alek." He offered them cigarettes, lit a match for them, then pushed Ratoff a little distance down the street. Kyra stood squeezing her hands. Keto kept repeating in wild curiosity, "Where, where, where do you think?"

Ratoff's exasperated voice reached them at intervals. "You're simply insane. What for—unthinkable."

Then Jan was back. "Look here, before I say anything, swear yourselves to secrecy. All right? Then you can decide if you want to come. We are on our way to the Persian quarter. There's an opium place there. We've always been lucky—so far this particular one has never been raided. I suppose you know what happens if it does get raided. If you're afraid—" He spoke in a hurried whisper.

"Oh, how—but that's awful! No, no, I won't go." Keto's tone was horrified, angrily disappointed.

"Well, then, don't. Sorry not to see you home."

"Don't be silly, Keto." In her dread of having him go away, Kyra interrupted Jan quite calmly. "Why don't you want to go? I want to."

"Kyra, it's so—you're mad, don't you see what you're getting into? You'll land in the Cheka. For God's sake, be reasonable." It was now Keto's turn to grab Kyra's hand and tug at it.

"No, I want to go."

"There's a brave little girl." Jan's fingers cupped her elbow, squeezed it. "Come on, Keto, don't be a ninny."

"You might as well go, both of you," Ratoff said persuasively.

Now that Jan has told us, we'd be much more likely to keep it secret if we were involved, Kyra guessed Ratoff was thinking.

"Oh, all right," Keto muttered disgustedly. "I always have been an easy one to persuade, but never this much against my better judgment. All right, I'll come along, but I won't touch the filthy stuff, and if anything happens—"

They took a cab to the outskirts of the Armenian bazaar,

then, so as to attract less attention, they started walking. It was a long way. The narrow black alleyways zigzagged uphill and down, and it seemed incredible that one could find one's way through the maze. Kyra walked with Jan some distance behind the others. Whenever they saw the light of a lantern above a door or a gate, they lingered so as to lengthen the interval between Ratoff's and Keto's passing and theirs, then slipped by on the far side of the street. If they spoke it was in a muffled whisper. Crossing a tiny square with a well in the middle, they suddenly encountered two dark figures who saw them at the same instant. It was too late to turn aside; they had to walk on, their backs unprotected. All slowed down, watching, avoiding any sudden gesture, finally passing sideways, animal fashion. From under lowered eyelids Kyra made out two wood-dark faces with square beards and glittering eyes. They met no one else, and there was a crouching stillness about the sagging, blind houses, the warped fences, the shuttered entrances to windowless shops. When they were within a street of their destination, they caught up with Keto and Ratoff. Hidden in a deep gateway they stood whispering. Suddenly from somewhere in the dark, heavy boots came clapping, voices rose gruff, loud, Russian. Jan's hand in Kyra's turned stiff. Instantly all four of them sank backward against the gate. The voices, the clatter grew louder, more direct, then there was a pause and when the stamping resumed it was in the opposite direction, around a corner, fainter. Presently Jan murmured, "It's the patrol—but I have to—"

From where they stood, they crept on singly. Jan started first, then Kyra. As she had been told, she slipped through a tiny gate, felt her way with outstretched hand along a tunnel-like passageway till she was gripped, stopped. A rag was thrown over her face, she was led on, around a corner. Now she saw light through the rag. Securely held from both sides, she was led what seemed endlessly round and round, down some steps, through a door. The rag was snatched away. For a second Kyra tottered, seeing nothing in the misty semidarkness, breathing in a heavy sweetness, feeling faint. Jan's face swam out of the mist, he was holding her, letting her down onto something low. A draft of air touched her as a door creaked open, and when she could finally see, Keto and Ratoff were at her side.

In the low-ceilinged windowless room there were three men besides them. All three squatted on mats, wearing turbans, their long coats in tatters. One seemed to be blind, his eyelids red and nastily swollen; the next was a very old man with a yellow-gray beard; the third a young boy. Then from a corner came a moaning sound, and Kyra made out the outline of another body flat on a heap of rags. There was a lamp on the wall burning weakly.

She saw Jan lowering himself onto a mat in the middle of the floor. Another lamp was being lit, an odd metal one with a narrow, dainty flame. Jan took a pipe in his hand. The young boy crouched at Jan's feet, holding a long needle to the flame of the lamp, something sputtering at the end of the needle.

"Kyra, come and lie here by me. You'll have the pipe next." Jan's mutter was scarcely audible, through clenched teeth.

She rose and went to him like a somnambule, and lay down. The spattering tiny black ball at the end of the needle came to rest in Jan's pipe. He was inhaling deeply, eyes closed. A sweet stupefying smell hung thick all around. One little black ball was rolled after another, held to the flame. No one moved but the boy. The two old men never changed their squatting positions, the blind one with his head thrown back, the very old one bending forward, watching the boy. From the corner the moaning sigh kept repeating itself.

"Now you."

Ratoff was at her other side, explaining. Obediently, head resting, mouth ready, Kyra waited, then inhaled. At regular intervals she went on inhaling. Slowly, slowly, someone was saying, slowly and deeper, your stomach, not your chest, wait now, another pipe, let yourself go, close your eyes, deeply, deeply, another. In her head deeply, deeply, heavily, turning slowly, twisting a gray and a red, sinking deeply, too deeply, sweetly like sweet ice, cold everywhere. Sweeter and icier and heavier in her breast, in her legs, weighed down, way way into a sweet icy depth past recalling, emerging, further ever further, another tinkling and jingling, eluding, uncatchable, pink red moving, violet on gray, eluding eluding in the depth—

Afterward Kyra could never remember exactly what happened. The tinkling and jingling grown violently loud made her open her eyes. There was still gray movement about her, a scuttering elusive movement. There was a dreadful banging continuing. Then there was a crash and light and air coming and voices screaming.

Kyra was no longer on a mat in the middle of the floor, but huddled in a corner against Keto, held in Keto's shivering arms. For a moment she knew soldiers were entering, then she forgot all about them, not caring, sleepy, wanting only to sink back to wherever she had come from.

After a long time someone was carrying her through cool air. Afterward they were riding and Jan was next to her. She was supremely happy. If her knees would only stop trembling, she thought to herself, she would be more supremely happy. Then Keto was bending over her in a room which was not her own, and there was only Keto and she was crying. Kyra did not want to see Keto cry. She patted her hand, tried to speak comfortingly. "I do like you, Keto, thank you, thank you very much." It did not sound right, but she really did not care as long as Keto stopped crying.

Then Keto was shaking her. "Kyra, for God's sake, make sense. Come to. Don't you know what has happened. Can't you understand, for God's sake. Oh, what am I to do. Look here, listen, the place was raided. Jan bribed them to let us go. Oh, it's horrible, horrible!"

27. Jan

Kyra pulled the sheet tighter round her face and pressed the pillow against her ears. If only nyanya would stop puttering about. Her broom banged Kyra's bed, swished about under it, knocked the armchair. She had opened wide the shutters and sunlight was pouring in. It was uncanny how nyanya guessed when there was something to disapprove of, and she never failed to show her disapproval. Nyanya was unhappy about all of them, but most of all of course, Kyra. Poor dear, Kyra thought, I'll make it up to her when I get up, I'll ask about her pains, and I'll talk about when we were small in Slavnoe and went picking mushrooms. If only she'd go away now.

Jan, my beautiful, capricious, exquisite one. Last night you were gentle with me, you lay with your head on my breast, you held my hands. It was as if Ratoff wasn't there. I smoked five pipes. You said it was gallant of me to get Riza's room for the evening and take such risks for your sake especially after last week's raid of the opium den. I did not tell you that I felt like a mangy dog lying to Riza and perhaps getting him into trouble, even though, true enough, he had been dispatched on an official mission which was to last several days. I knew that, but you had not even bothered to ask, and yet you are supposed to be his friend. I love you, Jan, even for everything that is unlovely in you. Jan, I want you so.

Nyanya has slammed the door. When I get up I'll go down to the kitchen for a while, and we'll talk about a long time ago. Jan, how would it have been if I'd known you in the long time ago? You wouldn't be as you are today, cruel and twisted. Your gray, haughty eyes, your thin nervous fingers.

Yes, you would still be proud, but also chivalrous, considerate. When you came to visit in Slavnoe, nyanya would approve of you. She would think you wonderful, no doubt about it. You and I would walk in the birch grove and stop to watch the sunset. I am very happy. I know you want to take me in your arms and kiss me. You do kiss me. Not the way you did in real life, but in some other better way, perhaps. And then it's all very simple and joyful because we are engaged. You want me to love you. Mother is happy because she knows you are sensitive and intelligent, which you are, even today. I, too, would be quite different. Jan, Jan, even though I know you are not wonderful at all, I love you.

She walked through intolerable brightness, yet she did not hurry. In a little while she would see Jan in his dance studio, she would be with him. She took side streets to delay her arrival, then climbed the narrow staircase to the studio and knocked without giving herself a chance to hesitate. Ratoff opened the door. He was in a dirty silk dressing gown and naked under it. She peered past him into the room and Jan was there, lying on the couch.

"Oh, it's you. Come in."

She went in, smiling a little, and did not cross directly to Jan, but stopped by a table to leave her purse on it, and to lean against it and look at Jan from that distance.

"How are you? You're smiling so I suppose you're well. Alek, have you seen anything like it? She's had the stuff only twice and it's never made her sick. There must be something wrong with her. Is there something wrong with you, Kyra?"

What was wrong with her, Kyra knew, was her crazed longing for Jan which obliterated all physical symptoms of ill-being. She could not tell him that. Jan turned to Ratoff. "Alek, tell her if she's in your way. Do you want to dress?"

"No hurry."

Kyra leaned harder against the table.

"Look out, you'll tip that table and break the lamp. Sit down."

"I'll only stay a minute. At home it was so noisy." She went over and sat at Jan's feet on the couch. He changed his position, making room for her.

"The armchair is really more comfortable," Jan suggested.

"I'm very comfortable. If I'm not in your way, stretch your legs as before, Jan, I don't have to sit way back."

"Alek, that tango keeps singing in my head. 'Marseille is loud at night. Inside the haunt "Three Tramps."' Play it, will you?"

> There life is not too dear
> and dangerous is love
> each morning not in vain
> a negro washes stains of blood
> from the darkened floor.

Kyra felt herself drifting away with the music. She tried to hold on to herself and suddenly knew that there was a scratching in her throat and hot tears under her eyelids. *There life is not too dear and dangerous is love.* Jan, don't do this to me, not today Jan, it should be easy to be a little kind if you remember last night. You had your head on my breast. Touch my hand, just put your hand on mine, please. Jan, Jan, I need you so today, don't be cruel to me today, not with my guilt about Riza. "Jan, are the pipes and things hidden here?" Her question was an idle one for she had to talk if she was to keep herself from crying.

"I don't think I better tell you for safety's sake. The dvornik * is always eyeing us. I'd wager he is in the pay of the Cheka. The door does not bolt properly. Can't one ever be left to himself in our freedom-loving country!"

"Need I remind you, my friend, that we are known as 'suspicious characters'?" Ratoff was playing the piano loudly enough to cover his voice while he laughed uproariously. "It's our little Kyra who can borrow a room for the night and have

* Dvornik: man in charge of the yard.

the dear folk believe it's for an innocent girlish love affair."
He turned around and smirked at Kyra.

Jan frowned. "We better be grateful for that." He
stretched out a hand, found Kyra's, pulled it toward him, then
let it drop. Kyra remained half leaning over him, not touching him, but achingly aware of his body just those few inches
away, of her desire to crumble down against Jan and throw
her arms around his neck. But he was not even looking at her
any longer. She made herself sit upright and stare ahead into
the room. She faced a long mirror set between the windows
and could see herself in it and also Jan's curled up legs.

"That's me," she said aloud, and laughed unexpectedly.

"What's you?"

Kyra gained control of herself. "That's me in the mirror
there."

"I suppose you like yourself."

"No, I don't think so," Kyra answered reasonably enough.
The bright blue jumper she wore and the drug of the previous
evening made her face even paler than usual, and her staring
eyes seemed to have turned jet black; a curly strand of hair
hung over one ear. Her feet did not reach the floor. The gray
American shoes were too long and too narrow for her feet,
and in her habitual way, she dangled them on her toes. She
looked like a lost gnome, quite hopeless.

"You are quite attractive," Jan said, and Kyra did not
know whether he was mocking her or not. "You have cat's
eyes and lovely hair, a good forehead, a pretty good nose
and mouth, but you're entirely too pale, especially today of
course, even your mouth is pale, and you hold yourself badly.
You may grow up, though, into a very attractive woman. You
have a charming body."

She turned to him. His half-closed eyes were on her
breasts clearly outlined by the knitted fabric of her jumper.
She wanted to press her arms to her sides, but did not. Instead,
she stared straight into his face.

Ratoff had stopped playing. "I'm going to the kitchen to

persuade one of our kind neighbors to offer me a glass of tea." He went out.

Jan had begun to stir about restlessly. Kyra knew she should leave. Jan did not want her here. She also knew that as soon as she walked out of this room, she would scheme to come back regardless of anything. She would walk along streets, sit on the old tombstones of the Georgian cemetery, stop in to see Lilly, and wherever she was she would not be without her obsession. She could not make herself leave. There he was, his legs almost touching hers, his breathing audible to her, and the hands which she never stopped thinking of moving in her field of vision.

" 'There life is not too dear—' " Jan was humming the tango again. Suddenly he sat up. "I have an appointment, I must be going. Alek will be back in a few minutes to entertain you. Will you excuse me?"

"Jan—"

"All right. I know you expect me to say something, to do something." Jan was standing now, looking down at her, talking rapidly and impatiently. "You did not have to go with us. Alek, you knew, was against it from the beginning. You wanted to go. I thanked you for managing to get the room last night. Frankly, I was surprised at your doing it. Do you want to hear me say I'm sorry or repeat my thanks?"

"It isn't that at all, at all."

Jan stood silent a moment, his face stiffening and when he spoke it was deliberately slowly. "Kyra, you should have understood by now that I have no more love for you than for anyone else. I am utterly indifferent to people, including those who choose to love me. If anything, those irritate me most, bring out the worst in me. Whether my instinct is normal or abnormal—and I have been assured it is the latter—my reaction is to punish those foolish enough to fall in love; provide them with their share of suffering. I assure you, I have had my full share early enough in life. When one is very young, dependence on a loved one is unavoidable and the loss pitifully cruel. But today the very idea of an emotional involvement is abhorrent, distasteful."

Fingers intertwined, clenched, stomach drawn in, Kyra kept up a silent plea, "Jan, stop Jan—" He stopped suddenly. "Forgive me for my rudeness, and thank you for not permitting yourself to cry. I won't be bullied into feeling sorry for anyone, and last night does not justify postponing what I am saying. This is not directed against you personally, Kyra. I am not rebuking you for your love, I am telling you in plain language that I have nothing to offer in return. Face it—I've treated you like a plaything, petting you when I felt like it, snarling at you or ignoring you at will. I really must be leaving now. Alek will be back any moment. Good-bye and, if you must, stop in again, but it would be better if you forgot me. Once again, forgive my rudeness."

Kyra listened to his steps descending the stairs.

Late that night, as she went up the steps onto the dark porch, a figure moved from the railing and came toward her.

"Kyra?"

"Levan, for heaven's sake, how you scared me! What are you doing in Tiflis, sitting alone here on the balcony at this time of night? Has anything terrible happened to you?"

"I've been waiting for hours for you, Kyra. It's not about me, but you. Kyra, listen, is it true? Come nearer and tell me what it is all about. There must be a mistake, but tell me all you know."

"About what, Levan?"

"Then it is not true? You weren't caught in a raid on some opium den? How did your name—"

"Levan, what are you saying? It is true, I mean it is true about us being caught. But what are you saying? How do you know about it?"

"Kyra, Kyra, oh, damn it, Kyra."

"But what?"

"Listen, Kyra. This is very serious, unfortunately it is extremely serious. I will tell you, but don't scream out or anything and wake everybody. Promise to stay quiet. Do you want a cigarette?"

"Thank you," Kyra whispered.

"Now, I have an acquaintance in the Criminal Inquest Division, a very decent chap, quite high up in the Party. I happened to see him yesterday and he said—he could not come right out with it, but the gist of it was that he warned me against having anything to do with you, being seen with you, even writing to you. They have your name in connection with a narcotics investigation they are conducting. A mass trial is being planned."

"But the militiamen let us go—Jan gave them a bribe—they let us go free."

"You don't understand. No one has been arrested as yet. It would constitute a warning to others. The arrests will come later, when they are ready for the trial. Are you—Kyra, my little Kyra!"

"Oh, Levan!"

"Poor little girl, how could you have—Jan, Jan Karitsky. That was how, wasn't it? The bastard, the loathsome bastard! But why did you do it, Kyra? You must have known how ruthlessly drug addicts are persecuted nowadays. Since when have you been doing this, Kyra?"

"It was the very first time."

"Oh God, Kyra! To wreck your life so senselessly, so stupidly! With your 'social origin' handicap, and no working permit, you fit right into their category of vicious offspring of class enemies. It is too late for recriminations, and don't cry because that's not going to help one iota. Maybe something can still be done. I must find some way out for you."

"When will they arrest me?"

"I have no idea when they will be ready for the public trial. But in the meantime we'll have to find a way—"

"I'll shoot myself."

"Your solution is quite premature. You'd better give me all the details. I don't know what can be done, but I must know the facts, the exact facts, if I'm to try to save you."

"There isn't much to tell. I met Jan by chance late one evening, and I said I wanted to go with him to the opium place. He did not persuade me, I swear to you, Levan, and Ratoff and Keto were frightfully against it. It was I who wanted to go, because of Jan. Well, we went, and there was a raid. I don't remember about it because I was smoking when they broke in. Then Keto took me to her room for a while, and when she got me awake enough, she took me home. I suppose they trailed us? Levan, I better shoot myself before Mother—"

"I understand, but I want your word of honor that you will do nothing to yourself until you hear from me. I will do everything I can, and in return I give you my word that I shall warn you in advance."

"I give my word of honor. I trust you entirely, Levan."

"Kyrochka, I must leave you now or I'll miss the train and my absence might be noted. You will understand that for your own sake, as well as for mine and our families', my coming to see you and warn you must be kept a secret. Nothing must be said to anyone, least of all to Jan. There are other counts against him such as, right or wrong, his homosexuality."

"I promise not to say a word to anyone."

"I must go. My little Kyra, insane, reckless little fool! Now is the time to be brave. Give me your hand, and do you hear me, be brave. Good-bye." The next second he was hurrying down the steps, and then the yard gate clicked shut.

28. Despair

Kyra knocked at Boris' door, half an hour earlier than she and Lilly had agreed upon. Barely pausing to say hello, Kyra beseeched breathlessly, "Please, please, Boris, you promised it to me, or you almost did."

"I did not. Stop pleading, will you? It's one thing for me to take drugs with that pain in my leg from the wounds, but you're scarcely more than a child. I know nothing about you, I do not know what prompts you, at your age, to turn to drugs. I won't give you any. And if Lilly ever found out—"

"I swore to you she never would." Kyra slid off the edge of her chair till she was half kneeling in front of Boris.

"I have to have it, Boris, I'll go crazy."

"Damn you, all right."

He did not get up at once, only uncrossed his long legs, and the frown on his face grew heavier. Kyra's eyes never left Boris'. She was aware that her stare was that of a wolf cub, yet she could not manage to change its expression or even to blink. It was as if her eyes, like a doll's, had been focused for eternity, glued rigidly. With all her being she was waiting. At last he did get up. When he had his back turned to her, opening a door of a cupboard, she, too, got to her feet. Her throat was contracting so that she could hardly swallow. With the palms of both hands she rubbed her throat, trying to ease the suffocated feeling. It frightened her. Boris came forward and handed her a slim vial.

"It's in tablets. You can crush with the edge of the bottle or here's my fountain pen. Tear a leaf of the calendar. You can take this bottle, but it is the last time, do you understand? Use half a tablet, it's plenty, the stuff is pure." He moved away. "I'm going to the kitchen to wash those grapes I got for Lilly."

After he had left, Kyra quickly uncorked the vial, slid a tablet into her palm, reached for the calendar leaf and placed the tablet on it on the bureau. Very delicately, taking care not to breathe on it, she pressed the tablet with the fountain pen holder, hesitated a second, then continued to crush the whole tablet. When it had all become powder, she gathered it into a little pile, and too cautious to try to lift the paper, bent over it, sniffing in gently and deeply, one nostril at a time, pressing a finger against the other one.

Presently she went to sit on the wide couch and there was the delicious cold numbness in and back of her nose. She watched Boris who had returned with grapes on a plate and was arranging things on a small table—a bottle of wine, glasses, little cakes. Boris' room suddenly took on a festive appearance. Kyra became aware that there were flowers on the bureau, she had not noticed them before. She was beginning to feel restless and alert and also ashamed of herself. After all, she had practically knelt in front of Boris. She had knelt in front of a communist to be given cocaine. But Jan had told her to get it and had given her money for the stuff. Not that that made it any bit better. Oh, to hell with it.

How nice the yellow grapes looked against the dark of the bottle, shiny damp grapes with the sun on them and the bottle out of the sun. Why was the bottle out of the sun? What made the sun fall on the grapes and not the bottle? Light yellow sun, afternoon sun, light yellow grapes, ripe. But wine in the bottle was after death and resurrection. That was it. The flowers too were in the sun. It was wrong for those half open rosebuds to be in the afternoon sun. They would age in their infancy.

"Boris, may I move the roses?"

It had been the vase with the roses that kept the bottle in shadow. Now the whole table was equally sunlit, grapes, wine, and flowers. In her exasperation Kyra fled from the couch. That's what comes from interfering with natural laws, she accused herself angrily. After all, those flowers were cut. Why hadn't she thought of something so obvious. Now she had ruined everything. Perhaps not. She simply must see more deeply. Yes, there was a law beyond.

Pacing up and down the room, Kyra heard Boris talking but she did not listen to him. Her thoughts soared, clearer and lighter, and their logic exhilarated her.

"I'm so happy, Boris, I'm beginning to understand—"

There was rapid knocking. It was Lilly.

"Be careful, Kyra," Boris said quietly, going to the door.

And suddenly Kyra remembered again. The abject terror in which she had been living since her conversation with Levan on the porch was returned to her in a peculiar new form. It was outside of her, entirely too heavy and limitless to fit in herself, it was now outside of her body, but she was attached to it. How could she have lost it for even a moment?

"Kyrochka, I haven't seen you for days. What's become of you? Gleb said he'd seen you a couple of times on Golovinsky, but you seemed too preoccupied to notice him."

"Really?" Kyra said stupidly, but it was all right, for Lilly was absorbed in Boris, her mocking black eyes suddenly soft, her mouth partly open, gentle.

She could not bear to stay here. She had to leave. Boris and Lilly were moving on another plane in space. Maybe the vast despair to which she was attached had made her vast too, for she saw them as if from above, their backs and their fronts and their sides all at the same moment, and also that part of the bureau against which Lilly now leaned to look in the mirror, and even the wall behind the bureau. She saw everything all at once and every petal of every rose and the preciseness of every petal. Even voices had three dimensions—length and width and volume. Lilly's voice was wider and fatter than that of Boris. All about her things crowded her consciousness, demanding attention, solution to their being. Gladly would she have pondered and solved and discovered further and further. Despair was forcing her out of the room. It was pulling at her, leaden, immutable. She had to free herself of all that was not it. She had to escape from this demanding room.

"I suddenly remembered I have to be home. It's very important." She moved toward the door.

"But Kyra, you can't go now with all those marvelous things Boris has prepared. It's crazy! What is it? Can't it wait?"

"It can't wait, Lilly, believe me." She escaped quickly from the room and went out into the street.

Well, Despair, she began half-aloud and laughed, well, you've got me all to yourself now. Don't crush me down with your *entire* weight, let's talk calmly. Calmly, do you hear? Now, what comes first. First of all, let's imagine how it's going to happen. Let's visualize every detail. My mind is so clear that I can see details as clearly as the leaves on that tree. Let's have the relevant details, then the whole, then connotations, annotations, conclusions. Afterward I shall give myself wholly to you. I shall merge with you, lose myself in you. I begin: I am sitting in my red armchair. Tassia and Sonia are each in her customary place at the long table, intent on homework. Next door someone is talking and laughing and there are shrill voices as usual in the yard. It is becoming darker in the room. A tram goes clanging down Golovinsky. Then there is loud knocking on the front door. Tassia and Sonia start up. The knocking is too bold and ruthless to mean anything but the Cheka. None of us moves. We hear the front door being opened, maybe by Nika's mother. Then abrupt speech and knocking on our door from the hall. Still we three do not move. In the dining room Olga Ivanovna takes a few steps. I know Tassia and Sonia think they have come after Olga Ivanovna. Everything is buzzing so in me that I can't hear what is happening in the dining room. But Tassia and Sonia are listening with all their might, and presently I see their faces turning toward me. I avoid looking at them. Olga Ivanovna appears in the doorway and tries to speak, but ends up by just waving her hand at me. I get up, I walk. Tassia and Sonia have not budged yet from their chairs. From the door I see two men in boots, breeches, black leather jackets, peaked caps. I am stepping toward them. One says, "You don't mean it's she?" Because I look too young. Then there are rapid steps, and Mother's voice as she returns from work, and then voices all around me, and I just stand. There is the spasm in my throat and waves sort of glide before my eyes—red, brown, and hot. I do occasionally see a face, Tassia's stretched out of shape by terror, mother's bluish, as though starched. Mother's arms are around me, she holds me so tightly that she hurts me. Presently she is talking to me. I would like to understand and answer, but I can't get words together. I say, "Mother." I stop. I say, "It's you, Mother." I try terribly, "Mother, forgive me, I'll be all right. It's only you." Because from now on I am really not caring what happens to me. I am crying. With my outward self I am crying; inside I remain like a falling rock. One of the men speaks in a tone of command. I become aware of nyanya because she is moving away. Now Tassia and Sonia as well as Mother are hugging me. They are crying. Mother screams out, "This cannot be true, she's a child." I feel I'm being pushed toward the door. Mother's arms strain. I lift my head and stare around to remember how things look. I am being pushed more strongly. Nyanya thrusts something at me. It is a soft bundle. I clutch it. Mother's arms are holding me back and as she lets go of me, I almost fall forward. My elbows are clasped from both sides— I am between the two Chekists. I am dragged through the hall and I know that behind the other doors neighbors are listening. I look back to see Mother, and I see her face. Now I cry with my whole self. I cry so that I can't stand up. I am half carried across the sidewalk into the black car.

We do not need to advance time beyond this, Despair. The worst is over. That which is about to happen has happened.

Now for the whole. We'll treat it briefly. As a syllogism. Major premise: all malefactors end up in prison. Minor premise: I am a malefactor. Conclusion: I end up in prison. I am tempted to proceed: no nice girls go to prison. I am going to prison. I am not a nice girl. We won't question the premises, that's beyond the point. Some little girls go to prison; some little girls do not go to prison. Halt! Our minds seem to be running away. Back to earth. Now for the annotations, but let's not be formal about it. The trial. The trial, I cannot imagine it but there must be testimony and a trial. The sentence. The sentence is ten years' forced labor. Jan said so. It means being sent to a forced labor camp, in a sealed boxcar, squeezed in with other criminals across the whole of Russia to Siberia, to Solovetsky Island maybe. Ten years of forced labor in the sub-Arctic, which probably means death for me.

Now we shall dwell on the connotations: shame and despair for Mother. That I ended up in prison for opium smoking implies that I have been led up to it by other rotten acts and rottenness in me. Nice girls don't end up in prison for opium smoking. In truth, that first time was meant as a harmless escapade motivated solely by longing for Jan, but that is beyond the point for we are dealing with connotations. I am not defending myself, for what I have been doing since that night justifies the above connotation. It's the connotations that will kill Mother: that that's the kind of person I have been led to become, and that there is no hope for me, either in or out of prison. For what future is there for me, even if I do live to get out of prison?

Kyra stopped suddenly, hands clenched.

The one thing I can't accept is what I shall do to Mother. That is the conclusion: anything, anything, to spare Mother some of this. But what, what, what? The only obvious alternative is to kill myself. I discount running away, for where shall I go without money or passport—I'll be caught instantly. Bezprizorni are no longer tolerated. Well, from the point of sparing Mother, what is better? What is easier? A dead daughter, or a daughter in prison? My death does not necessarily mean she won't know about the opium and that I was to be arrested. This needs careful thinking out. I must think it out. It's the only thing left for me to think about. Oh God, help me! I don't know what to do, I don't know what to do. What should I do?

Kyra raised her head, grown aware that she was standing in the middle of a sidewalk and that someone had just bumped into her and cursed her for being in the way. She could not recognize the street she was on. It was somewhere below Erivansky Square in the Armenian quarter. Walking on again, she thought how long it had been since she left Boris', and wondered what time it could be now. The heat sucked in by the narrow street still lay heavily, but the sun seemed to be low. I must go home immediately, I must hurry and get home before Mother does, Kyra thought frantically. It might have happened in the meantime. They may be there waiting for me, they may have been and left and will be coming back. I must know. She started to run, sweat trickling down her cheeks, down her back.

The shutters were closed, leaving the room in semidarkness and not so suffocatingly hot as the street. Kyra closed the door painstakingly and stood leaning against it. The familiar room seemed oddly unfamiliar, almost uninhabited in its still obscurity. Where were Tassia and Sonia, Kyra wondered idly, not really caring, actually glad not to have to confront them. Still if she had found them sitting there it would have been a comfort. The room was like a shut-in desert. On Sonia's bed, leaning helplessly forward, sat a teddy bear. Curiously, Kyra stared at its yellow soft body, sorry for its helplessness, its unwantedness, its not belonging in this empty room. She moved away from the door and sat down on Sonia's bed. With her forefinger, gently she stroked the teddy bear's back, then she picked it up. She held it to her face. Quickly she put it down again. This would not do.

Something scuttled across the floor, along the wall under the table. Leaning with her elbows on her knees, Kyra watched. There it was again, a mouse. A mouse running like one demented, around and around. A small, velvety gray mouse which evidently could not find its hole. Rising, she went toward it. Now it hid under Kyra's bed, but no sooner had she lifted the counterpane than it was skipping over Sonia's bed and then across the top of the bureau, without a sound, delicately avoiding the combs and the nail file and the scissors. How did it ever jump so high, Kyra wondered. Teeth set, Kyra went after the mouse. When she'd caught it she'd let it out of the window. It had no business running about so senselessly. By the bureau she finally cornered it, holding it down with her handkerchief, but when she gathered up the handkerchief the mouse had disappeared. Wildly Kyra glanced around. There it was. It was running on the table. Kyra dashed to the table just as the mouse slipped over the edge into her drawer of the table.

"What is the matter, Kyra?" She had not heard nyanya entering.

"There's a mouse here," Kyra cried out desperately.

"Where do you see it?"

"It's in my drawer, it jumped into my drawer."

"Well, let's see now. You open the drawer and I'll hit it as it jumps out with this shoe brush here. The vermin!"

Trembling, Kyra pulled open the drawer. All was quiet inside. After a moment nyanya poked around with the brush. There wasn't any mouse.

"But, Nyanya, I saw it jump in."

"It does not seem to be here. Did you close the drawer right after it got in? You're sure you got it before it jumped out again?"

"But I did not close the drawer."

"Now, what are you telling me, Kyrochka? Who could have closed the drawer? It couldn't have jumped in with the drawer closed."

Kyra could find no answer.

"It seems to me like you're seeing things." Nyanya peered into her face.

"There was a mouse." Kyra tried to avoid nyanya's eyes.

29. Deliverance

She was so cold; her hands were stiff from being cold, and shivers kept gliding down her back. Try as she might to huddle and squeeze herself into the armchair, arms crossed, fists pressed into the armpits, knees up to her chin, the cold shivers came and went and came again. Sun filled the room, the windows stood open and flies were buzzing. From upstairs came the sound of a piano, the same scale played over and over again. If she did not stop being this cold, she might die from cold right in the middle of this scorching summer day. She tried to pretend she had a blanket tucked all around her, a heavy blanket that would have to keep her warm. If only someone would bring her a blanket! It would be simple for someone to just walk up with a blanket or even a coat. She would be terribly grateful. If only Sonia would get up from the floor and without saying anything, fetch a coat and put it over her. Sonia, Sonechka, can't you see I'm almost dying? A single tear trickled down Kyra's left cheek. Wanting to brush it away against the upholstery, she raised her head a little and immediately pain clutched her nape as with iron pincers. It was odd that there could be such pain when earlier it had seemed that she almost had no head, or at least not her own, so light and yet stuffed it had felt, like a torn rubber ball packed with cotton, lying there on her shoulder but not part of her icy body. If I live through today—Kyra knew that her lips were moving as if in supplication—I won't touch cocaine again.

But maybe I shouldn't live. Mother, Mother, what have I done? And now what is best? Mother, please help me somehow. Don't let it happen. Take me away, take me away, hide me. I'm going crazy. I can't stand it any more. Jan. No, I can't think of Jan. I'll go crazy. I can't think at all.

Sonia, please cover me up with something. Get up from the floor and fetch something to put over me. You love me, Sonia, I know you love me a great deal. You once said you'd give your life for me. Remember how at Alexandropol we walked in the plains together and I talked to you? Yet you can't guess about me and that I'm sick. And if you did guess or if I told you, you would be very frightened, the way you were when I fainted and we were alone in the room, as we are now, and you tried to lift me up and you cried and cried. So I can't ask you. How badly it feels in my chest as if something heavy was being dragged from there, especially on the left where the heart is. Oh, someone, please help me!

"What, Kyra? Did you say somthing? I thought you were asleep and that you'd be very lame after sleeping in that funny position."

"Sonia—"

"What?"

"I think I'm not well—"

"You know what I can get you? There's a bottle of wine in Olga Ivanovna's trunk, in the small empty one. It's standing up, opened and almost full. Then I can fill it with water."

"Thank you, Sonia."

She heard Sonia jump up, upsetting something, maybe dropping it off her lap, then skipping out of the room. With an immense effort, eyes still closed, Kyra raised herself into a sitting position. But after Sonia had returned with the wine, a large tumbler of it, and she had drunk, she suddenly began to feel very much better. It was as if new warmer blood had been poured into her.

"That's helped already."

"Would you like some more? Of course, we may be found out but I don't care," Sonia offered generously.

"Yes, just a little more. And, Sonia, would you bring me Mother's shawl?"

"You don't mean to say you're cold. How funny when I'm so hot. All right, I'll get it right away."

With the woolen shawl tucked around her, Kyra watched Sonia who had returned to her place on the floor, sitting shoeless, legs apart, tongue slightly out, a brush and a shoe in her hands. She was trying to cover the worn patches on it with polish to make them less unsightly. She dabbed at the flat yellow tin of polish with an already brown-smeared finger, not wanting to waste it by using the brush except to polish.

"Kyra, you're not falling asleep again or anything? Listen, you know Varia Rutnik—she's our pioneer leader—well, she again walked home from school with me today. That's the second time. It's not just an accident—I bet I'll be asked to join the pioneers."

"Oh, Sonia—"

" 'Oh Sonia' what? Think how useful it would be. For example, you wanted to go to the University, now, didn't you? And you couldn't. Tassia'll never get in, either. But I would be able to. So why shouldn't I?"

"But Sonia, you're you, nothing can change that."

"What am I?"

"You're a noblewoman."

Brush in mid-air, Sonia stopped short. "Shsh, Kyra, don't say a thing like that so loud."

"I do see your point of view. It's sad though."

Sonia bent once again over her shoe. "Anyway, I probably won't."

"You won't? Why?"

"There is something more important to me than anything, anything. Maybe I'll tell you. I've never told anyone. You won't laugh at me, will you? It's a person. He might hate me if I joined the pioneers. Oh Kyra, he's so wonderful, you can't imagine anyone like him. The very first day I saw him in school, I knew he was wonderful, and ever since he seemed more and more so. Of course, he does not know. But, Kyra, since school started this fall, he has begun to talk to me sometimes during recess, and once he lent me a book. It was a book of poems and I copied them out and learned them by heart. He's two grades ahead of me, and very clever. He explains all kinds of things. Kyra, is it possible no one has noticed the change in me? It's like being two different people, before I talked to him and since. How is it nobody noticed? Did you, Kyra?"

"Sonia, Sonechka dear, I never suspected. As you grew, I should have given you more attention. But, you know, you used to be such a brat. Now you've changed, you're altogether different."

"Kyra, you're not laughing at me?"

"How can you think that?"

"Kyra!"

Levan was leaning in over the windowsill. She had not heard his steps on the porch, and turned around blankly, aware only of hard sharp splinters being driven into her heart. "Come out here."

As she skirted Sonia, she tried to think of something to say. "Good-bye, Sonia," she said.

"Why on earth are you saying good-bye?" Sonia asked, puzzled.

"I didn't mean to—" Kyra closed the door and stepped steadily along the short corridor, past the **back** door of the apartment of Nika's mother, past the always stinking toilet, to the heavy porch door, through the door, across the porch. Levan came toward her and drew her against the railing, then let go of her arm and thrust his hands hard into his trouser pockets.

"Well, it's all been fixed," he said quietly.

Kyra stared.

"It's all fixed. You don't need to fear and sicken any longer. You do look sick, a ghost of yourself. I can't tell you how I did it because it involves—Kyra!"

Wet bright streaks were sliding past Kyra's face, muffling Levan's voice and her sight of him. She put out a hand to grab the banister but it tottered away from her, and she, too, started to totter, then plunged head forward into a humming, whirling blackness.

Her elbow fast in Levan's hand, Kyra walked stiffly into the tea garden and toward the table the waiter had pointed out. Levan did not let go of her till she had sat down, then unhurriedly he ordered a bottle of wine, opened a box of cigarettes, all the while not speaking to her, almost not looking. Unable to break the silence herself, Kyra could only glance up humbly.

I'm safe, she kept telling herself; nothing is going to happen to me, I'm safe, I don't have to be desperate any longer. I don't have to be desperate. Yet she could not grasp the meaning of this—it eluded her like the goldfish she had once, as a little girl, tried to snatch out of a fountain. She drank from the glass Levan had placed in front of her.

"Levan, I am—"

"I did not bring you here to talk to you, Kyra, but to get you away from the house before you gave yourself entirely away. Don't talk unless you want to."

"I'm so sorry, Levan."

"Sorry? What do you mean by 'sorry'?"

"About you—all this trouble." She realized she was being ridiculously inadequate.

"If that's all—" Levan stopped abruptly, his wide lips stretched into a single flat, harsh line, his eyes narrow and bright black with anger.

"Oh, please don't hate me, Levan."

She listened to his growl, a short fierce threat. "Levan, it was all my doing, hate me if you must, but it's no use shifting the blame on Jan. He did not make me do anything against my will." She dared ask the question: "And Keto, and Alek and Jan?"

"Keto, it turned out, was not implicated. It was you who chanced to be caught in the act. As for those two bastards, those pederasts, they are not likely to escape Siberia if only because there are other charges against them. We all know about the one-time bezprizorni forced into a life of crime. It's recent history. But in Jan's case there is a difference—he seems to take delight in leading others to their ruin. The thought never crossed my mind when I introduced him to you that Easter Eve, but now I'm convinced of the evil in him."

"I'm not disputing you, but I'm so in love with him."

For a long while they were silent, Kyra conscious that Levan, calm again, was studying her curiously. Stretching both hands far across the table, he suddenly leaned toward her.

"Kyrochka, little girl, what has happened to you? You mustn't, you simply mustn't give up like this. Whatever the odds, one just does not give up. You've always been courageous, is it too difficult to be brave any longer? I'll help you, I'll do anything to help you, you know that, you know I'll never leave you, whatever happens. Just a couple of years ago, wasn't it, you were such a little girl, such a bright, eager little girl. Remember how I used to walk up and down your room with you in my arms? I won't let you change, do you hear? I won't allow it. Forget all about this, forget it entirely as if it had happened to someone else. Be again the Kyra I cherish." Levan added almost inaudibly, "You had such trust in me when it seemed no one else had, not that you were aware of it at the time, but it helped."

"Oh, Levan, you have saved me this once, but I still have to live on as before all this happened. You have saved me, but where am I to go from here? I remember you saying that you felt like a hunted rabbit running in circles with no way out, no hope of escape. It's this gnawing fear that there's no way out. I keep having this dream—have you had dreams like it? Just wandering and wandering through dark corridors, endless corridors, searching for a way out, for some door that would lead out, and there is no way out, running and running and screaming and never being able to escape from those dark tunnels." Kyra's voice rang out so shrilly that it jarred on her own ears.

She snatched Levan's hands and squeezed them with all her might, then let them go, slumped forward, head on her folded arms. It was very quiet in the darkening tea garden, empty but for themselves. There was another long silence between them before Levan spoke. "Irakli Georgiani has been shot." Starkly the words reached her.

"Levan, you know for certain?"

"His body was returned to his mother."

Presently she said, "I saw him some two months ago. Why was he shot?"

"They couldn't have really thought he took part in the revolt, he was too ill to lift a rifle. But the accusation was his inciting peasants to revolt. As if in their desperate misery and brutal oppression our peasants needed inciting to rise up. Only despair gives birth to such futile heroism when one knows the massacre which is to follow."

"I saw Irakli two months ago," Kyra repeated softly. "He walked all bent over and his clothes were in tatters. We sat on some steps not far from his former house. We sat there for a long time, and he talked. He had said, 'I have stayed away from Tiflis and seen no one from here. I did wonder how you were growing up. I hoped you would understand something, and understanding, would forgive my ruthlessness with you.

That's when I let you go then when you were fifteen. I did it to spare you.' I asked, 'Spare me what, Irakli?' 'Spare you my unhappiness,' he said. . . ."

"Irakli!" Kyra whispered aloud, racked by pity. A wineglass standing on the edge of the table tottered, fell, ringing thinly, to the ground. Motionless, Levan and Kyra stared at the fragments.

When, later, they got up to go, Kyra stopped to stare into Levan's eyes. "I am going to try, Levan, I promise you I'll try very hard." She swallowed her tears and took the plunge: "I swear to you, you who have in truth saved my life, that I shall never take drugs again." Levan bent down and kissed her hair.

She kept her promise to Levan, even when, some weeks later, the news seeped through that Data and Sandro had been killed by the frontier guards as they were illegally crossing the mountains in their attempt to escape to Turkey. She also learned that the trial had taken place and Jan was on his way to Siberia. What made her resolution more bearable was her growing awareness that in her search for pleasure, she had actually reaped too much pain. Herself their victim, she had somehow chosen to love the victimized, Irakli and Jan. Even her early love for Levan had sprung from great pity, from her admiration for his selfless gallantry when, wounded and hiding in the cellar, he had dashed from his shelter in an attempt to save a stranger. She had become what Eva might have stigmatized as a masochist, *une souffre-douleur*, one irresistibly drawn to suffering, at first to that of others in pity, then to her own in heedlessness. Her zest for snatching from life all that was within reach with the intention of enriching a gray existence had somehow led to the reverse—loss and blundering into nearly wrecking her life. Did she regret it? No, a hundred times, no! But now she must revise her assumptions, certainly not to accept a humdrum day-to-day survival, but to seek for something brighter, a more luminous future. She was only seventeen. Her whole life was before her. What was she to make of it? She did not know the answer.

30. Hope Born of Despair

A swift autumn evening breeze kept blowing through the room, carrying whiffs of sound from distant streets. Kyra, Tassia, and Sonia, each on her side of the table, sat, elbows forward, taut-faced. Their mother had stopped walking up and down the room and had sat down on the piano stool. Now, absent-mindedly, she began to play. As she went on playing, the children's heads turned in her direction and their bodies leaned with more ease against the table. Tassia's mouth steadied itself, and her swollen eyes lost their despairing stare. As Kyra looked toward her mother, Tassia's face was in her field of vision, and incredulous, Kyra thought, one day soon she just won't be here.

Tassia is going to America. When one says it aloud, it's simply untrue; when one thinks it, one's mind cannot reach its significance, one's mind doubles up, snatches at the present, at the known, lets go of the unimagined. Tassia will go to America. It means Tassia will be here no longer. What is Tassia thinking of now? What did she think when she agreed so simply? First, she had nodded, then said "Yes," then begun to cry as if this abrupt, unsought change of fate created no disbelief. When their mother had stopped talking, when there was nothing more for her to say in matter-of-fact explanation, and she had paused suddenly, seeking to keep up her self-control as she opened her arms to Tassia, Tassia had nodded and whispered "Yes" before throwing herself forward in tears.

Their mother, who now worked as an interpreter for the Americans at their Tiflis headquarters, had often mentioned departures and arrivals, but obsessed as Kyra was with her own present, she paid little attention, hardly ever listening. But today it had been a very different matter. Their mother came home with a thick packet of documents and instructions delivered to her by the latest newcomer to the Near East Relief staff. Those papers all concerned Tassia's departure for the United States. They were definitive but for some necessary signatures.

Nyanya was entering the room with the samovar, her cheeks still red and wet in patches, her breathing short. Avoiding looking at anyone, she trudged heavily through to the dining room and thumped the samovar down. Their mother let her hands drop from the keyboard but remained slightly bent forward. Presently she got up. She did not speak till she was at the door.

"It's still entirely up to you, Tassenka, remember."

After the door had closed behind her, the children continued to stare at that door. They listened to what she was saying to nyanya, only bits reaching them between nyanya's sobs.

". . . it's what's best for Tassia . . . what's to become of her here? There's Kyra without a . . . bad for them . . . It isn't forever, she'll return, she'll come back well educated, with a profession, healthy, strong, a useful person . . . what can I do for my children?"

Kyra stretched out an arm along the table, not quite touching Tassia.

"Tassia, do you believe it?"

"I know what you mean, but somehow I think I do."

"Well, can you imagine it really?"

"I suppose not really the way it will be. I don't know what a college is like or what America looks like, of course, but I can imagine, well, sitting and studying, then talking to people who are entirely different from us, and everything going fast and very easily and just right. And seeing, oh, all kinds of things— And when I've finished all the studying and I've become a doctor, then I'll come back." Tassia spoke slowly as if from the depth of a trance.

"Tassia, I've just stopped understanding you." Sonia banged her fist on the table.

"You seem so unsurprised, somehow," Kyra added reflectively. "I know you're just pretending to be calm, make the best of it, but I also can't understand you."

"Kyra, I'll try to explain." Tassia's voice was unsteady. "You see, long before Mrs. Woodcock spoke of it, I believed, I've always believed something like this would happen to me. It isn't so much that any particular thing would happen, as what would *not* happen, by which I mean, just nothing. I had this faith—so there it is."

"You could not have thought you were going to America." Sonia was beginning to wriggle on her chair. "If we hadn't gone to Alexandropol you'd never have known Mrs. Woodcock, you'd never even have seen her. I wish you never *had* seen her, too. And now she wants to adopt you. I wouldn't get adopted for anything!"

"But she isn't adopting me. I don't want to be adopted either. It doesn't count if it's only on paper to get me out of the country before I am sixteen. You know I wouldn't really get adopted. But she is going to send me to college to study to be a doctor! And I will see Chicago, I will see Constantinople and Paris, and all the places in between!"

"I'm going to get into a University here, just see if I don't. Maybe I'll go to Moscow. Wait and see!" Sonia had tilted her chair, one knee jammed against the table for balance, her cheeks pink, her blue eyes shining with challenge.

"Keep quiet, Sonia," Kyra interfered. "Before you get to the University you might have to join the comsomol. Anyway, Tassia knows she must go. We've been talking about just that for how many hours now? Of course, she ought to, otherwise it will be as with me—"

"Well, would you go?"

"Me?" Kyra hunched her shoulders uneasily. "That's a nonsensical question really, because I'm too old, as you know."

"You just don't want to answer!"

"Obviously there's a big difference. It's idle to discuss it. I'm just too—oh, old by now." Kyra thrust all ten fingers into her hair and a hairpin slipped out of her knot, tinkled against the floor. Quickly she bent down to look for it. The question had been present in her mind long before Sonia had asked it. Would she go? If the opportunity had presented itself, she would be sitting here now thinking only of Jan in Siberia and what she was going away from. Only what she was escaping from would matter. Tassia is thinking where she is going, what she is going toward. If she were going to America, she'd just be running away. Even safe in America, she would still only be escaping. Kyra frowned. But, then, perhaps what was wrong with escaping? Escaping from what was holding one in an implacable grip? She had used those very words "running away" and "escaping" when she last talked to Levan in the tea garden such a short time ago. She would be escaping from a present and future that seemingly held no hope for her in the Motherland. She certainly did not want to go, but Jan was in Siberia; Irakli, Data, and Sandro were dead. Eva had left for a more fulfilling life. As she herself had asked Levan, where was she to go from now on? Until Alexandropol had been mentioned this evening, she had all but forgotten an episode that took place during the last days of their stay in Armenia. Since then there had been nothing but despair. But she had not always felt desperate. Then, not so long ago, she, too, had conceived a better future. That fantasy, that daydream first arose because of Sir Galahad.

"Tassia, Sonia, you do remember Sir Galahad?" she exclaimed, gladdened by the recollection.

Her sisters nodded. "Of course—the horse you escaped on." Their surprise at her sudden question showed that they had not connected it with their discussion of the future. To Kyra it was anything but irrelevant, for Sir Galahad was the very embodiment of escape.

By far the handsomest horse in the stable was the thoroughbred which belonged to a Captain Blackstone, adviser to the Near East Relief Mission. Sir Galahad and Kyra understood one another perfectly. A day had come when trotting within the confines of the compound became unbearable to both. Galloping suddenly past the startled sentry, they dashed joyously down the dirt road in the direction of Alexandropol and the last American outpost, some three miles away. Halfway, a mounted marauding band came into view, emerging from behind a hillock, evidently attracted by the sound of galloping hooves. The band's rifle shots were perfunctory, Kyra realized, for fear of damaging the horse, the prize they were after. Maddened by the shots, Sir Galahad easily outdistanced their pursuers on the miserable half-starved mountain ponies, and he and Kyra reached the entrance of the outpost with nothing worse than a few scratches on Sir Galahad's flanks and Kyra's legs from the barbed wire fencing at the gate. Captain Blackstone had faced Kyra sternly the following day. "I forbid you to touch Sir Galahad again; you broke strict security orders. You do not qualify for ransom—they must have seen that for themselves—otherwise they would have shot at the horse. It was the thoroughbred they wanted. It happened to end well enough. You're a plucky kid, I have to admit. You must have kept a grip on the bridle and your senses about you to steer Sir Galahad into the camp. But however plucky, you acted irresponsibly."

How could she have forgotten Sir Galahad, their shared delight and their shared frenzy? Yet, she had accepted as just Captain Blackstone's recrimination. She could not blame him. On the contrary, she admired him. At the time she became determined to "hitch her wagon to a star." She would marry a younger Captain Blackstone, she would be taken to America, she would own a Sir Galahad, and would study at a University all the subjects she so wanted to. Was it within probability? Miracles did happen, as in Tassia's case.

This brought her back to the present. Tassia was saying, "You are wrong, Sonia, it is not that simple, that easy. You accuse me of wanting to go to America. Don't you realize it's so very far away, and for so many, many years away from

Mother and you both and everyone and everything I know. Nobody else from Tiflis has ever gone to America to school. It's such a lonely feeling. I wish I were not going alone."

Kyra moved back in her armchair, then pushed the armchair away from the table to be able to see the whole of Tassia —the old blue sailor blouse, the skirt fallen back above the knees, the long boyish legs still in socks, the smooth light head with the hair parted in the middle and a stumpy braid over each shoulder, the sunburned scratched hands, the thin neck. Kyra could see how it would happen in Batoum on the day of Tassia's departure.

They drove up to the barbed wire fencing off the harbor. The foreign boat was there in the harbor. By the gate to the enclosure they said good-bye. There were guards waiting at the gate. Once Tassia was through the gate, a guard took her suitcase and closed the gate. Through the barbed wire they watched Tassia being led off to the Customs shed and did not move their eyes from the shed where Tassia was being examined, searched, stripped. They hoped for another glimpse of her. Presently they did see her, standing at the door of the shed. She too looked in their direction. One was not allowed to talk to anyone after the examination. Then again there was a guard leading her off. Kyra, Sonia, and their mother waited. It was night when the whistle blew and the boat started to slip away . . .

"Children." Their mother opened the dining room door and was standing holding on to the doorknob, smiling. "Come and drink your tea or the samovar will be cold."

"Tassia, when you come back . . . let's imagine how it will be. Let's imagine you're already back and it's many years from now. We'll all be together, and how will it be? Can you imagine how nice it will be having tea together once again?"

"I wish it did not have to be for so many years and so very, very far," Tassia repeated, as she got up. "Here there's Mother and you and Galia and Nina, but what do I know about what's ahead?" Tassia pulled at her braids sadly. "Mother, I should put my hair up, shouldn't I, for America?"

"Mother, don't you think I'll get to a University too?" Sonia jumped up. "You know, I'm sure I will."

Kyra did not get up but lay lower back in the red armchair. It was best, just now at least, not to wonder about the future. If she had to think, it must be of herself as a whole—past, present, and future. Then it would not matter so much where she was, but what she was. At some point, like everyone else, she must have become conscious of an identifiable "I." That "I" was undoubtedly still an integral part of herself, even though deformed, cowed, by events. There was a thread she had to grasp and this thread held together the things that mattered in life. She was groping for the thread when, from some warm depth in her, a memory arose instead.

She was sitting on the windowsill in her mother's bedroom, turning the pages of a picture book. It was winter in St. Petersburg, and looking upward, she could see the white heavy sky. Her mother stood in front of the tall mirror in a new dress while Masha, pins in her mouth, squatted on the floor doing something to the hem. In the nursery next door, nyanya was putting baby Tassia to sleep. She could be heard humming a lullaby and pacing to and fro. Masha left the room. Presently her mother, too, left the room. Kyra remained alone. She sat, at first aware only that she was alone, and then she became conscious of something more—herself in herself. She was in herself. Sliding down from the windowsill, Kyra stood stock-still. Gooseflesh tightened her arms. She was shivering. The staggering realization was forcing her on to something. Its implications were within her reach. Exhilarated, her mind reached out—I, I, I want, I do. What could she want and do? Kyra arched her back, stared around. She started to run. She ran down the corridor and into the dining room, flung open the sideboard, snatched a gingerbread cookie, and stuffed it into her mouth.

She returned to the bedroom, her exaltation suddenly

gone. Bewildered, frightened, she tried to climb back onto the windowsill. Without help, she could only get one leg up, her shoes smudging the wallpaper under the window. Howling, she dashed from room to room in search of her mother.

There Remain the Scars

Il me restent:
Les circatrices
des pures brûlures
de
Tiflis.

                    Kyra Karadja

Epilogue

Kyra left Tiflis on her way to the United States sooner than she had envisaged. She was not quite eighteen on her arrival in this country. Unable to take her diaries out of Russia, she almost immediately began recording her reminiscences to make up for their loss. Basically this was an attempt to preserve her sense of identity, so severely threatened throughout her young life. She started by reconstructing various episodes, thoughts, visual impressions, and emotional reactions. Later it occurred to her to put those into a coherent whole. The result is this book, until recently unavailable for publication.

Graduating Summa Cum Laude from a venerable New England college, Kyra then continued her higher education. Married, both she and Tassia followed professional careers. They were unable to return to their homeland despite repeated efforts to see their mother again.

The Editor